Working Women in Mexico City

Working Women in Mexico City

Public Discourses and Material Conditions,

1879–1931

Susie S. Porter

The University of Arizona Press

Tucson

331.40972
P84w

cau

The University of Arizona Press
© 2003 The Arizona Board of Regents
First Printing
All rights reserved
∞ This book is printed on acid-free, archival-quality paper.
Manufactured in the United States of America

08   07   06   05   04   03   6   5   4   3   2   1

Library of Congress Cataloging-in-Publication Data
Porter, Susie S. 1965–
Working women in Mexico City : public discourses and material
conditions, 1879–1931 / Susie S. Porter.
p. ; cm.
Includes bibliographical references and index.
ISBN 0-8165-2268-5 (cloth : alk. paper)
1. Women—Employment—Mexico—Mexico City—History.
2. Industrialization—Mexico—Mexico City—History.   3. Mexico
City (Mexico)—Economic conditions—19th century.   4. Mexico
City (Mexico)—Economic conditions—20th century.   I. Title.
HD6101.Z6M446 2003
331.4′0972′5309034—dc21
2003008303

British Library Cataloguing-in-Publication Data
A catalogue record for this book is available
from the British Library.

Chapter 6 was originally published as "And That It Is Custom
Makes It Law: Class Conflict and Gender Ideology in the Public
Sphere, Mexico City, 1880–1910" in *Social Science History*, 20: no. 1
(spring 2000): 111–48. Copyright © 2000 Social Science
History Association. All rights reserved. Used by
permission of the publisher.

Contents

Illustrations

Figures

Map

Tables

Acknowledgments

As I moved from collecting archival sources to writing the dissertation upon which this book is based I received funding from several University of California institutions. The Center for Iberian–Latin American Studies (CILAS) at the University of California at San Diego provided me with pre-dissertation (1992) and dissertation (1994) research grants. The UC–MEXUS Center provided both pre-dissertation research grants (1990 and 1991) and a dissertation research grant (1994). The Department of History at the University of California, San Diego granted me a Graduate Fellowship (1993). When it came time to transform the research into a dissertation my work was generously supported, both financially and intellectually, by the Center for U.S.–Mexican Studies at the University of California, San Diego (1994–1996). The Tanner Humanities Center at the University of Utah, Salt Lake City, provided the financial and intellectual support to write the book.

Financial support is nothing without the proper tools and guidance, and for these I am indebted to many people. First of all, the members of my dissertation committee, Eric Van Young, Christine Hünefeldt, Stephanie McCurry, Stephen Haber, and Paul Drake, taught me more than perhaps I have been able to absorb. I am especially grateful to Eric Van Young for his continuing support. I hope the many ways his generous intellect has inspired me is evident on the pages that follow. In transforming the dissertation into a book, Jerry Root read every word many times, and all the words I cut out as well. His influence is on every page of this book. In my writing and in my life more generally, he has given me space to speak. This book is also the result of the support of my colleagues at the University of Utah: Raúl Ramos, Janet Theiss, Beth Clement, Rebeca Horn, Megan Armstrong, David Igler, and Kathryn Stockton. Thanks also to Wesley Sasaki-Uemura and Tom Wolf for helping me into the public sphere and to Jeff Cowie for, among so many other things, a dictionary. I am particularly indebted to Patrick McNamara and Joel Wolf, whose belief in this project have made this a much better book than when it first arrived in their hands. I would also like to thank my senior colleagues in the Department of History, University of Utah, for reminding me of the profound and ongoing importance of feminism.

During the writing of this book I relied on the infinite generosity of Doris Fillion, Yves Sauvé, Patrick Gaillard, Tom Stillinger, and Disa Gambera. Thank you also to Cecelia Root for keeping me in her prayers.

Patti Hartman of the University of Arizona Press gave me important guidance from the moment she took on this project. Her clear and concise advice helped make this book into something people might want to read. Thank you also to Al Schroder and especially Ruth Steinberg for their editing.

In my house, faith came in mundane, practical activities like making pies. My mom Karen taught me that one must have faith that flour, water, and shortening can make a flaky crust. Without faith, one is tempted to add more water or more shortening, so that the ball of crumbs sticks together better; but if you do that, the crust turns out hard. It is not obvious that the crust will stick until it is already rolled out. I learned from her that given the right basic ingredients one must have faith that good will come out of what appears to be nothing. Without this faith I would have never begun to write this book, let alone finish it. Since his presence in my life, my mother's husband, Joseph Barletta, has only reinforced that faith. To my father, Leo Porter, I owe my affinity for history and the desire to discover the humanity and dignity in every story.

To my sister, Sara Porter, I dedicate all my hard labors. It has been through her example that I have learned to labor hard and to love hard, no matter the context.

Introduction

In 1896 a group of seamstresses in Mexico City wrote a letter to a women's journal in which they asked for support in their struggle against wage cuts that had led to "moral and material" suffering. The seamstresses nicely articulated two categories essential for understanding working women throughout the period of early industrialization in Mexico: morality, and the public discourse surrounding it, and material conditions. This book will trace the way these two categories shaped the history of working women in Mexico City. In 1879 the material conditions of working women situated them primarily in the female-dominated industries of cigarette and clothing production. By 1930 women worked in a wide variety of industries, not only those that were female dominated. This transformation of material conditions mirrored a transformation in public discourse. At the beginning of the period, clothing and cigarette production were perceived as women's work by the public. Female-dominated industries were understood as conducive to protecting female morality. Indeed, in the 1880s the lack of "respectable work for women" was thought to represent a threat to female honor and sexual morality. The Mexican Revolution ushered in new ways of speaking of working women in the public sphere and opened a space to speak of women as workers in terms less closely associated with morality. Nevertheless, material conditions transformed more rapidly than did cultural understandings of working women. The public discourse that saw factory work as compromising a woman's honor continued to inform labor relations well into the 1920s. However, the places where that discourse came into play shifted. Although the Federal Labor Law (1931) did not evoke morality when regulating conditions of work for women, as this book will show, on the factory floor morality remained a key category in shaping relations at work.

In 1879 Emiliano Busto published *Estadísticas de la República Mexi-*

tuna, a broad survey of the Mexican economy that included a special focus on Mexico City industry. His study marked a moment of transition that centered on the rise of industrial production in Mexico. Busto noted the benefits to the Mexican economy of mining and commercial agriculture. However, he saved his praise for industry, which benefited the country not only economically, he wrote, but in terms of "moral principals."[1] For Emiliano Busto, and for many Mexicans at the time, industrialization was simultaneously an economic and cultural event, with financial, political, and moral implications. To understand the relationship between gendered notions of morality and work, *Working Women in Mexico City* follows Emiliano Busto in his conception of industrialization as an economic and cultural process. However, while at the same time being sensitive to how historical actors conceived of industrialization, this book also takes a critical approach to the relationship between material conditions and the discourse of morality.[2]

The history of Mexican working women has been shaped by the particularities of Mexican industrialization. Porfirio Díaz ascended to the presidency in 1876, and under his leadership a series of incentives were passed to encourage investment in Mexico. In the post-independence period, political instability had hindered economic growth, especially in those sectors that had driven the colonial economy, mining and agriculture. Díaz and his followers sought to overcome political instability and a stagnating economy by facilitating economic investment, especially from abroad. Investors from Europe and the United States, who at the time sought new opportunities beyond the saturated markets of their own national borders, looked to Mexico. These investors were encouraged by the expansion of the Mexican railroad, the elimination of regional and national tariffs, and the favorable terms of investment offered by the Mexican government. Initially, foreign investment was concentrated in mining, which in turn spurred the growth of commercial agriculture. By 1890, investment in industrial production of consumer goods, which had begun in the 1830s, was expanding rapidly.[3]

Rapid economic expansion brought large numbers of women into Mexican manufactories and industrial production, although, as Margaret Towner shows, the number of women as a percentage of the economically active population actually declined with industrialization.[4] During the period 1895–1910, for example, this percentage went from 17 to 14 percent. Beneath this modest decline, important differences existed in women's employment.[5] The census category "industry," for example, included extractive industries, gas and electric workers, and other occupations that hired very few women. The category "transformation industries," on the other hand, included "workers in industrial establishments," manufactories, and the artisanal production of consumer goods. Nationally, the number of women in transformation industries jumped between 1895 and 1900, although by 1910 that number had dropped again, though not to 1895 levels. At the same time, the percentage of the economically active female population employed in transformation industries grew from 21 percent in 1895 to 26 percent in 1910. The number of women in industry also jumped between 1895 and 1900, but by 1910 had dropped, representing a 1 percent overall decline for the period.

Mexican industrialization was an uneven process, both in regional variation and the impact it had on women. A brief comparison of Mexico City with other regions of the country shows the differential impact of industrialization on women and gives us an idea of the parameters of this study. Industrialization was both a rural and urban phenomenon. In rural Mexico—for example, Morelos, Veracruz, Oaxaca, and Chiapas—the expansion of capitalist agricultural production forced many men and women off of the land. Mechanization of agricultural production provided more wage-earning opportunities for men than for women, the major exception being food processing where women sorted raw materials like coffee.[6] Not all industrialization in rural Mexico occurred in agricultural production, however. Investors established the first modern industrial textile factories in rural areas, often in former haciendas. In these factories employers hired mostly former male artisans and a small percentage of women.[7]

Urban industrialization differed from city to city. During the Porfiriato, Mexico City, Monterrey, and the geographical swath containing Puebla-Tlaxcala and Veracruz became the leading industrial centers of Mexico. These regions were little affected by the violence of the Revolution and so remained industrial leaders.[8] Throughout the period, Mexico City factories hired a greater percentage of women than in other cities. According to 1920 census data, Mexico City had the largest number of clothing, cigarette, knitwear, and silk textile factories. These were by and large female-dominated industries.[9] Clothing and cigarette factories had developed as female-dominated industries in the early nineteenth century, while silk textile and knitwear producers, in the absence of an artisanal tradition, had hired predominantly women when they set up shop in the 1880s and 1890s. In addition to large modern industrial factories, Mexico City had many small factories, artisanal workshops, and home production units. Mexico City also had the largest service sector, both in aggregate numbers and in rate of growth, beginning at the turn of the century.[10]

In comparison, industrialization in Monterrey, Nuevo León, was characterized by large-scale production in metal works, breweries, and carpentry, industries that collectively hired no more than a handful of women. Puebla textile factories tended to be larger than those in Mexico City, though they were fewer in number and hired fewer women.[11] Mexico City also had a greater diversity of small manufactories than Puebla.[12] Mixed economies like that of Mexico City have historically provided more work opportunities for women, which explains the migration of women to places like Mexico City or New York City, instead of Monterrey, Nuevo León, or Detroit, Michigan, where large industry offered more work opportunities for men.[13] The conclusions of this study, then, pertain above all to Mexico City. Its economy was marked by industries that tended to hire women, industries new to Mexico that could not depend upon a male artisanal tradition for workers, and diversity in the scale and organization of production.

Christine Stansell and Anna Clark have used the term *metropolitan industrialization* to describe early-nineteenth-century New York and London, respectively, and while I do not mean to make a strict comparison, reference to the term aids in understanding Mexico City.[14] Stansell and Clark use the term to describe economic development that is dependent upon a division of tasks rather than upon modern industrial technology, especially in the production of consumer goods. Such a division of labor allowed employers to assemble a variety of handicraft workers as low-wage labor under one roof. The arrangement well describes Mexico City cigarette manufactories and clothing producers, major employers of women. *Metropolitan industrialization* also included the street vendors, laundresses, and other women and men who greased the wheels of industrialization—by producing goods for demand not met by factory production, by distributing goods, and by taking up some of the domestic work left behind by working women. The industrialization of late-nineteenth-century Mexico City differed from that of New York and London in the early nineteenth century in that, by the 1890s, Mexico City was home to large, mechanized factories as well. All these types of work contributed to industrialization by the goods that were produced, workers' participation in the labor movement, and their presence in public discussions of working women. Thus, the subject of this book is women during industrialization, both those in factories and those beyond the factory walls.

How did cultural understandings of women and work figure in these material changes? The *obrera* (working woman) appeared sporadically in Mexico City newspapers before the 1870s. By the 1880s she had become an important topic of discussion. Women's habits of work, consumption, and socializing brought them into factories and public places in new ways. Newspapers printed articles that pitied the exploited female worker, expressed disdain for her habits, and mused about her family life. Other articles rallied in her favor when she strove to improve her lot, but also condemned her for some of the ways she chose to do so. Female street vendors, pickpockets, shoplifters, and prostitutes also inhabited Mexico City's streets. While we might not think of such women as occupying the same space as the obrera who worked in a factory, Mexican social commentators wrote about all of these women in similar terms that centered around notions of female weakness, both moral and material, in the struggle for survival.

These discussions were intimately intertwined with the evolution of class relations. As a material and cultural process, industrialization resulted from and gave new life to new relations of work, the rise of a class-bound society, and new places for women within class distinctions. John Lear estimates that the Mexico City middle class, consisting of bureaucrats, merchants, professionals, teachers, and the military, represented 22 percent of the economically active population.[15] The rhetoric of middle-class identity, however, reached beyond those whom we might argue belonged to it in a material sense. While scholars frequently discuss class as an aspect of materials conditions — occupation, salary, living standards — and, indeed, it is often treated as such in this study, class also functions on an ideological level.[16] Many Mexicans, from *artesanos cultos* (artisans who fared well, despite increasing rates of proletarianization) to the wife of the President Porfirio Díaz, participated in this conversation about the middle class. As Mexicans sought to define the contours of middle-class identity, they utilized discussions of working women to do so.[17]

These class-based discussions were important because they created new paradigms within which working women interacted with co-workers, employers, and representatives of the Mexican government. In effect, gender functioned as a marker of class distinction in these discussions. For example, the term *respectability* identified an occupation as middle class. It thereby placed virtue and gender at the center of class distinction. At the same time, these discussions also shaped conceptions of working women. Because gender delimited the parameters of the middle class, women, as a discursive category, fit only within certain occupations deemed virtuous in the public eye. Thus, within public discourse virtue became central to female worker identity. During the 1910s and 1920s, the Mexican government attempted to ameliorate the adverse effects of industrialization on women, and did so informed by those categories of understanding that emerged at the turn of the century.

Cultural understandings of women have a well-developed place within Latin American historiography. Historians have long understood gender both in oppositional terms—male versus female—and as identifying normative behaviors that include a series of qualities that define masculinity and femininity. The *macho* is defined by his relationship to women, and by his relationship to other men. So, too, the *female* is defined by qualities that distinguish her from men, and from other women who do not conform to societal norms. For Latin America, scholars have identified these norms as self-denial, motherhood, chastity, religious piety, and domesticity. In 1973 Evelyn P. Stevens first used the term *marianismo* to describe normative femininity, tracing its cultural origins to the veneration of the Virgin Mary and the culture of chastity. Since Stevens's article, scholars have debated the basis of her argument, the gap between normative and lived femininity, and the similarities of marianismo to the "cult of domesticity" in the United States.[18] Scholars who eschew the term *marianismo* continue to speak of "gender right," "gender reciprocity," "gender traditionalism," and the honor/shame code, all of which contain both an oppositional and normative model of gender.[19]

While analytically separate, both oppositional and normative definitions of gender were operative in the creation of norms for women in late-nineteenth- and early-twentieth-century Mexico. In Mexico, as well as the United States and Europe, oppositional gender relations have been invoked to explain occupational segregation by sex, wage differentials, and the distribution of rights and resources.[20] These have emerged alongside the second, related aspect of gender ideology—normative femininity—which also informed workplace discipline and state legitimation of rights. Men and women have identified with or invoked both normative and oppositional modes of understanding gender, regardless of their own gender.[21] While analytically separate, the intimate relationship between the two modes of understanding gender meant that a series of words and phrases created a web of meaning that entangled Mexico City working women. In turn-of-the-century Mexico, these words and phrases were rooted in an understanding of industrialization as a material and moral event. Thus, different words contained meanings that connoted both moral and material states: *debilidad* (debility and weakness), *deseo* (desire), and *honor*.

While not all of these words have been explored by historians, an extensive literature on honor has been developed, for both the colonial and modern periods of Latin American history. The term *honor* has been so persistent and pervasive that its force is diminished if it is not grounded in a specific time and context. The term has been used in personal relationships and in public efforts to establish hierarchy, to claim and delimit rights, and to define the meaning of nation and modernity.[22] I argue that in late-nineteenth- and early-twentieth-century Mexico working women acted within a discourse of female honor, the meaning of which was tied to shifts in women's participation in the workforce. As increasing numbers of women worked in mixed-sex environments, the factory (and work spaces more generally) came to represent a sexualized space. And female honor was one of the concepts, along with others mentioned above, used to map out the space available to women in the work environment.

Recent studies have painted a rich picture of Mexico City in this period as a community of men and women, workers, criminals, bourgeois voyeurs, and reformers.[23] In the years between 1880 and 1930 Mexico underwent profound changes in demographics, spatial organization, relations of work, and politics. Some have identified those changes with "modernization," "imaginings of the nation," or the Revolution of 1910. The history of working women in Mexico City clearly relates to these processes. But no single force affected the work women could or could not do quite so much as industrialization. And where women labored shaped a particular cultural understanding of working women, influenced by the nature of the work they performed, how they organized, and how people talked about them. Furthermore, public discussions regarding working women associated changing gender roles directly with industrialization. Industrialization is, therefore, the lens through which this study views the working women of Mexico City. Like other recent studies, then, this book examines the Mexican Revolution from the perspective of other processes important to inhabitants of the city.

A note about what constitutes Mexico City. A study of Mexico City could be about geographical space, political power, or community, imagined or otherwise. John Lear, Mauricio Tenorio, and others have theorized and described the role of space and community in Mexico City society and politics.[24] This study differs from theirs in that, given its focus on working women, it considers Mexico City in a loose sense, less geo-graphical and more as a cluster of factories, neighborhoods, and conver-sations about the women who lived and worked there. Given this con-cern, the geography of this study encompasses the central areas of the Alameda, southwest of the Alameda, Guerrero, and the swath of land reaching around the northeast and southern portions of the city that be-came the heart of industrial and working-class Mexico City. At times it also includes workers from suburbs like Contreras, who joined Mexico City women in their protests. But beyond geography, this study includes those people who inhabited women's world of work and who participated in conversations about that work.

The geography of this study is also defined as a space of engagement, or public sphere. Historians, inspired by Jürgen Habermas, have de-bated what constitutes the public sphere, taking as a baseline the coming together of individuals to form opinion regarding issues of common con-cern.[25] As François-Xavier Guerra and others have argued for eighteenth-century Hispanic America, it was not only in the press but also in the streets and public plazas that different groups carved a place for them-selves in the public sphere. Mary P. Ryan has shown that in the nine-teenth century this was particularly the case for disenfranchised groups, like middle-class women, in the United States.[26] It is important here to distinguish between the "public sphere" as employed by historians in-spired by Habermas and its use by historians of women, for although they may be related, they are not the same thing.[27] For women's histori-ans associate the public sphere with the early stages of industrialization, the separation of home and work, and the emergence of a middle class. For these historians the public sphere encompasses a wide range of places and activities that historically have been considered gendered masculine. The Habermasian public sphere includes physical places where people come together—the press, coffee houses, salons—but more importantly, it represents the forming of public opinion. In late-nineteenth- and early-twentieth-century Mexico City, working women made streets and plazas, as well as the press, the space of that engagement.

Some historians argue that, historically, participation in the public sphere has been denied to working women, that while male workers have held property in their labor, women have held property only in the virtue of their person.[28] I argue that it was precisely based on conceptions of female virtue that Mexican working women legitimated a place for them-selves within the public sphere. And furthermore, they participated in creating the language of that engagement, the language that legitimated their voice as relevant to public opinion. In this regard, I have adopted the concept of "paradigm of reason," as elaborated by Geoff Eley, as necessary for participation in the public sphere.[29] The language of morality, honor, and female nature gave "reason" to and facilitated working women's entrance into the public sphere, both as a legitimating force and for the connections with the wider public it allowed them to make.

A dichotomized paradigm of femininity provided working women the space to do so. In his study of Northern Mexico, William French has succinctly described the two poles of this paradigm of femininity as inhabited by "prostitutes and guardian angels."[30] Within this dichotomized vision, as women left the private sphere they left behind all that was associated with inhabiting that sphere, especially sexual morality. Working within the paradigm, one might argue that the obrera entered into the struggle for survival and therefore into the public realm, and that in so doing she put at risk that which defined her as a woman. And yet, within this dichotomized vision of femininity the obrera was neither figuratively nor literally a prostitute. Rather, she embodied the ideological contradictions of industrialization. Industrialization heightened the distinction between the public and private spheres while at the same time creating the female worker. When women entered factories in the 1880s, they inhabited a space that had been construed as masculine. Within public discourse, the "mixing of the sexes" that resulted posed a danger to female sexual morality and respectability. However, many observers also recognized the need of women to work and sought to protect their rights as workers. Those rights were defined as both economic and moral.

The Mexican Revolution occasioned a shift in the discourse of female morality. Women's presence in the work force and as labor organizers influenced the relative power of the language of female morality. Public discussion of working women focused less on morality and more on the rights of workers generally, established in the 1917 Constitution, and on motherhood.[31] Though the power of morality in the public sphere declined, it did not disappear entirely. It is in this regard that the Mexican Revolution does not represent a pivotal moment, for as women went to work they were accompanied by discursive constructions of working women. Mexican working women had to negotiate factory discipline informed by normative femininity. This book observes Mexican women in their world of work and shows how some women accepted the concept of honor as relevant to their rights as workers, yet also argued against sexual morality as the basis of that honor. Still other women spoke of female morality as inclusive of publicness, thus countering upper-class conceptions of separate spheres as essential to female honor. Despite the different positions taken by working women, a discourse of female sexual morality and honor became a language or way of talking about social relationships that set out the central terms by which interaction occurred.

Thus, discourse consists of language and of how that language resonates with, shapes, and is shaped by points of coincidence in politics, work relations, and labor organizing. Configurations of words and phrases, such as "respectable occupation," "morality," or "honor," resonated with individual acts and collective movements. William Roseberry qualified the relative place of discourse in a way that reflects the approach I take in this book when he wrote that people resist words, but that those words are stand-ins for larger social, material, and political power relations.[32] When women resisted the discourse of female sexual morality at work, they engaged in a larger process of defining their rights as working women. Furthermore, while discourse may shape the terms of many social relations, material conditions—such as women's disadvantaged position in the workforce—gave coercive power to discourse.

Entering and Exiting the Archives: Sources

As a historian, I enter and exit the archives, as do the people of whom I write. What I can claim to know as a result of my comings and goings is dependent upon the processes by which the people I write about came to leave their mark on the written record. Often that mark was made only in fragments. The research I conducted for this book is the result of casting a wide net, and my catch is a part of the history I tell. I combine published and unpublished censuses, newspapers, and government documents generated in the inspection of factories and the mediation of conflicts. None of these sources extend throughout the entire period under consideration. Certainly, this limits what kinds of arguments I can put forth. However, the stringing together of these different sources is suggestive of the changing means of mediating social relations in Mexico. Just one example: whereas during the Porfiriato working women engaged the public via the press (among other places), after 1911 much of this engagement was redirected through the newly formed Department of Labor. Thus, women's engagement was rechanneled from the public sphere to a government institution, and yet women continued to utilize a discourse of female morality in making their claims.

While each chapter that follows includes a discussion of sources, two further points are worth mentioning here. First, whereas other studies of Latin American working women rely on oral history, given the time period under consideration, this book is based entirely on archival material.[33] Although letters and petitions may not provide the voice of working women themselves, they are the only access we have to these women. Historians have been rightly hesitant to claim that such sources provide a "true" voice of these women. They point to the shaky handwriting of petitioners, which reveals the mediation of a public scribe, or to the lack of power of petitioners. How public scribes shaped the words of petitioners is unclear; nevertheless, petitions written in the same hand used the same language as those that were not. Regardless, this book takes petitions as evidence of the language used by working women, a representation, at least, of language that reflected both their material conditions and the rhetorical possibilities available to them. Second, the use of censuses to write labor history has come increasingly under question and yet remains an important tool for those historians, like myself, who hope to write both social and cultural history.[34] This book takes statistics both as representation and as evidence of actual events. This is particularly the case with chapter 1, which charts transformations in the workforce based on the numbers contained in industrial censuses, while also telling a story of the cultural categories that informed the creation of those documents. Rather than undermining the argument based on taking statistics at face value, by questioning the categories of the census, I reinforce my assertion that by the time of Department of Labor investigations in the early 1910s Mexicans had come to think of working women as much more problematic participants in industrial labor than in the time of Emiliano Busto in 1879.

Finally, I acknowledge two absences in this book. First, ethnicity appears only in passing. The sources I consulted rarely raised ethnicity in relation to working women. Photographs from the period show physical differences among subjects that might have been interpreted as racial differences, but how that may have played out in regard to working women is not clear. The absence of any substantial discussion of race is significant in and of itself, for it suggests the power of class to delineate distinctions that in other places and times were more closely associated with race.[35] Second, domestic service provided a major source of employment for women in Mexico City.[36] However, these women appeared infrequently in newspapers, workplace census materials, and petitions. Furthermore, despite what the reality may have been, public discourse did not construe domestics as vulnerable to the same threats as women who worked in factories. The employment of domestics was construed as a private, not public space. Given these circumstances, the claims I make regarding working women are qualified by the absence of domestics.

Chapter Organization

The chapters in this book are organized thematically, each evolving with an emphasis on change over time. The thematic organization reflects my argument regarding cause and effect, which could be described as a revised materialism. Imputing worker consciousness from objective conditions such as occupation and wages has been rightly discredited as overly simplistic. I do, however, attribute historical force to material conditions. Transformations in the sphere of economic production and class formation gave rise to a discourse that in turn informed those same processes. Simply stated, I examine how, despite changing material conditions, the past is carried forward.[37] In 1879 Mexico City women worked in a limited number of occupations, many in female-dominated manufactories. Within public discussions, this occupational segmentation of the work force was understood as appropriately safeguarding female sexual morality. By 1890, economic investment in Mexico City transformed production so that increasing numbers of women worked in mixed-sex factories, as well as in the still female-dominated clothing industry. In seeking to understand this transformation, observers both relied on older notions of female respectability and work, and developed new understandings that emerged within the context of changes in the organization of production, women's labor activism, and the Mexican Revolution. Thus, I argue that economic structures, and the political and cultural formations that accompany them, are the product of both the past and adjustments to change over time. Instead of disappearing, gender discourse shifted as Mexicans attempted to interpret transformations in the economy, class relations, and women's position in the work force.

Chapter 1 examines the shifts in working women's position in the Mexico City industrial work force from 1879 to 1930. In 1879 the women who appeared in industrial census material worked primarily in tobacco processing and clothing production, plus a handful of occupations in both factory and handicraft production of consumer goods. The chapter argues that the rapid economic development that began in 1890 built upon this gendered organization of production and gave form to occupational segregation, sex-typing of occupations, and gendered wage differentials. The Mexican Revolution did not significantly alter the industrial base established at this time; however, by about 1926 women declined as a percentage of the industrial work force. Throughout the period, women's work was marked by occupational segregation, gendered wage differentials, and the persistent abuse of apprenticeships.

This material process was accompanied by a shift in cultural understandings of working women, the subject of chapter 2. Accompanying this transformation of the Mexico City workforce, a constellation of cultural conceptions of the female worker evolved centering on female weaknesses, both moral and material, and appropriate practices of femininity in the public spheres of work and the streets. Many of these concepts continued to hold sway despite the increasing recognition of the rights of working women that occurred with the Mexican Revolution of 1910.

Both the position of women in the workforce and cultural understandings of work shaped women's labor organizing — the subject of chapters 3 and 4. Chapter 3 focuses on the Porfiriato and shows how female-dominated industries gave life to a vibrant, work-centered culture for women. It argues that despite similarities between men's and women's organizational activities, working women's language of engagement in the public sphere was bound up with conceptions of female morality. Chapter 4 examines women's labor organizing after 1910 and shows how the voices of women in the public sphere became stronger as they joined with the larger working-class movement, and more muted in their capacity to speak to the specificity of working women.

If public discourse construed the factory as posing a threat to female sexuality and honor (chapter 2), and if that discourse shaped women's activism (chapters 3 and 4), what was the place of sexuality, sexual morality, and honor at work? Chapter 5 examines how Mexican working women fought against the insertion of sexuality into work relations and the connection made, and used against them, between private morality and their rights as workers. While the Mexican Revolution represented a shift in the formal power of the language of morality in the public sphere, the relevance of morality within the factory persisted. This chapter also discusses the possible means by which women defended their rights as workers, utilizing the language of honor and sexual morality. In so doing, these women participated in creating a consciousness unique to working women.

Chapter 6 examines the working conditions of *vendedoras* (female vendors), women who worked at the physical and symbolic forefront of public space, as their sales literally put them in the street. As the government attempted to deal with changes in Mexico City wrought by industrialization, it marginalized many vendedoras from a legal means of making a living. Discursive constructions of female sexual morality and the contingent rights of women in public shaped material conditions of work on the streets just as they did in the factory. In the letters they wrote to city officials, vendedoras articulated an identity that, like other working women, refuted the link made between sexual morality and legal rights.

Chapter 7 examines the evolution of conceptions of the female worker within Mexican government institutions and in legislation between 1880 and 1931. While Porfirian law made little distinction between male and female workers, government support of mutual aid societies, charitable institutions, and vocational training did. Within these institutions, female sexual morality served a legitimating role in women's access to resources. With the Mexican Revolution the government legislated formal recognition of the rights of working women as mothers and passed a series of protective labor laws that, while not explicitly about female morality, had their origins in such concerns. This chapter also examines how the daily work of inspectors for the Department of Labor, established in 1911, was marked by cultural conceptions of working women based in privileging female sexual morality as relevant to women's rights as workers. In their investigations, inspectors worked out the meaning of women's work that informed a series of laws culminating in the Federal Labor Code (1931).

Two important themes run through these chapters. First, several chapters raise questions regarding the material, rhetorical, and historiographical relationship between Mexican women and the domestic sphere. Rather than denying the relevance of the public/private dichotomy, I hope to contribute to the reorientation of how we use it to explain working women's history.[38] The position of women in the domestic realm has been used to explain women's workforce participation, gender ideology, and the reasons for and methods of women's labor activism.[39] Women's position in the domestic sphere may have informed a woman's decision to seek waged labor, however I argue that which jobs they took was largely shaped by transformations in the workforce. Similarly, I elaborate on scholarship that has identified the powerful poles of discursive constructions of Mexican femininity as the public woman and the angel of the domestic sphere. The working woman as a discursive construction was located between these poles and embodied the evolution and contradictions of Mexican industrialization. The prominent role of foreign investors, the precarious position of the middle class, and the move of women from female-dominated work to work in mixed-sex settings all informed cultural constructions of the working woman. Finally, though women may have participated in consumer protest and seconded the strikes of male relatives, they also organized for reasons related not to protecting family and community but to protecting their rights as workers.[40]

Second, the coming and process of the Mexican Revolution has been a central orienting event in Mexican historiography. Recently, scholars have begun to suggest the defining importance of other events, events that temper our claims that the Revolution was as much of a watershed event as historians have claimed.[41] While the Revolution included a dramatic transformation in the relationship between workers and the state, for working women that relationship retained certain continuities with the past. Stephen Haber has demonstrated that industrial development initiated during the Porfiriato remained after the years of revolutionary upheaval.[42] The continuities across political change inherent to industrialization contributed to the persistent importance of honor, morality, and conceptions of female nature to the rights of working women. Though the Mexican Revolution has been positively associated with maternity benefits and protective labor legislation, much of this legislation was informed by the association of women with gendered conceptions of honor and morality that had developed in the previous two decades.[43] Furthermore, the relative significance of the Revolution is put into question by the existence of similar social reform movements, without Revolution, throughout the Americas.[44] The rhetoric of revolution did open a political space within which women formulated their demands in new terms; nevertheless, honor, morality, and female nature continued to inform their rights as workers and participants in the public sphere.

Working Women in Mexico City

CHAPTER 1

Women in Metropolitan
Industrialization

Between 1879 and 1930 women's participation in the Mexico City industrial workforce shifted from concentration in a small number of female-
dominated occupations to a wide range of work in mixed-sex factories.
By the 1890s working women occupied the city in new ways, transiting
the city streets to work in small workshops and factories. The following
story nicely illustrates how women came to be involved in that work, why
they took the jobs they did, and the material and cultural significance of
work for women.

In 1910 the Torres family—Marcela, who was expecting her seventh
child, her husband Agapito, and their six children—celebrated the cen-
tenary of Mexican Independence in their hometown of Guanajuato. Before Marcela gave birth to their seventh child, Agapito, a thirty-one-year-
old employee at La Valenciana mine, died. Marcela Bernal, now Viuda
de Torres, sent her two smallest boys to live with her sister and brother-
in-law. A woman on her own, with two working-age girls, she had a
choice to make: stay in Guanajuato—where virtually the only source of
non-agricultural employment for women was domestic work—or move
to the capital, Mexico City, where there were more work opportunities
for women. Some sixty years later, at seventy-seven years of age, Señora
Ignacia Torres Viuda de Alvarez recalled that her mother Marcela told
her and her sisters, "Well I'm sure not going to let you end up as maids."[1]

In Guanajuato, as in other provincial cities, people knew of the work
opportunities in Mexico City. In an interview in the 1970s, Torres Viuda
de Alvarez pointed out the uniqueness of factory work for women when
she recalled, "As far away as [Guanajuato], news arrived that in Mexico
City there was a factory where women worked." And so Marcela Bernal
Viuda de Torres and her daughters moved to Mexico City. After arriving
by train at Buenavista station, Bernal Viuda de Torres approached a *tor-*

tillera (tortilla vendor) and asked her about work for her girls. The next day the tortillera's niece took the eldest daughter to La Cigarrera Mexicana, a cigarette factory, where she found work. The second eldest daughter, Ignacia, initially worked in the tobacco factory as well, but went on to become a seamstress. Ignacia Torres Viuda de Alvarez described these events:

> Here [in Mexico City] there are factories; here there was a means of putting the young girls to work, so we came . . . and once here, this woman . . . took me to a [cigarette] factory, but I earned very little. She said: "No, at this rate you will not be able to help your mother." She then took me to other factories and to another, and we went from factory to factory. This woman spoke with the owner, the overseer, everyone, and finally she took me to a sewing shop that was on San Antonio Abad. . . . I did not know how to sew, but this man paid well and only hired poor yet honorable people, right? He paid two people who taught us; that was how I learned to sew pants, jackets, soldiers' uniforms. . . . In short, I remained a seamstress until I married.[2]

While the Torres women's story is illustrative, many aspects of it remain unexamined in Mexican historiography.

In seeking to understand the position of women in the Mexican work force, historians have either left unexplained why women worked where they did, or have echoed historical claims that women's jobs were, if not a natural extension of female domestic duties, certainly a logical one.[3] The domestic origins of women's occupations provided an explanation for the unskilled nature of women's work, the wages they received, and the value placed on that work. This chapter challenges the "natural" link between domestic skill and waged labor by examining the shape of the labor market and the cultural factors that circumscribed the choices women had when they went to look for work.[4] This shift in perspective moves us away from explanations which rely on seemingly unchanging cultural factors. For example, seamstresses did not sew in sweatshops because they learned to sew from their mothers, but because they were not allowed to be shoemakers, steelworkers, bakers, or printers. Ignacia Torres did not seek work in a clothing factory because she sewed at home; as she states in her own words, she learned to sew at work.

Upon arrival in the city, the possible jobs the Torres women might have found were the result of the historical development of Mexico City industry. Throughout the period 1879–1928 women remained approximately one-third of Mexico City's industrial work force; however, the nature of women's employment changed. In 1879 women were restricted to work as *costureras* (seamstresses), *cigarreras* (cigarette factory workers), and in no more than a handful of other occupations, such as thread spinners. This chapter argues that the rapid economic development that began in the 1890s was shaped, though not determined, by this positioning of women in the workforce. Women's declining participation in tobacco processing at the turn of the century coincided with their increased occupation in factories producing silk and woolen textiles, knitwear, and processed food. The gendered division of production was associated with wage differentials and the continued abuse of apprenticeships in the early 1920s. In going to work, women entered new spaces that included both the factory and the streets they traveled to get there.

"The Largest Proportion of Women"

Before examining the changing shape of the labor market into which women entered, it is worth discussing briefly why women went to work. Marcela Bernal Viuda de Torres sent her young daughter looking for work for several reasons. The death of her husband made her responsible for sustaining herself and her children. Faced with limited job possibilities in the provinces, Bernal Viuda de Torres moved to Mexico City. She would stay home and tend to the house while her older girls worked. While this particular combination of circumstances and decisions was not atypical, migration, civil status, parenting, and household maintenance strategies all played a role in women's entrance into waged labor.

Throughout the period 1880–1930 Mexico was primarily a rural country and most Mexicans worked in the countryside, whether on their own land or someone else's. Regional variation in economic development meant that women worked in varying capacities in the countryside. In provincial cities and rural towns, women worked in artisanal production and as domestics. Other women worked the land either for subsistence or to market crops such as coffee, corn, and wheat. Women's labor on haciendas has been more difficult to determine. Archival documents do not give a clear picture of women's work processing raw materials, preparing tortillas for workers, and working in agriculture under the authority of male family members. Despite such research difficulties, historians have found that the expansion of capitalist agriculture has decreased work opportunities for women. And while some *hacendados* hired women to process raw materials because they were "cheaper than machines," the limited employment opportunities in agriculture led women to migrate to urban areas in search of wage labor.[5]

Mexico City was one of the places where women were likely to migrate. Census takers in 1910 considered it noteworthy that "[the] entity with the largest proportion of women is the Federal District, which in the three censuses (1895, 1900, 1910) has remained in first place in this respect." The Federal District remained the census region with the largest percentage of women until 1921. Women made up roughly 53 percent of the Federal District population between 1895 and 1910. The percentage of women continued to increase throughout the violence of revolutionary battles and subsequent years of demographic recovery. While many women were born in Mexico City, like men, they were more likely to have migrated there. In the year 1900 a mere 33 percent of Federal District residents were native of that city. Most came from the surrounding state of Mexico (28 percent in 1900), as well as from Guanajuato, Hidalgo, Puebla, Querétaro, Michoacán, and Jalisco.[6]

Civil status influenced who sought work and where. Unmarried, widowed, and divorced women worked to support themselves, as well as to contribute to household income. The 1900 Federal District census found that 10 percent of the population was widowed, 79 percent of whom were women. In this same year, almost half the population of the Federal District was either single or widowed, a fact much lamented by municipal authorities. They compared what they termed "horrible" statistics to those of the United States and Europe, and found Mexico wanting.[7] Municipal authorities feared the lack of family integrity (that is, the lack of male heads of household) and identified it as the cause of social instability and an apparent "lack of morality" in Mexico. The number of widows in Mexico City was slightly higher than in the rest of the Mexican Republic. Nationwide, 8.92 percent of the population was widowed in 1895. The national figures had declined to 7.53 percent by the eve of the 1910 Revolution. The bloodshed of civil war resulted in an increase in the number of widows in Mexico, to 8.92 percent in 1921. Between 1900 and 1930 the number of widows continued to increase as the number of widowers decreased. In 1914 Venustiano Carranza amended the Constitution of 1857 and made divorce legal. Divorce statistics first appeared in the 1921 census, in which women made up 85 percent of divorced individuals. In 1930 the number of divorced women in Mexico City had declined to 62 percent of the total number of divorced individuals.[8]

While it is clear that single, widowed, and divorced women worked to support themselves, married women also worked. Lanny Thompson found that during the Porfiriato working-class families frequently required not only the wages of daughters but those of wives as well.[9] This pattern continued into the revolutionary period. A 1913 Department of Labor survey of three hundred working-class families found that the majority of women worked for a wage in addition to performing household work.[10] According to 1920s industrial census figures, married women continued to work. For example, at La Perfeccionada knitwear factory women were more likely to be married than the men. Twenty-four percent of the men and 33 percent of the women were married. By the 1930s Mexican women were less likely to work outside of the home. This should not overshadow the reality that married women continued to work in a wide range of industries. For example, 14 percent of seamstresses in Mexico City in the 1930s were married, and 9 percent were widowed.[11]

Married or single, many women were either the sole support of their families or crucial contributors to the household economy. Family arrangements varied, often with women supporting some combination of parents (especially a mother), siblings, and children. During the Porfiriato journalists reported on the large number of women who were supporting their mother and children.[12] Thompson, in his study of working-class neighborhoods, found that 23 percent of households consisted of a grouping of relatives, many of whom were "sisters, aunts, and grandmothers [who] make a life together."[13] After the Revolution government inspectors frequently commented on the number of female heads of household working in factories. Regarding a complaint made by a group of women who objected to being paid on Saturday evening, one inspector wrote, "You have in the shops . . . many widows for whom Sunday is barely long enough to clean their clothes and those of their children."[14] Throughout the 1920s inspectors reported on female heads of household, like seamstress Margarita Portella, who lived and worked out of her home with her two children and her mother. She earned 1 peso a day and paid 30 pesos a month in rent. Thus, women all across town lived and labored as the primary support of their households well into the 1930s.[15]

The Gendered Organization of Production
before 1879

Population census takers reported on the disproportionately large female population, journalists on the number of single female heads of household, and government factory inspectors on the plight of working widows, but the roots of women's circumscribed participation in the labor market lay in the shape of the work force, not in the life circumstances and choices of individual women. Guilds, which had restricted women's work until 1799, had a lasting impact on female employment. During the early nineteenth century women made up approximately one-fourth of the Mexico City work force, the majority working as domestics. However, Silvia Arrom found that between 1811 and 1848 domestics as a percentage of the female work force declined from 60 to 43 percent.[16] During this period, increasing numbers of women found work in manufacturing, commerce, and the service sector. The largest number of women labored in the production of goods not regulated by guilds: cigarettes and clothing.

Artisanal production, governed by guilds, was based on a gendered division of labor. Guild regulations admitted women into protected trades only if their deceased husbands had been members. And even in these cases, widows were required to transfer to a man all rights and responsibilities of membership, as well as the tools of the trade, within one year's time. The economic activities in which women participated in any significant numbers were excluded from guild status. Because work processing raw materials was not regulated, women salted hides for leather workers; spun wool, cotton, gold, and silver into thread for weavers; did finishing work in printed cloth factories; and starched clothing in laundries. A 1799 royal decree lifted guild restrictions on women and encouraged their participation in "labor and manufactures compatible with their strength and the decorum of their sex."[17] Arrom tells us that guild restrictions had a lasting impact on female employment. Twelve years later, in 1811, only 5 percent of working women engaged in trades that had been formerly regulated as guilds.[18]

Restrictions against women's participation in guilds made them attractive to employers in the tobacco industry. When the Spanish Crown established the Estanco del Tabaco (tobacco monopoly) in 1765, employers drew upon non-guild workers, a number of whom were registered as tribute-paying Indians, and eventually they came to hire primarily women.[19] Between 1795 and 1809 women went from 43 percent to 71 percent of Mexico City tobacco workers, becoming the largest group of tobacco workers in the country.[20] Most female workers were either single or widowed, while male workers were married. At roughly this time (1791), tobacco workers made up 55 percent of all manufactory workers in Mexico City, making women a substantial portion of the early working class.[21] By the early 1800s the Estanco del Tabaco had become the single largest employer of women and one of the most profitable manufactories, along with silver mining and textile production, in New Spain.

Cigarreras worked under what would come to be thought of as model conditions for women, both because of the large numbers of women employed and the way employers organized work with a concern for female sexual morality. From the moment workers arrived at work until they left at the end of the day, employers attempted to separate men and women. Male and female workers entered and exited through separate doors on opposite sides of the factory. The names of the streets onto which workers walked to and from work spoke to this practice. To this day, two Mexico City streets, Estanco de Mujeres and Estanco de Hombres, remind us of employers' efforts to shape working-class people's habits of work and socialization. Attesting both to colonial administrator's efforts to separate the sexes and resistance to those efforts, one administrator wrote, "In these factories there are a multitude of people of both sexes, and no matter how much supervision there is . . . who would not be embarrassed by the perverse and dangerous conversations among such licentious and debauched men and women who, although they leave work through different and separate doors, upon turning the corner join up again."[22]

Despite administrators' apparent lack of success at controlling workers on the street, they could do so within the factory. Administrators hired men and women for different jobs and divided work departments accordingly. Men carried tobacco throughout the factory, while women rolled tobacco. Cigarreras sat on benches at long wooden tables divided by partitions. At each workstation a woman stemmed and rolled tobacco leaves into cigars, or stemmed, cut, and rolled tobacco into cigarettes made with paper or leaves. The sexual division of activities extended beyond work to the lunch hour, when workers ate in separate lunchrooms.[23]

With Mexican independence, government officials debated the future status of royal monopolies, a future complicated by questions of female poverty. In early republican Mexico women of precarious economic status had limited options. Mexican government representatives expressed astonishment at the number of indigent women of "questionable morals," filling *recojimientos*—church-supported charitable institutions.[24] Support-ers of the tobacco monopoly argued that if the government retained con-trol of the manufactories it would provide a respectable means of keeping women off the street. The state monopoly survived independence but was dissolved in 1853. Termination of the monopoly resulted in the prolifera-tion of small cigar and cigarette factories in urban centers throughout the country, including Mexico City.

Though many women worked as cigarreras, the largest non-domestic occupation for women in the mid-nineteenth century was costurera. Women sewed clothing in a variety of arrangements: in countless small clothing businesses, for merchants who contracted outwork, as indepen-dent sewers, and as servants in convents. Sewing was divided along lines of gender, just as in Europe and the United States.[25] Men constructed garments for men, while women sewed clothing for women and children, linens, and some items for men such as neckwear. Both tailors and seam-stresses hired women to work as apprentices or as inexpensive labor to perform the less skilled tasks involved in their trade. Men performed the skilled work of cutting patterns and cloth and of fitting, while women did most of the sewing of seams and attaching of buttons. While *sas-tras* (female tailors) appeared occasionally in historical documentation, the majority of *sastres* (tailors) were men and the majority of women worked as costureras. According to the 1879 Mexico City industrial cen-sus women were 67 percent of sewers of military clothing and 100 percent of those employed in the production of shirts, linens, and mattresses (see table 1.1).

The first modern textile factories in Mexico hired male weavers, many former artisans, who then hired men, women, and children to work for them within the factory.[26] Most efforts to recruit workers, such as those of the Fomento de Artesanos established in 1843, focused on men. Puebla industrialist Estéban Antuñano published two pamphlets in the late 1830s in an effort to mobilize workers in the Puebla area. One pamphlet en-couraged male artisans to work in factories, while the other discussed the benefits of employing women. Despite such efforts, no more than 10 per-cent of Antuñano's workers were women.[27]

The division of labor that resulted from guild restrictions and gov-ernment monopoly reliance on female labor was manifest in the first in-dustrial census of Mexico City (see table 1.1). Emiliano Busto's 1879 cen-sus found that women constituted 37 percent of the adult industrial work force in the Federal District. Women were 32 percent of that workforce,

TABLE 1.1
Industrial Census, Federal District, 1879

Industry (Number of Establishments)	Women as a Percentage of All Adult Workers	Number of Men	Number of Women	Number of Children	Total
Mattresses (10)	100	0	60	0	60
Shirts and linens (14)	100	0	210	0	210
Shirts and linens, outwork (200)	100	0	200	0	200
Cigars and cigarettes (20)	85	357	2,100	250	2,707
Military clothing (4)	67	100	200	0	300
Matches (7)	50	70	70	0	140
Paper (7)	50	150	150	0	300
Textiles, cotton (4)	25	691	228	54	1,073
Textiles, wool (2)	25	235	80	70	385
Chocolate (11)	24	100	32	0	132
Shoemakers (80)	23	980	290	580	1,850
Hatmakers (79)	16	400	75	0	475
Acids and chemical products (2)	0	50	0	10	60
Arms and projectiles (1)	0	—	—	—	—
Bakeries (50)	0	765	0	0	765
Beds, metal and brass (4)	0	130	0	90	220
Beer (7)	0	60	0	10	70
Bookbinding (25)	0	100	0	50	150
Candles, wax, and tallow (27)	0	128	0	0	128

TABLE 1.1
Continued

Industry (Number of Establishments)	Women as a Percentage of All Adult Workers	Number of Men	Number of Women	Number of Children	Total
Cardboard boxes (3)	0	30	0	0	30
Carpentry, common (120)	0	300	0	100	400
Cars (6)	0	130	0	50	180
Copper works (5)	0	40	0	10	50
Fine crockery (3)	0	50	0	50	100
Gun carriages and cars (1)	0	68	0	0	68
Gunsmiths (7)	0	30	0	0	30
Metalworks (2)	0	80	0	20	100
Mint (1)	0	152	0	0	152
Needles (13)	0	12	0	0	12
Pastry shops (18)	0	100	0	8	108
Pharmacies (64)	0	94	0	0	92
Printing (33)	0	264	0	66	330
Seltzer water (4)	0	15	0	5	20
Starch (5)	0	30	0	0	30
Tailors (79)	0	513	0	0	513
Leather works (16)	0	600	0	40	640
Wheat mills (14)	0	320	0	0	320
Woodworkers (2)	0	40	0	10	50
Total		6,379	3,695	2,228	11,635
Women as a percentage of the adult work force					37

TABLE 1.1
Continued

Industry (Number of Establishments)	Women as a Percentage of All Adult Workers	Number of Men	Number of Women	Number of Children	Total
Women as a percentage of total work force					32

Source: Busto, *Estadística de la República Mexicana.*

if we include children as a category of worker not distinguished by gender. While women made up a significant percentage of workers, their employment continued to be restricted to a limited number of occupations.
Women worked in twelve of the thirty-eight census categories. The cigarette and clothing industries employed 70 percent of all female industrial
workers. Not only were women concentrated in a restricted number of
occupations, the industries in which they worked hired primarily women.
The cigarette and clothing industries were female-dominated, employing
women as 78 percent or more of their work force (85 percent of adult
workers). In the cigarette industry, the percentage of workers who were
female was probably higher, given that girls were hired as apprentices. At
the same time, women worked in some mixed-sex industries. Women were
half of all workers employed in smaller establishments like match and
paper manufactories, and they were a smaller though significant percentage of workers in the production of chocolate (24 percent), hats (16 percent), and shoes (23 percent). In these industries employers paid women
piece-rates to grind chocolate, sew hats, cut shoe leather, dip matches, and
gather rags to make paper. Of the adult workforce, Federal District textile
factories employed women as 25 to 31 percent of their workers (see tables
1.1 and 1.2), less than the 36 percent Dawn Keremetsis found nationwide,
and even less than the percentage of women in early textile production in
the United States and Europe.[28] Most other industries at this time were
closed to women (see table 1.1).

The results of the census reflect certain assumptions about what constituted industry in Mexico, and about women's work. In drawing up

TABLE 1.2

Composition of the Cotton Textile Factory Workforce, Federal District, 1879

Factory	Women as a Percentage of Adult Workers	Number of Women	Number of Men	Number of Children	Total
La Hormiga	29	100	250	50	400
La Magdalena	29	80	200	40	320
San Fernando	14	18	110	14	142
La Fama Montañesa	18	30	140	50	220
La Minerva	15	20	110	30	160
Mercado de Guerrero	17	50	250	60	360
El Aguila	32	60	125	40	225
Sin Nombre	40	10	15	5	30
Totals	31	368	1,200	289	1,857

Source: Busto, *Estadística de la República Mexicana*.

the census, Emiliano Busto included clothing produced as outwork, thus identifying the significant number of workers outside of the factory with the category "industry." The industries included in the census ranged from modern industrial textile factories to small-scale manufactories like hat making and bookbinding. The census also tells us something about how Busto may have thought about the differences in men and women's work. While Busto distinguished between men, women, and children in his count of workers, he did not distinguish between the wages of men and women. His reasons are not clearly stated; perhaps for Busto the concentration of women in female-dominated industries provided sufficient distinction, or perhaps he accepted gendered wage differentials as unremarkable. Thus, for Emiliano Busto, industry was not necessarily identified with modern machinery or a particular arrangement of production; and it included women, though not all of them, who worked both inside and outside factory walls.

The Expansion and Publicness of Work for Women, 1879–1910

During the Porfiriato, national economic growth transformed industry in Mexico City. The national railroad system, the banking industry, and legislation to promote development were all part of this transformation. Scarcely industrial in 1879, production was conducted primarily in small enterprises and a handful of modern factories. Most goods were consumed within the capital itself, although some manufacturers extended their markets beyond the city limits. Beginning in 1880 and accelerating dramatically in the 1890s, new factories appeared in Mexico City. While among the most industrialized regions of the country, the Mexico City economy was characterized by a variety of different forms of production.[29] The co-existence of workshops, manufactories, and factories in Mexico City brought women not only into new occupations but to new spaces within the city.

The expansion of industry meant a transformation of the spatial organization of production that brought qualitative changes both to the lives of Mexico City women and to those who observed them. While women had been present on the streets of Mexico City since the colonial era, their public presence increased significantly as central neighborhoods became populated with factories employing large numbers of women. Downtown, in the area southwest of the Alameda, and in the neighborhoods of San Antonio Abad and Guerrero there were numerous factories, often female-dominated, where women worked in an array of occupations. While some of these neighborhoods were clearly peopled with members of the working class, others, like Guerrero, were also home to Mexico City residents of precarious middle-class status. Julio Sesto, a Spanish resident of Mexico and a diplomat, noted the changing appearance of Mexico City in 1909 when he described the working women who made a "beautiful contrast" with the working men as they came and went on "the cigarrera . . . avenues."[30] He found it noteworthy to comment on "[the mix of] hats and shawls, the freemason's apron and hair combs, the hairy arms of men and the women's mother-of-pearl hands." For Sesto, changes associated with industrialization contained a change in gender relations in public space.

This mixing of "hats and shawls" was the result of new factories in central locations in the city. New tobacco processing factories brought more than a thousand cigarreras into the downtown area. In 1894 Ernesto Pugibet's El Buen Tono cigarette factory reopened in new premises in the city center. Situated to the southwest of the Alameda, just five blocks off Juárez Avenue, El Buen Tono sat on the Plaza San Juan, a central marketing center and the site of many comings and goings of city life. A sizeable enterprise, El Buen Tono dominated the neighborhood, not only due to its size and the hundreds of women it brought to the factory daily, but because of the advertisements on the exterior walls of the factory and the company's efforts to influence vendor practices in the market (see map).[31]

Several other large cigarette factories also brought women to the downtown area. Two blocks away from El Buen Tono, west of the Alameda on Puente de Alvarado Street, sat La Tabacalera Mexicana. And just southwest of the Zócalo, La Companía Cigarrera Mexicana filled an entire city block. In fact, the factory of La Companía Cigarrera Mexicana had engulfed a smaller city block earlier in its development, becoming the largest of cigarette manufactories. Smaller tobacco factories included La Principal on Zaragoza Street, and both La Rosa de Oro and Del Rio on Calzada de la Teja. In the smaller factories male and female workers lunched together in the patio or on the factory steps rather than in segregated facilities. Cigarreras working throughout the downtown area filled the streets as they began their workday at eight in the morning, and between six and eight in the evening when they left for home.

Still other industries opened up within the city. By 1910 there were twelve textile factories employing 5,088 workers in the Federal District. Among these were six new factories built within the city limits between 1884 and 1906. For example, La Carolina cotton textile and clothing factory opened in Colonia Guerrero in 1910 and by 1921 would come to employ more than two thousand workers. The silk textile and knitwear industries also brought women into Mexico City factory production. Swiss-born Hipólito Chambón built a silk *rebozo* and textile factory in 1880 in the ex-convent of Teresitas on Plaza Villamil. Chambón moved the factory to Fresno Street in 1894. In 1910 he employed 220 men and women. And eight hundred women made their way to La Perfeccionada knitwear factory after it was built in the 1890s in Colonia Obrera.[32]

Thousands of seamstresses worked throughout the city in a variety of circumstances. The Palacio de Hierro workshops, some of the largest, were located on beautiful, tree-lined Cinco de Febrero Street in the southern section of the city. The factory was built gradually after the turn of the century and came to encompass two city blocks. By the early 1920s the almost six hundred men and women who worked there made furniture tapestry, women's clothing, shirts, *passementerie* (gimp, lace, and bead

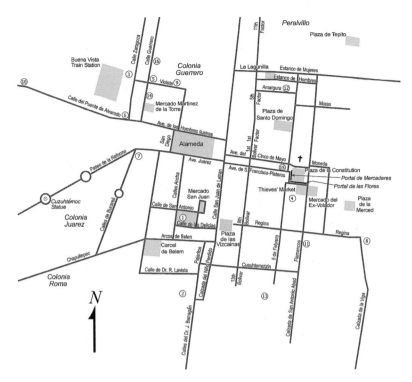

Map of Selected Industries, Mexico City, circa 1910

Key

1 El Buen Tono Cigarette Factory
2 La Perfeccionada Knitwear Factory
3 La Carolina Woolen Textiles
4 San Antonio Abad y Anexas Cotton Textile and Clothing Factories
5 Zolly Brothers Hat Factory
6 La Tabacalera Mexicana Cigarette Factory
7 La Companía Cigarrera Mexicana Cigarette Factory
8 La Victoria Woolen Mill
9 La Constancia Clothing Factory
10 Fábrica Chambón Silk Textile Factory
11 Cluster of Clothing Workshops
12 Cluster of Clothing Workshops
13 El Palacio de Hierro Workshops
14 La Concordia Clothing Factory
15 La Tampico Shirt Workshop
16 Fashionable Shirts and Knitwear
17 La Principal Cigarette Factory

and ribbon embroidery), hats, umbrellas, and textiles. Workers sewed on electric machinery, with the exception of women who sewed passementerie on pedal machines. Occupational segregation by sex kept men and women in separate workspaces. The Palacio de Hierro furniture shops, which employed mostly men, were located on the adjacent block to the north.[33]

The growth of female-dominated industries contributed to the visibility of working women. Downtown was filled with upscale dressmaker shops, clandestine sweatshops jammed into old buildings, and small living quarters where a woman might sew for relatives and acquaintances. In 1910 La Tampico clothing factory was established in Colonia Guerrero. At La Tampico over one hundred women worked to make ready-to-wear clothing on electric machinery. Converted from an apartment building into a factory, La Tampico occupied a three-story building. Hundreds of women worked just a half mile south of the Cathedral, along San Antonio Abad Street, where La Sinaloense, La Concordia, Fábrica de Corbatas, and other clothing producers employed anywhere from sixty to over two hundred costureras per establishment. These women, too, entered into an industrial environment. Just one example, La Concordia clothing factory was surrounded by its parent company Industrial San Antonio de Abad y Anexas, a major textile producer.[34]

Women worked not only in these larger factories but in small workshops as well. Around the corner from El Buen Tono were *pulquerías*, milk vendors, dressmakers, and small producers of candles, bread, charcoal, pottery, and shoes. Employers converted apartments and homes in the city center into work space, especially for sewing workshops, the largest of which included La Constancia and Zolly Brothers hat factory on Violeta Street in Colonia Guerrero. Small workshops had an element of chance to them. More than anything else they were an expression of an investor's concern for conserving money and space rather than plans for future expansion. The transformation of downtown dwellings into work places often meant uncomfortable and unhygienic working conditions, narrow corridors, decaying walls, and the overcrowding of workers. In such establishments, the sex-segregation of workers was not a priority. A woman might sit on a *petate* on the floor, pulling bastings or attaching buttons, her work illuminated by a single lightbulb hanging from the ceiling to warm the dark corner, while men would cut cloth at nearby tables.[35]

Women all across the city worked for wages at home, though the nature of their work also drew them into the streets. Even if their work was conducted in the home, seamstresses were responsible for picking up cut cloth at the factory and returning goods upon their completion. Other women worked as employees in shared apartments, rooms, or the common patio of their buildings, where fewer than a handful of women could work. In the face of possible regulation, most women claimed the other workers in their shops were family members or friends who merely helped them pass the time. Such was the case with Maria Becerríl, who claimed only to sew enough clothing to survive. Sara Guzmán combined running a sewing shop with selling doughnuts from her home. Some of these women earned very little. Angela Pineda, resident of Amagura (Bitterness) Street, earned fifty centavos a day. In their comings and goings, these women walked on the streets past workers lunching on factory steps, vendors selling their wares, and other women going to work.[36] And there were women who worked on the street. These were not vendors and street-hawkers, but women who sat on the steps of their home or small workshop, working late into the evening.[37]

Continuity and Change: 1895–1930

Margaret Towner has argued that industrialization, which she locates as having occurred in Mexico between 1895 and 1910, pushed women out of the work force.[38] Census data for Mexico City show high levels of female employment, although the data also show a decline in women workers as a percentage of the total industrial workforce. The 1910 population census reports that women made up 35 percent of the paid labor force, far above the national average of 12 percent. Industrial census material for the Federal District report a modest decline in women as a percentage of the workforce between 1879 and 1921, from approximately 32 to 28 percent.[39] These numbers should be regarded cautiously. As Mexican's ideas about industrialization changed, so too did censuses. Nevertheless, these numbers establish the significance of women as a percentage of industrial workers. That said, important shifts in women's work lay beneath the aggregate numbers.

Whereas in 1879 women had worked primarily in female-dominated industries, with the economic expansion of the 1890s they worked in an increasing variety of locations. Mexico experienced an economic crisis in 1907, but the industrial base established between 1890 and 1907 remained until a new wave of investment in industry in the 1940s.[40] How that industrial base was utilized influenced women's employment levels, wages, and conditions of work. During the 1910s and 1920s many tobacco, textile, and clothing factories continued to rely upon the technology that had been installed before 1907. Given the capacity for overproduction of much of Mexican industry, employers sought to increase the productivity of cigarreras and costureras, hiring women as inexpensive labor in the production of these and other consumer products. A closer look at three industrial occupations — cigarrera, costurera, and obrera — shows the declining role of women in the tobacco industry, but also the persistence of other female-dominated occupations, along with an expansion of mixed-sex workplaces that were shaped by the sex-typing of occupations.[41]

Cigarreras

The cigarette industry played an important role in the history of working women, both for how it figured symbolically in discussions of appropriate work for women, and, until the 1920s, for the substantial employment opportunities it provided. Throughout the Porfiriato cigarette work stood as an ideal employment for women because, as a female-dominated industry, it purportedly protected female morality. Despite its enviable reputation, efforts on the part of industrialists to dominate the market and increase worker productivity led to declining working conditions for cigarreras. The history of that decline is marked by employers' efforts to increase worker productivity, in part by relying on the long-established reputation of cigarette work as a female-dominated occupation and the cigarette factory as a moral space for female workers. Employer's efforts were reinforced by the increasing domination of production by three companies and the political ties among the stockholders in these companies. As a result, despite the fact that the cigarrera occupation was a lucrative one for women, they earned less than the men who increasingly came to dominate the industry.

The changing position of women in the tobacco industry occurred within the context of the more general transformation of the industry. During the late 1890s and early 1900s, cigarette factory owners sought to expand production and dominate the market. They enlarged their facilities and installed imported machinery from Germany and the United States. This enabled them to introduce low-cost, machine-produced products that quickly outsold hand-rolled cigarettes and cigars. Companies advertised their products by painting murals on the sides of buildings, taking out newspaper advertisements, and by participating in social

FIGURE 1.1
"Smoke number 12. There is no better pleasure."
Lupe Velez, El Buen Tono advertisement, 1926.
Source: Fototeca Nacional, Mexico City.

events. El Buen Tono's advertising campaign in the 1910s and 1920s featured well-known actresses and singers, who lounged in coy poses, bedecked in the latest fashions while smoking delicate cigarettes (see figure 1.1).[42] The combined effect of increased capital investment, advertising, and expansion of the market led to an increase in production. Between 1877 and 1892 annual production in the Federal District reached 23 million boxes of cigarettes. Production jumped from 108 million boxes in 1899 to 277 million boxes in 1911.[43]

Between 1890 and 1926 three companies came to dominate the production of tobacco products: El Buen Tono, La Tabacalera Mexicana, and La Cigarrera Mexicana. This domination was facilitated by the formation of joint-stock companies made up of Mexican, French, and Spanish investors beginning in the 1890s. For example, El Buen Tono, established as a family enterprise by Ernesto Pugibet in 1875, was reorganized as a joint-stock company in 1894. This reorganization tied Pugibet to Enrique Tron, owner of the Palacio de Hierro clothing workshops; Pablo Macedo, president of the Mexican Congress; and Manuel González Cosío, Secretary of War.[44] Then, in 1906, Pugibet, the owner of El Buen Tono, purchased the major interest in La Cigarrera Mexicana, further reducing competition. Combined, the two companies controlled over 60 percent of the national market. By the 1890s such market domination had led to the closure of smaller producers such as Moro Muzo, El César, El Faro, El Borrego, El Modelo, El Premio, La Niña, La India, and La Sultana. By the first decade of the twentieth century, the number of tobacco factories had declined from 43 to 14. These closures put hundreds of women out of work.[45]

Within the context of increasing competition, employers raised worker productivity. They were able to exert pressure on cigarreras in part because it was generally agreed that cigarette production was women's work. This identification was the result of several factors. To begin with, the industry had developed within a sex-segmented labor market. As it was one of the few occupations available to them, the many potential women workers competed for a limited number of jobs. By the 1890s, many Mexicans recognized that limited employment options for women had caused a successive decline in wages. On the occasion of a strike at El Premio cigarette factory in 1893, a journalist for *La Convención Radical Obrera* wrote: "The cigarrera, who has not been able to break this circle in which she has been circumscribed since a most tender age, because she has not been considered apt for any other form of work, has had to suffer the progressive decline of her wages, to such an extent that it is almost impossible for her to survive, and this, with such admirable patience that it causes astonishment."[46] The journalist recognized that stereotypes about appropriate work for women limited not only their options but their earning potential as well. One can only imagine that these same limited work options would have also explained women's "patience."

Cigarette work was identified as women's work because of the work culture that existed within the factory. Separation of the sexes had existed during the colonial era, and it persisted into the late nineteenth century, albeit not in its earlier form. For example, at El Buen Tono only women worked in pressing, grading, sorting, and rolling, jobs which relegated them to all-female spaces. During the 1890s much of this work was performed on newly installed machinery, but it continued to be dominated by women. At El Buen Tono most cigarreras worked in two large rooms: one with 19 machines that was dedicated to low-wage work (cleaning, separat-

FIGURE 1.2

El Buen Tono Cigarette Company, wrapping room. Source: Figueroa
Domenech, *Guía general desciptiva de la República Mexicana*, vol. 1.

ing, and stripping), and another containing 120 recently imported *Decouflé*
cigarette machines. These rooms looked out onto an interior passageway
that had been named for Porfirio Díaz. Meanwhile, men worked in the
lithography, carpentry, and paper box shops, and in the large bodegas
where goods were stored.

The identification of cigarette work with women was also reinforced
in discussions about that work. An 1899 government-sponsored guide to
industry displayed a photograph of El Buen Tono to show off the interior
of a Mexican factory (see figure 1.2). José Figueroa Domenech, author
of the guide, highlighted the female-dominated environment at El Buen
Tono when he wrote: "The machines move silently, and what is more as-
tonishing is that the hundreds of female tongues that belong to the many
girls who make the cigarettes, also remain silent, as if it were not a characteristic of women to be chatty, and as if an air of strict discipline permeated
the workshops."[47] He also praised the two factory schools for workers'
children, the showers which workers were allowed to use three times a

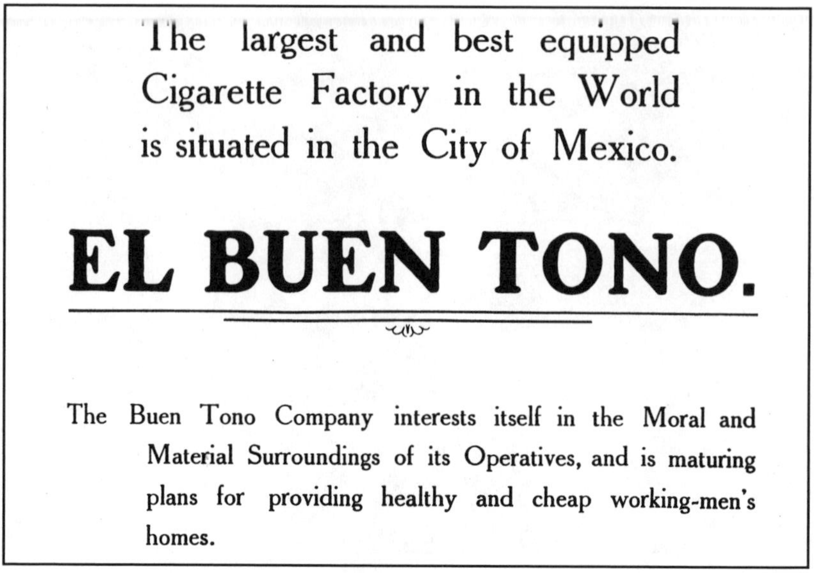

FIGURE 1.3
Advertisement for El Buen Tono. Source: México, Department of Finance,
The Mexican Yearbook . . . 1912.

week, the pharmacy, the company doctor, and the Catholic church which women were expected to attend.

Throughout the 1910s and 1920s, management continued to promote El Buen Tono as an establishment that protected worker morality, which included separation of the sexes. An advertisement in *The Mexican Yearbook*, a publication of the Mexican Chamber of Commerce intended for a national and international readership, relied on this image as a means of promoting the cigarette manufacturing business (see figure 1.3). This gendered organization of work persisted into the 1920s. Men worked in a separate department of the factory drying tobacco. Women stripped the dry tobacco, which was then transported by men to the main room of the factory. Whereas earlier women had shredded, bunched, and rolled the tobacco by hand, in the 1920s they did this work by machine.[48] Each woman had her own mark that she put on the cigars she rolled so that her work could be properly accounted for. Male workers continued to manufacture the labels and boxes in the paper box and lithography departments, as well as the adhesive for the labels. Male mechanics kept the machines in running order.[49]

Industrialists' desire for greater control of the market led them to de-

mand greater worker productivity, which threatened the viability of cigarette work for women. The tobacco industry stagnated between 1877 and
1892, and in order to compensate for losses management either reduced
wages outright, or more frequently raised production quotas.[50] In 1881
cigarreras and management agreed upon a wage of 4 reales for every 2,185
cigars produced. Quotas reached 2,400 in early 1885, and later that year
management raised them again. Some factories attempted to raise quotas
to 2,600, and others up to 3,200, while at the same time reducing salaries
from 4 reales to 3 reales.[51] The protests occasioned by increasing production quotas are discussed in more detail in chapter 3.

Beginning in the 1880s employers repeatedly sought to undercut the
value of cigarette work by hiring cheap, unskilled labor. In a reversal of
the more familiar story of women undercutting skilled male labor, in 1885
employers utilized men to undercut skilled female labor. Because the tobacco industry had been considered a female work space since the early
nineteenth century, employers could hire male labor to work in separate
departments, in which different conditions of work prevailed. El Buen
Tono and other factories hired captive and free male labor at lower wages
and higher production quotas, progressively laying off the higher-paid
cigarreras.[52] As a result, in 1895 many employers were paying the same
wages as they had paid in 1885. Even with these worsening conditions,
overseers also levied fines on workers, further reducing wages by 12 to 15
percent.[53] As a result of these processes, between 1879 and 1921 the number of women as a percentage of Mexico City tobacco workers declined,
from 85 percent to 68 percent of adult workers, and by 1929 women represented only 52 percent of the workforce in cigarette production (see
tables 1.3 and 1.4).[54]

Despite the fact that in the 1890s men had been hired to undercut
women's wages, by the 1920s men's wages had risen above women's. This
was due in part to the efforts of unionized labor, a topic discussed in chapter 4. A 1927 national study found that male cigarette employees earned
3.9 pesos to 2.6 pesos for cigarreras. Women continued to dominate the
poorly paid cornhusk cigarette industry, where they were 96 percent of
all workers. These women's wages were 63 percent of what cigarreras
earned in the paper-wrapped cigarette industry. The 21 percent of women
who worked in cigar production earned less than either the male cigar
makers or the cigarreras (see table 1.4).[55] Despite the decline in work
opportunities in the tobacco industry, wages in the Mexico City manufactories continued to be considerably higher than wages in the prov-

TABLE 1.3
Women as a Percentage of the Adult Workforce, Selected Industries, Federal District, 1921

Type of Factory	Percentage of Women
Baked goods/pastries	44
Bakery	5
Barbershops	3
Baths	34
Beauty salons	98
Beds	16
Bookbinding	48
Breweries	0
Brushes	48
Butchers	0
Cabinetmaking	25
Candles	17
Cardboard	34
Cardboard boxes	55
Cards	62
Carpentry shops	0
Cigarettes	68
Cloth and thread textiles	35
Coal and firewood depositories	0
Cooperage	0
Dairies, goats' milk	0
Dry cleaners	68
Foundries and metal works	0
Furniture making	3
Garages	0
Glass	0
Hats	41
Inhumations	3
Jewels and watches	14
Knitwear	95

TABLE 1.3
Continued

Type of Factory	Percentage of Women
Laboratories	24
Lamp factories	23
Laundries	44
Leather works	0
Lithography	18
Matches	71
Mattresses	43
Mechanics shops	0
Mills, coffee	36
Mills, grain	0
Mills, nixtamal	44
Neckwear	95
Needles	0
Newspapers	4
Oils	0
Paint	0
Passementerie	72
Perfume	73
Petates	13
Pianos and musical instruments	3
Plaster of Paris	0
Plumbing	17
Pottery	17
Preserved foods	60
Printing press	25
Rag	51
Rebozos	76
Restaurants *(fondas)*	78
Shoe factories	17
Shoe shops	14
Soap	25

TABLE 1.3

Continued

Type of Factory	Percentage of Women
Sweets	54
Tailors	12
Tanning	6
Thread	62
Tin cans	0
Tinsmiths	0
Tortillerías	99
Transportation	0
Umbrellas	85
Upholstery shops	19
Vulcanization	40
Wine and alcohol	12
Woodworking	0
Total*	25

Source: Censo Obrero, Distrito Federal, AGN, RT618: 1 (1921).

*Total is for entire census and includes categories not listed here.

inces. In addition, cigarreras earned more than many other female factory workers. The women who remained in cigarette production in the 1920s had worked there their entire lifetimes, attesting to the relative desirability of the work. The decline of opportunities for work and of earnings for women in this industry meant a major shift in female work culture in Mexico City.

Costureras

The occupation of costurera remained the single largest occupation for women throughout the period under consideration, yet the nature of that work changed with industrialization. The conditions the costureras labored under became increasingly associated with the factory. The transformation of "the needle trades" began with the production of ready-to-wear clothing by government contractors in the late nineteenth cen-

TABLE 1.4
Gendered Composition of the Workforce and
Wage Differentials, Federal District, 1929

Industry	Number of Men Employed	Male Wages (Pesos)	Number of Women Employed	Female Wages (Pesos)	Women as a Percentage of All Workers	Women's Wages as a Percentage of Men's
Matches	346	2.33	1,012	2.07	75	89
Cigarettes	534	3.90	581	2.60	52	67
Men's shirts and intimate apparel	52	2.92	421	1.93	89	66
Sweets	263	2.31	277	1.37	51	60
Stockings/socks	77	2.75	263	2.00	77	73
Textiles/wool	420	3.37	227	2.50	35	74
Thread	102	2.53	221	2.12	68	84
Preserved food	60	2.29	218	1.16	78	51
Yarn	467	2.16	218	2.00	32	92
Shoes	553	2.42	181	1.83	25	76
Sweaters	89	2.56	139	1.87	61	73
Fine ceramics	355	2.72	133	1.32	27	49
Printing/ bookbinding	301	4.80	93	2.16	24	45
Paper bags	80	2.70	88	2.58	52	96
Textiles/cotton	1,411	2.75	83	2.44	6	89
Mattresses/ cushions	26	2.17	73	2.10	74	97
Handkerchiefs	37	2.25	53	1.50	59	67
Cardboard boxes	17	2.68	46	1.93	73	72
Umbrellas/ parasols	35	2.75	46	2.12	57	77
Garters/ suspenders	4	2.62	45	1.50	92	57
Buttons	61	2.25	45	2.00	42	89
Paper	250	3.00	45	2.75	15	92
Perfume/ toiletry	3	3	40	1.87	93	63
Pharmaceutics	5	2.33	22	1.83	81	79
Furniture	169	2.63	19	1.35	10	51

TABLE 1.4

Continued

Industry	Number of Men Employed	Male Wages (Pesos)	Number of Women Employed	Female Wages (Pesos)	Women as a Percentage of All Workers	Women's Wages as a Percentage of Men's
Matches	346	2.33	1,012	2.07	75	89
Tents/curtains	19	2.25	16	1.87	46	83
Chocolate	22	2.16	16	1.12	42	52
Paint/varnish	29	2.15	6	1.25	17	58
Bread/pastries	947	2.47	5	1.83	1	74
Tanneries	398	2.51	4	1.50	1	60
Soap	75	2.77	2	3.55	3	1.28
Cement products	293	4.31	0	—	—	—
Industrial machinery	42	3.30	0	—	—	—
Plumbing	81	3.08	0	—	—	—
Total*	10,247	2.59	5,567	1.42	35	55

Source: México, Secretaría de Comerico, Industria y Trabajo, *Monografía sobre el estado actual de la industria en México.*

* Totals include industries not listed in the table.

tury. By the first decade of the twentieth century women were working as seamstresses in the clothing, knitwear, mattress, and other consumer goods industries. Gender divisions of labor evident in the late nineteenth century continued to shape the evolution of the industry. Women worked as seamstresses and low-wage apprentices in domestic production, as out-workers contracted by factories, in small and large workshops, and in factories. Sex-typing of jobs, extended periods of apprenticeship, and low wages characterized that work.

The expansion of the clothing industry in the late nineteenth century was intimately tied to the granting of exclusive government contracts for the production of military apparel *(munición)*. With the expansion of the police and military under Porfirio Díaz, demand grew for ready-made uniforms and military goods like tents. In order to meet this demand, as early as 1877 the Secretary of War and Marine granted exclusive rights for the production of munición.[56] In the 1890s a Señor de la Barrera held the contract. By 1901 he had passed it on to Ricardo Otero, who was soon the owner of one of the largest clothing factories in Mexico City, La Sinaloense.[57] Señor Otero's success suggests there was a close relationship between the development of military and civilian ready-to-wear clothing production in Mexico. Exclusive production rights would give such employers considerable leverage over their workers.

The ready-to-wear clothing industry expanded as an integral part of investment patterns typical of Mexican industrialization. Investors in Mexico sought control of various aspects of production, from raw materials to the distribution of the final product.[58] This was especially true for investors in textiles who sold cloth to jobbers, at rates they controlled, to be sold throughout the country. Investors in the textile industry also invested in major department stores built in the final decades of the nineteenth century. An unexplored link in this chain is the clothing industry. The owners of the largest Mexico City department stores—Al Puerto de Veracruz, El Palacio de Hierro, La Ciudad de Londres, El Puerto de Liverpool, El Correo Francés, and La Gran Oriental—were shareholders not only in textile factories, but in clothing production as well.[59] The expansion of the clothing industry was fueled in part by the efforts of these men to gain an edge over their competitors.

The ready-to-wear industry was given added impulse by smaller investors of both national and foreign origin. French, German, and English investors, as indicated by their names—Louis Sarre, Paul Elle, Chastell Brothers, Dubernard, Cassaubons, Louis Lack, Mr. Kips, Arturo Lederman, and Féderico Dreinhofer—owned many of the principal clothing shops established between 1880 and 1901. Men and women employed in the sewing industry saw the arrival of the U.S.-financed New England Shirt Company in 1903 as a transitional moment in the development of clothing production.[60] The New England Shirt Company set up shop in the old Bank of Montreal building, dedicating its efforts to the manufacture of ready-made clothing on a scale until then not seen in Mexico. So rapid was the expansion of production that the New England and other companies recruited workers from throughout central Mexico.

Producers of ready-to-wear clothing relied on subcontracting, which had developed in the 1890s. Contractors who held rights to supply the government with military apparel sold these rights to subcontractors, who in turn hired workers and oversaw production. The press reported that many subcontractors paid well below the government-established tariff and then pocketed the difference as profit. This practice, they claimed, reduced the seamstresses' wages by 20 to 50 percent. When in 1901 subcontracting did not sufficiently reduce labor costs, employers threatened to move production to the United States where, they liked to claim, they could hire cheaper labor.[61]

The practice of subcontracting entered a new phase after the 1910s, when commercial houses and department stores began auctioning off their shops, along with production contracts, to those willing to oversee production. These shops and contracts were usually sold on credit to displaced tailors and small businessmen. For example, the Taller de Camisas at number 198 Guerrero Street was established with the machinery of La Britania (est. 1911), which had previously been known as La Casa 'High Life.' Señor Eugenio Morales, an employee of a major clothing manufacturer, purchased the entire shop, which had employed over two hundred women, along with a production subcontract. Morales, like other middlemen, did not have the capital to build a new factory, but he was able to enter, or remain in, the business by subcontracting. According to a 1936 study of Mexico City *maquiladoras*, subcontracting accelerated after 1931 when producers sought to avoid providing worker benefits stipulated in the Federal Labor Law.[62]

The clothing industry continued to grow throughout the 1920s, based on a gendered division of labor. Production was divided into *prenda grande* (large garments), also known as *prenda de manga* (sleeved garments), and *prenda chica* (small garments). The difference between prenda grande (or prenda de manga) and prenda chica was in what was produced and in how much was paid for the product. Higher-paying prenda grande included the manufacture of jackets, smoking jackets, coats, and suits, all items which required fitting, while lower-wage prenda chica included pants, blouses, workers clothing, military clothing, intimate garments, lingerie, and the less expensive women's clothing. Except for the production of expensive women's dresses, costureras mostly worked in prenda chica. Those who worked in prenda grande sewed while men performed the higher-paid task of cutting cloth.

While much of this work was done in workshops located across the city, many sewers, both male and female, worked out of their homes. Employers benefited from outwork by transferring certain costs of production to the worker. Working out of her home, a woman would have to pay for workspace, gas for heat, and paraffin for light when she worked into the night. Seamstresses often purchased their own thread and needles, both when they worked at home and in a shop. Management held outworkers responsible for transporting cut material home and finished pieces back to the factory. In addition, these workers suffered from the lack of work during slack times more than workers in other industries. During periods of unemployment, seamstresses had to rely on taking in laundry and other "catch-as-catch-can" work opportunities.[63]

The implications of the gendered division of clothing production multiplied with the implementation of new technology. The introduction of pedal sewing machines in the late 1870s and of steam- and then electricity-powered machine at the turn of the century marked distinct moments of change, with similar effects. In the late 1870s the government eliminated the payment of import taxes on sewing machines. The removal of the tax, in combination with newspaper advertisements announcing their availability, led to their proliferation. Employers attempted to place the expense of purchasing a sewing machine on the worker herself. However, the cost of a sewing machine proved to be prohibitive for most women. In the 1870s a basic sewing machine cost between 50 and 70 pesos. While some middle-class women may have been able to afford a sewing machine for personal use, seamstresses, who earned roughly 1 peso (approximately 12 reales) a day in the 1890s, and only 50 centavos in 1901, were unlikely to be able to afford such a purchase.[64] This increased women's dependence upon factory employment.

The arrival of electric sewing machines only exacerbated this dependence. Employers could now assemble anywhere from a hundred to three hundred women into workshops filled with row upon row of machines. All operating at once, they must have made the air tremble. In this increasingly regulated workspace, women wore uniforms that slipped over their clothing, and head-coverings (see figure 1.4). Overseers constantly paced the rows of workers, watching for any machine that slowed. Employers combined factory work with outwork as a means of both reducing wages and addressing the seasonal nature of the industry.[65] Outworkers often suffered from the competition posed by large workshops utilizing electric machinery. In 1913 a group of seamstresses who worked out of their homes using pedal machines complained to the Department of Labor that such shops were leading to a reduction of their earnings by half.[66] And yet technology was implemented so unevenly in the clothing industry that in the same year another group of seamstresses who did handwork made the same complaint regarding the competition posed by women working on pedal machines.[67]

Given this downward pressure on wages, by all accounts costureras made less than many working women. In 1891 newspapers reported that

FIGURE 1.4
Clothing factory, circa 1920. Source: Fototeca Nacional, Mexico City.

cigarreras made 4 reales a day, whereas seamstresses earned from 2 to a maximum of 4 reales a day. By 1901 wages had declined further, so that after all was said and done, if employers did not impose fines, a seamstress might earn between 30 and 40 centavos for a twelve-hour day.[68] The Department of Labor's official publication, *La Gaceta del Trabajo*, reported in 1921 that many industrialists preferred to hire cheap labor and utilize "machinery imported in the '70s" rather than purchase new equipment.[69] The role of women sewing for low wages either by hand or on pedal machines continued to be significant at least until 1936, when a government study of sweatshops found that 25 percent of seamstresses worked by hand and 19 percent sewed on pedal sewing machines.[70]

Despite the low wages, and within a context of a limited range of employment opportunities, women continued to seek work in clothing production in large numbers. Between 1885 and 1910 the number of seamstresses in Mexico City rose by 34 percent, and the number of dressmakers by 174 percent. By 1910, these two groups combined almost equaled the number of factory workers. Women also worked in a variety of related occupations. For example, in the year 1900 nearly 10,000 women worked in the Mexico City needle trades as costureras (6,328), needle pointers (578), dressmakers (1,220), sewers of passementerie (47), and embroiderers (237).[71] The number of workers in clothing production continued to grow. One government factory inspector estimated that in 1921, 10,000 women and men worked in the clothing industry. And a 1936 study counted 17,000 seamstresses in Mexico City sweatshops alone, giving some idea of the growth that occurred in this industry.[72]

While sewing had not always been the provenance of women, with industrialization commentators spoke of sewing as if women had a particular aptitude for the work, thus reinforcing the gendered division of production. Some industrialists argued that women were more apt than men as sewers, due to their agility, sense of taste, and docility as workers. A 1921 issue of the Department of Labor's *La Gazeta del Trabajo* explained the predominance of women in the sewing industry: "In general it is noteworthy that industrialists are satisfied with the constancy and punctuality of the women workers, much more so than among men — as well as in their care in the work with which they are charged and in the good taste of that class of work which is required of them."[73] Department of Labor inspectors also found it "of great interest that the majority of these working women know how to read and write, or at least to read, and that in any case the percentage of them who are illiterate is less than among men."[74] The degree of dependability and level of education of female seamstresses resulted from limited work opportunities for women. Education did not open more doors for women's work.

A constant tension existed in Department of Labor reports, as inspectors sought to understand the perennially low wages of seamstresses. In 1921 an inspector noted that some seamstresses earned so little that they must have only worked for trinkets or spent their earnings on frivolous pleasures, "stealing that from which their sisters in need should benefit."[75] Inspectors held these women responsible for lowering the wages of women "truly in need."[76] Such commentary contributed to the stereotype that women did not belong in the workplace, yet it is difficult to imagine that women would work under such conditions if they did not have to.

Concerned about the proliferation of sweated labor, in 1921 the Department of Labor produced a study aimed at evaluating outwork. Juan Peza, a factory inspector and the author of the report, initially intended to focus his attention on male heads of household. However, the preponderance of women in the industry forced him to include them as well. Peza found that tailors' wives were essential to production and the sustenance of the household. While tailors cut and fit the clothing, women pressed seams, sewed buttons, and did other sorts of finish work. The wives of tailors were known to work exceedingly hard, so much so that Peza considered it unnecessary to even describe conditions "all too well known."[77]

In addition to investigating the living and working conditions of tailors and their families, the report also included seamstresses. In his report, Peza found that women worked as master seamstresses *(maestras)*, apprentices *(aprendizas)*, and family members. Many seamstresses, in turn, employed extremely low-wage labor in order to earn a living. For example, one maestra earned just under 2 pesos for each pleated skirt she produced, making her total monthly earnings 33.30 pesos. After paying 24 pesos to four apprentices for a month's work, she kept 9.30 pesos. Apprenticeships were ubiquitous in the industry, and while they gave women the necessary training to do industrial sewing, they also served to keep wages low. Inspector Peza noted that employers frequently violated the legal three-month limit of apprenticeships. He lamented that "true injustices are committed, because the women work for months without receiving a full salary, or if they do it is 10 centavos a day for nine or ten hours of work." Still other seamstresses worked together as family members, as did five sisters who sewed fine cashmere skirts out of their home. In one week the sisters made forty skirts. Receiving 50 centavos per skirt, their weekly earnings came to 4 pesos, or 80 centavos per day per sister. Sewers of workers' clothing and military apparel fared similarly. A seamstress could earn 2 pesos for a dozen work shirts, which took two ten-to-twelve-hour days to complete. A woman working alone could sew a dozen pair of jeans in a week, for which she would earn 1.87 pesos, a measly sum considering the physical effort needed to sew the stiff and awkward material. As a point of comparison, in that same year of 1921 cigarreras earned an average of 1.50 pesos a day.[78]

According to the report drawn up by Inspector Peza, such wages would not even have been sufficient to provide the most modest of housing or buy the cheapest of shoes, and women earning such a wage would be ill-fed at best. When wages were compared to living expenses, women

TABLE 1.5

Average Daily Earnings and Expenditures by Sex-segregated Occupation, Federal District, 1921

| | Earnings | Expenditures | |
		Food	Other
Tailors, male (prenda de manga)	$3.35	$2.32	$1.03
Tailors, male (prenda chica)	$2.71	$1.73	$0.83
Tailors, female, and seamstresses	$1.14	$1.39	-$0.29
Seamstress of mechanics shirts	$1.00*	$1.39**	-$0.39

Source: "Tailoring and Related Work, Study of Outwork," AGN, RT294: 15 (1921).

* Based on a ten-hour day at 8–10 centavos per hour.

** Inspector Peza stated that women exaggerated these amounts by at least 20 percent.

were always left in debt (see table 1.5). Peza suspected that, out of pride, the women he interviewed had exaggerated their food consumption by 20 percent, thus explaining the negative numbers in the last column. He noted that "almost every single one of them has a mother, small siblings, or children to maintain, and it is truly admirable how one could live on such miserable wages."[79] Many women, he mused, could expect little more from life than a hospital bed. Indeed, as a group, seamstresses likely suffered from exhaustion, malnutrition, and a number of other physical ailments. Some of these ailments would have been those associated with poverty, such as tuberculosis—described as endemic among seamstresses—and some would have been specific to female poverty, such as dysmenorrhoea, "deviation of the organs," metritis, menorrhagia, dispareunia, and sterility. Due to the constant, close nature of the work they performed, seamstresses often suffered from rheumatism and poor vision as well.[80]

With the increase in mass production of clothing, women's labor continued to dominate in the industry. In a 1920 industrial census women made up 74 percent of sewers of hats and clothing for women, 83 percent of sewers of general outerwear, 60 percent of those making clothing for men, 48 percent military tent makers, and 71 percent of mattress makers. In addition, women worked as sewers in other industries, often within factory walls. Women made up more than 70 percent of the workforce in rebozo, neckwear, knitwear, and mattress factories, many though not all of them working as sewers. An increasingly restricted definition of what constituted "industry" in national censuses meant that women working in these occupations went uncounted in the national statistics. In the 1930 census no specific information was recorded for sewers within these industries.[81] Just as in other industrial contexts, wages in female-dominated industries tended to be lower than those in mixed-sex industries. Costureras earned 66 percent of what men earned in the same industries. In 1929 the average daily wage in the manufacture of men's shirts and men's intimate apparel was 2.92 pesos for men and 1.93 pesos for women (see table 1.4).

Obreras

By the 1890s women found new occupations within both new and well-established industries. Women remained a significant minority in textile production until 1921. Women also worked in new occupations in the production of consumer goods. In these industries employers drew upon gendered divisions of labor established during the previous decades. By and large, women worked supplying raw materials, processing finished goods, and doing work that was qualified as unskilled. There were two important exceptions to the predominance of women in unskilled work: knitwear and silk textiles were industries new to Mexico that were not able to draw on an artisanal tradition and so hired significant numbers of women.

The Mexican textile industry expanded between 1890 and 1910, and in the process created new work opportunities for women. Between 1884 and 1906 six new textile factories were built within Mexico City. The Compañía Industrial Manufacturera, a consortium formed with Spanish and French capital, established the first modern industrial textile factory, San Antonio Abad in 1882. San Antonio Abad and subsequent new factories utilized modern machinery (installed between 1898 and 1906), required increasing amounts of raw materials, and hired a growing number of workers. Mexico City was second only to Puebla in the number of textile factories, amount of capital invested, and annual production.[82] The number of textile workers rose steadily from the 1890s until the recession years of 1907 and 1908.[83] By 1910, only employment levels in Mexico City textile factories (compared to those in Puebla and Veracruz) had recovered to 1907 levels.[84] Despite years of recession, in the Federal District the number of workers per factory grew. If we combine cotton, wool, and silk thread and textile production, women made up 48 percent of the work-force in 1921.[85]

However, distinctions among and within these branches of production were significant. In cotton textiles, the percentage of female workers declined from 29 percent in 1895 to 21 percent in 1921. With the decline in consumer demand between 1925 and 1932, the number of textile workers declined, with women comprising 15 percent of the national textile work force in 1928.[86] In Mexico City women made up only 6 percent of cotton textile workers in 1929.[87] However, in woolen textile production women fared better, increasing their participation in the workforce from 21 per-cent to 35 percent between 1921 and 1929.[88] In addition to the differences between women's workforce participation in the wool and cotton textile industries, within each of these branches of production women's work was in specific occupations. For example, women played only a small role in producing printed cotton cloth (13 percent), whereas they nearly domi-nated thread production (77 percent).

Women's employment also grew as a result of the arrival of new indus-tries to Mexico. When Hipólito Chambón established the first Mexican silk textile mill in 1880, there was only a limited tradition of silk weaving from which to draw workers. Miguel Hidalgo y Costillo had introduced the silk worm in the late colonial period but had met with little success in its cultivation. In the absence of skilled male artisans, Chambón directed his recruiting efforts at women. He established a sericulture school in Jalisco to train young women, and an agricultural colony in Tenancingo, Mexico State. Chambón also sponsored promotional evenings, including one at the National Theater in Mexico City, at which Carmen Romero Rubio de Díaz was an honored guest.[89] A journalist lamenting the dearth of jobs for women encouraged the government to establish a silk factory like the one owned by Hipólito Chambón. Silk textile production, he ar-gued, provided "respectable" work for women. The appropriateness of this work was, in part, due to an organization of work that distinguished between male and female workers. The Chambón factory was divided into various departments, where women worked in the preparation of the silk, cleaning, bobbin preparation, dyeing, warping, and basting. Men worked in the mechanics shop and weaving room, the latter located on the top floor. By the early 1920s Chambón employed 240 workers, 63 percent of whom were women. Some of the women had worked at the factory for over forty years.[90]

FIGURE 1.5
La Unión knitwear factory, 1899. Source: Figueroa Domenech,
Guía general desciptiva de la República Mexicana, vol. 1.

The *bonetería* (knitwear) industry also hired large numbers of women
in the absence of an artisanal tradition (see figure 1.5). The French, who
brought knitwear production to Mexico, also drew on their own tradition
of employing women in that industry.[91] The largest knitwear factory in
Mexico City, La Perfeccionada, was backed by French capital and opened
in 1895. La Perfeccionada employed 643 women and 168 men to make
intimate apparel, socks, stockings, sweaters, and other cotton knitwear
on electric machinery. Men dominated the occupations of dyer, mechanic,
and overseer, while women worked as weavers and in all finishing work,
including as seamstress, loopers, and in quality inspection. Unlike some
industries, in knitwear production men and women might work in the
same job category, as was the case with weavers. Nevertheless, aggregate
data for the industry indicate women earned approximately 73 percent of
men's wages in the early 1920s.[92] In 1931 Mexico City knitwear factories
surpassed those around the country in value of total production, number of workers, and the percentage of female workers. (In most regards,

Puebla came in second.) In Mexico City fifty-four knitwear factories employed 2,146 women and 438 men; women earned an average wage of 1.77 pesos, and men, 2.81 pesos.[93]

Women also took jobs in the rapidly expanding consumer goods industries. Indeed, Mexican industrialization was characterized by an emphasis on consumer goods, including shoes, processed foods, books, perfume, and pharmaceuticals. That women entered industries previously dominated by men did not always mean that women took specific jobs occupied by men. Women were generally employed not in the actual production of goods, but rather in the packaging, papering, boxing, bottling, and labeling of those goods. In cookie and cracker factories men worked as bakers while women stood sideways to conveyor belts and selected baked goods to be placed in boxes kept at small wooden work stations. Women found work in bookbinding as early as the 1890s as sewers and folders. Whereas there were no women employed in bookbinding in 1879, by 1900 Mexico City had 375 male and 110 female bookbinders. In 1921 women represented 40 percent of bookbinders, though by 1929 their participation had declined to 24 percent.[94] Male bookbinders interpreted women's entrance into the profession as the cause of the decline of the craft, as did typesetters.[95] Other employers as well hired female workers to participate in the production of hats, pharmaceuticals, and shoes. In hat making women worked as sewers and apprentices. And whereas men had dominated shoe making in the nineteenth century, by 1906 women worked cutting soles and assembling parts in the newly established United States Shoe Factory and in Carlos Zetina's Excelsior shoe factory.[96]

In 1920 and 1921 the Department of Labor produced two separate censuses. The 1920 census was a census of industry that included, in addition to information on median annual production, mechanization, and geographic location, a count of workers differentiated by gender. Included in the census were large, modern factories, small workshops, and outwork. The 1921 census was a census of workers. It included similar industries, though not all those in the 1920 census, and it often exhibited slight variations in the way it categorized industries. Although the two censuses reported on women's workforce participation slightly differently, they both came to similar conclusions.[97]

The most noteworthy shift in women's workforce participation since the 1880s was their entrance into an increasing number of consumer goods and service industries. The 1921 census found that women dominated in

FIGURE 1.6
Shoe factory, circa 1920. Source: Fototeca Nacional, Mexico City.

several areas of the economy, including but not limited to knitwear, neckwear, rebozos, umbrellas, perfume, dry cleaners, tortillerías, and beauty salons (see table 1.3). Large numbers of women also worked in the production of cardboard boxes, matches, cigarettes, passementerie, preserved foods and sweets, and in mills (nixtamal, coffee, and grain), small restaurants (fondas), and rag processing. At the same time, many industries still hired no women: foundries, woodworking, plumbing and carpentry, and transportation, for example. It is also noteworthy that with the mechanization of some kinds of work formerly thought of as "women's work," women's participation in those industries declined, at least according to the figures in the censuses. This was the case with laundries, and to a lesser degree with chocolate (included in the 1920 industry census). It was also the case with the production of tortillas, which was divided into

FIGURE 1.7
Print shop, circa 1920. Source: Fototeca Nacional, Mexico City.

two kinds of work: the grinding of the corn (at nixtamal mills), which had
come to be dominated by men (54 percent), and the actual making and
selling of tortillas, which continued to be a virtually all-female occupation
(see figures 1.6, 1.7, and 1.8).

Gender distinctions marked which jobs employers offered to women
and the wages they paid. The prevalence of piece-rate work for female
workers contributed to women's low wages. Like cigarreras and costureras, obreras in the packaging and processing of prepared foods received wages based on output. (After the passage of minimum wage laws,
employers manipulated piece-rate wages in order to avoid compliance,
a practice that would be formally addressed in the 1931 Federal Labor
Law.[98]) Women's work was lower paid than men's, whether this work
occurred in large factories or small workshops. Though aggregate cen-

FIGURE 1.8
Packaging baked goods at an industrial bakery, circa 1920.
Source: Fototeca Nacional, Mexico City.

sus data did not make such distinctions, individual census returns show
that small workshops employed fewer workers and used older machinery. Such was the case in the domestic production of rebozos, which in
the 1920s were still produced on small wooden looms. Men wove while
women worked as spinners, spoolers, and embroiderers. In one workshop
the five male weavers were paid 1.50 to 2.00 pesos a day, while the four
female embroiderers earned from 75 centavos to 1.25 pesos; the eight spinners, also women, earned from 40 to 80 centavos a day.[99] Family production units in workers' homes also followed this same division of labor, and
Department of Labor inspectors noted similar wage disparities.[100]

   In larger textile factories mechanization meant an expansion of low-
wage jobs for women, while men worked in higher paying positions as
weavers and dyers. In the first decades of the twentieth century textile
overseers of artisanal background hired workers, and in so doing retained
aspects of the artisanal organization of production and social relations.[101]
Female workers continued to work in the preparation of raw materials,

work done by hand, and thread spinning.[102] Workers in the highest-paid position, weaver, averaged 1 peso a day in 1896, while those in thread production were mostly children and were paid 40 centavos a day; both women and children were employed in carding and were paid 50 centavos a day.[103] Mechanization often exacerbated wage disparities for female and male piece-rate workers, as when in 1893 the owner of La Fama Montañesa installed new machinery which produced a wider cloth with an increased thread count, without raising the piece-rate wages of his workers.[104]

Women's wages were also the result of the sorts of work for which they were hired in factories. The 1921 worker census reveals that many of the factories included within the textile industry category did not produce textiles exclusively. And so women's role as skilled labor in textile production was less than the aggregate numbers given above would seem to suggest. For example, El Surtidor produced textiles, mattresses, and beds, while La Hormiga produced textiles and knitwear. La Union, established in 1889, produced textiles, mattresses, matches, and cardboard boxes, and did lithography as well. The variety of items produced within one factory meant jobs for women, but they were hired to fill and sew mattresses, spin thread, produce knitwear, finish rebozos, and package matches.[105]

Whether we compare overall wages for both sexes or men's and women's wages in the same work categories, men might earn as little as women, but women never made more than men. Women frequently earned half of what men earned in the same job category.[106] While the job categories might suggest equal work, equal wages did not correspond to that work, as the following example for mattress makers, *colchoneros* and *colchoneras*, shows. At a particular mattress factory both men and women earned a minimum of 2.50 pesos a day, yet while males could earn up to an average of 6.66 pesos a day, women never earned more than an average of 3.33 pesos a day.[107] This factory owner was thus able to take advantage of the less costly labor of women by hiring just two men compared with seven women. Even a skilled working woman in the hat industry, an *oficiala*, would earn significantly less than an *oficial*. And yet, even a comparison of job classifications and wages does not tell the full story, for the meaning of work was constructed in various ways. Several Department of Labor inspectors jotted down *"mujer"* (woman) as the job description that paid the lowest wage in a particular factory, implying that to be a woman was to be cheap labor, like *mozo*, boy, connoting not only age and gender but servile status.[108] The first aggregate numbers that appeared to distinguish between male and female wages were for 1929, when women overall earned 55 percent of what men earned (see table 1.4).[109]

By 1926 Mexican industry was suffering from decreased consumer demand. Investment slowed and many industries either reduced the size of their labor force or slowed their rate of hiring. The number of women as a percentage of the industrial workforce declined during this period. Between 1921 and 1930 the number of women in industry grew at a slower rate than that of men. Women's participation in the industrial labor force went from 20,000 in 1921 to 24,000 in 1930, whereas the numbers for men nearly doubled, from 55,000 in 1921 to 100,000 in 1930, so that by 1930 women made up 24 percent of Mexico City's industrial workers.[110] The growth of women in commerce was equally slow, increasing by only 1,000 during the same period.[111] In 1930 women represented 17 percent of the city's economically active population.[112]

Census Categories
and Comments in the Margins

Archives shape the historical narratives we create. And because many women made their way into the written record only in fragments their history can be difficult to capture. When and how women's stories enter and exit the archive can serve to tell a history that complements the one based on aggregate data. The categories created for the 1921 industrial census defined industry in terms that were more likely to include men than women. While the census counted workers in the transportation and construction industries, and in mechanical workshops, it did not count ragpickers, food processors, itinerant peddlers, and waitresses. These individuals, many of whom were women, were necessary for the functioning of industry: they produced and distributed goods and provided fast-food for workers. Working outside the factory walls, such women and men also contributed to industrialization as both an economic and cultural process.[113]

Historians have written about the rise of textiles as essential for understanding Mexican industrialization. Growing in the shadow of the textile industry was the paper industry. Paper producers obtained a portion of their raw materials from textile factories. In addition to the waste produced by textiles factories, paper manufacturers also relied on rag collectors who worked the city streets. During the Porfiriato the twenty or so Mexico City *traperías* (rag processors) paid ragpickers to gather the raw material that female workers later sorted and cleaned before it was sold to paper producers. The establishment in 1890 of San Rafael, the first modern paper factory, which used conifer pulp, meant the displacement of many women and men who had worked supplying this industry.[114]

Consumer preference meant that many occupations remained in the hands of women, despite mechanization of the food and textile industries. Mechanized production of chocolate arrived in the 1880s; however, consumer preference for metate-ground chocolate stunted the growth of a chocolate industry. Women did, however, dominate in the industrial production of chocolate as well. In 1920 only seventy-nine women and forty-four men worked in the industrial production of chocolate. Consumers were also slow to purchase tortillas made from mechanized corn mills *(molinos de nixtamal)* and tortilla machines. Although corn mills had been installed in regions of Mexico in the late nineteenth century, Arnold Bauer found that for several decades Mexicans resisted purchasing the industrial product: in the final years of the Porfiriato one could still find that "a corps of specialized *molenderas* (female corn grinders who worked on a *metate*) produced *masa* (tortilla dough) for markets and sidewalk stands."[115] By the late 1910s molinos de nixtamal were widespread in Mexico City, though this did not mean an expansion of work for women. In 1921 women made up only 48 percent of workers in corn mills. Women did, however, continue to dominate poorly paid work in *tortillerías.* Some cotton textile goods, such as the traditional *serapes* and *gabanes* could not be produced by imported looms and so remained within the domain of artisans. Women worked with the male weavers of these items as sewers and embroiderers.[116]

Other workers did not appear in industrial censuses at all. Yet, from the perspective of the worker, the impact of industrialization was similar. *Meseras* (waitresses), women hired as independent contractors to wait on tables and provide counter service selling anything from trinkets to baked goods, worked in conditions over which they had little control (see figure 1.9). Men dominated in service jobs in first-class restaurants, while women worked mostly in second-class restaurants, a division of labor reinforced by organized labor in the 1920s. Not only did women earn less in second-class restaurants, working conditions often lowered their take-home pay. Employers held the mesera responsible for the cash she collected and from which she made change. During the inflationary period of 1915 meseras complained to the Department of Labor about customers

FIGURE 1.9
Counter sales, circa 1920. Source: Fototeca Nacional, Mexico City.

who, because they did not have sufficient change or legal tender, would eat or take merchandise and leave with nothing more than the promise to pay. "Isn't it true that this is a refinement of the exploitation of women?" asked a journalist for *El Renovador*.[117]

Conclusion

Relations of work during the mid–nineteenth century shaped industrial development. The existence or absence of an artisanal tradition laid the groundwork for the continued gendered division of occupations, the cultural understanding of those jobs, and the wages women received. New manufactories relied on the abundance of women in search of work, both early in the history of cigarette production and with the establishment of the silk and knitwear industries in the 1880s and 1890s. In clothing production the division of work between tailors and seamstresses set the stage for increasing disparity between men and women's working conditions. In the 1920s men continued to dominate prenda grande and women dominated prenda chica, although women continued to do low-waged work in both. Subcontracting, mechanization, and a continued reliance on outwork kept a downward pressure on wages.

Despite the decreasing work opportunities for women in tobacco processing, women's overall employment in Mexico City industry remained fairly constant—a fact explained by women's continued dominance in clothing production and their entry into a wide range of consumer goods industries, including knitwear, silk textiles, and processed food. Employers hired women, for example, to do finishing work in mattress factories, package goods in industrial bakeries, and as loopers in knitwear factories. With the important exception of the knitwear industry, these were low-wage jobs construed as unskilled labor.

The organization of industrial work produced new goods, and it also produced new ideas about the male and female worker. Male and female workers were defined by where they worked, what they did, and what they were paid. The simple existence of female-dominated factories contributed to the belief until the late nineteenth century that, for example, the cigarrera was one of the few respectable female occupations. Within the factory, the division of physical space also re-created gender differences. Moreover, the meaning of work was also reinterpreted outside of factory walls. Obreras, cigarreras, and costureras filled the streets of the increasingly industrial sections of the city. This material transformation provoked a transformation in the discursive and cultural understanding of working women. Labor leaders, statesmen, journalists, and feminists would try to make sense of what these material changes meant.

CHAPTER 2

"She Has Moved Beyond Her Sphere"

Discursive Constructions of Working Women

As women streamed into the streets of Mexico City on their way to work, a growing stream of public commentary accompanied them. Journalists, statesmen, labor leaders, and men of letters discussed the moral and material consequences of industrialization, including the consequences for Mexican women. Such public conversations reflected both transformations in women's work, especially the decline of the traditionally female-dominated tobacco industry, and the rise of work in mixed-sex factory settings, as well as changing class relations.

Public discourse on women's entrance into factories began in the early nineteenth century as a discussion about changing gender roles. "Mixing the sexes," as many referred to it, posed a moral danger. By the 1880s this discussion of female nature had evolved into an expression of changing conceptions of class as well. This chapter discusses two paradigms of class. First, within the paradigm of paternalism, the existence of working women signaled the overturning of class and gender hierarchies. Second, within an emerging middle-class identity, the virtue of the working woman served as metaphor in the service of class distinction. Within both paradigms of class, female nature was associated with weakness, both material and moral, in the struggle for survival. The Mexican Revolution created a political environment in which talk of workers' rights included the rights of women, and in which female virtue played a decreasing role in public discussions of working women. Nevertheless, the normative assumptions regarding working women that emerged at the turn of the century persisted into the 1920s.

Scholars have elaborated the texture and importance of dichotomized models of femininity in Mexico. Silvia Arrom finds that by the mid–nineteenth century there was a resurgence of the celebration of women's role in the domestic sphere, especially her role as mother. This separate and unequal role for women coincided with the separation of work from the home and with liberal political philosophy, which construed domestic relations as fundamental to civic life.[1] In his work on Porfirian Chihuahua, William French has succinctly referred to the poles of this paradigm as "prostitutes and guardian angels" (of the home).[2] Debra Castillo and Jean Franco describe similar gender dichotomies in Mexican literature.[3] And what of the women in-between? In this chapter, I argue that the obrera occupied that middle space. Discursively, the obrera came to embody the seeming contradictions of industrialization: the separation of the public and private sphere and the simultaneous creation of the working woman.

From Mixing the Sexes to
Gender and Class Distinction

Knowledge about sex differences informed Mexicans' ideas about relations between individuals and was interwoven with their conception of social organization. In the nineteenth century, upper-class Mexicans widely believed that men and women had fundamentally different natures. Statesman Andrés Molina Enríquez was not unusual when he argued that women depended upon the protection of men for survival. He claimed that a woman's biology inhibited her from surviving in the struggles of the workplace.[4] Such reference to biological differences in strength, reproductive function, and temperament reinforced gendered understandings of psychology, morality, and social roles. Writers interested in delineating gender difference commonly organized their thoughts around the concept of public and private spheres. They discussed separate spheres as constituting complementary, not equal, activities, which formed the basis of felicity between the sexes, stability within the family, and well-being for society at large. Liberal conceptions of the relationship between the individual and society meant the actions of individuals influenced social stability.[5] Women's individual behavior in the private sphere naturally complemented men's activity in the public sphere and bore the weight of significance for social stability. Thus, the male world of competition, individualism, and public activity was complemented and necessarily balanced by the female world of emotions, moral sensibility, and motherhood in the private sphere.

The practice and symbolism of female seclusion were part and parcel of practices of class distinction. Though women's actual lives may have differed from public portrayal of their lives, seclusion, the practice of limiting women's entrance into the public sphere, was an integral aspect of femaleness in early-nineteenth-century Latin America. Upper-class women infrequently left their homes without a chaperone, and then only for certain activities that were deemed appropriate for women, such as religious observance. Even so, too-frequent outings to Mass might be questioned. The seclusion of young women became integral to courtship rituals, where playing with the boundaries of public and private became part of flirtation. A young woman might appear in the window of her house—creating an illusory publicness—in order to highlight her seclusion and thus her desirability as a woman. If the young woman received visitors in the family parlor, they were under the mother's vigilant eye. While such gatherings could include both men and women, writer Manuel Payno has described respectable interactions that occurred along same-sex lines. Men often gathered in taverns and cafes, whereas the *tertulia* was the provenance of women, where the mistress of the house utilized her social skills to put her visitors at ease. If a woman ventured out of the house, she rode in a carriage so as not to mix with the street crowds—as well as to show off her carriage.[6]

Mid–nineteenth century advocates of expanding women's sphere did so within the context of political instability. Mexico achieved independence from Spain in 1821; however, political turmoil persisted. The North American invasion of 1846–1848, Liberal/Conservative conflicts, and the imposition of a monarchy under the French pretender Maximilian (1864–1867), led politically engaged Mexicans to be concerned with citizenship and economic development during these crucial periods of state-building. Advocates of education for women argued that educated mothers would contribute to the project of nation-building by raising informed citizens.[7] Even when government officials or private citizens encouraged women to enter into the public sphere to work, their comments were directed at plebeian women. As early as 1799, the decree eliminating guild restrictions encouraged women and girls "to engage in all labors and manufactures compatible with their strength and the decorum of their sex, regardless of Guild Ordinances and governmental ordinances to the contrary."[8] Even with the establishment of the first mechanized textile factories in Mexico in the 1830s, most Mexicans still did not associate women with factory work. When industrialist Estéban Antuñano sought a workforce for his newly established cotton textile factory, he published a pamphlet with the aim of countering resistance to the employment of female factory operatives. The pamphlet title, "Political, civil, industrial and domestic advantages of also employing women in the modern mechanized factories which are being established in Mexico," suggests the tensions surrounding the idea of women in factory labor.[9]

In his plea for the employment of women in factories, Antuñano addressed widely held objections to women working outside of the home. Antuñano began by dismissing the idea that modern machinery required significant physical strength or long apprenticeships. The bulk of the text, however, addressed questions of public and individual female morality. Antuñano claimed that the presence of women in factories would improve public morality by contributing to a decline of public drunkenness, although he did not explain. Hiring women, he argued, would increase family income, which workers could then spend on housing, thus relieving industrialists of that expense. With so many benefits accruing to workers, Antuñano thought of his factories as "semi-public institutions with patriotic or philanthropic ends, rather than business concerns."[10] Antuñano further sought to legitimate the move of women into factories by reminding his readers that the same practices existed in industrially advanced nations such as England.

But more than public morality, Antuñano addressed concerns about the effects of factory work on women's morality. The entrance of women into a new sphere of activity implied new social relations, the details of which posed several problems for upper-class observers. The possibility of men and women working in the same factory raised fears about the impact that such interaction would have on women. Within public discourse, the public sphere was masculine—a place of competition and egoism, where women were not prepared to survive. Women's morality would be compromised in the face of male power. With the entrance of women into factories, the workplace became thought of as sexualized; in contemporary parlance, social commentators spoke of "mixing the sexes." The idea of the factory as a sexualized space became central to understanding working women over the next century.

Antuñano's pamphlet echoed concerns expressed in Mexico City newspapers. Fifty years later, in 1887, a journalist would write, "Let us suppose that she dedicates herself to waged labor and goes to work in a house as seamstress, or as an obrera and goes to work in a factory. In the former she is, usually, the pastime of one of the 'boys' or of the man of the house, and in the second the whim of her boss; and, either way, she joins the contingent of clandestine prostitution. The evil is in the blood, they used to say in olden times, and we say the same. The evil is in social exigencies, and these evils are difficult to remedy."[11] The very conditions of work turned virtuous women into prostitutes.

Estéban Antuñano had sought to address these very concerns. He held up his own factory, La Constancia, as an example of the successful integration of both male and female workers. Antuñano expressed concern for women's sexual morality, but contrary to popular perceptions, he argued that a young woman, idle and alone in her home, posed more of a threat to morality than one at work in a factory. Indeed, the very organization of the factory would protect women. Male overseers and directors would watch over young women in the factory, serving as safeguards to her morality. The continual movement of the machines, he argued, would keep workers in place and discourage idleness. Furthermore, Antuñano envisioned the entire family working together in the same locale. This domestic sphere reconstituted within the factory invoked an ideal of both artisanal work relations and of male authority that would purportedly safeguard workplace morality. In this regard, Antuñano was not unlike early U.S. industrialists who devised similar plans in order to attract women to work in their factories.[12]

We cannot say whether Antuñano's words described actual workplace realities; still, his need to write this pamphlet speaks eloquently to the tension posed by a mixed-sex workplace. As indicated by the solutions he suggested, industrial development altered the gendered expectations of work. Though men and women had worked together since the colonial period, the organization of work prior to the 1880s had been different, loosely adhering to a separation of the sexes or to the submission of women to male authority, if only symbolically. Those who expressed fears about women's entrance into factories construed artisanal production as organized within the family, where all the members worked together under the same roof. Domestics worked for families that, while not their own, did represent patriarchal space construed as private. Obrajes and early factories hired women related to husbands, fathers, or brothers. And, tobacco manufactories separated men and women in their work. It was not clear what the rules of interaction between the sexes would be in these new factory settings.

"Distinctions between Rich and Poor":
Paternalism and Gender

By the 1880s the question of whether women should enter into factory work had become a moot point. However, literate Mexicans kept the presses running over the impact of industrialization on Mexican society in general, and on women in particular. While earlier public discussion of women's presence in factories questioned changing gender relations, the symbol of the obrera had become integral to a new concern about class relations. Mexicans who construed class relations through the lens of paternalism saw working women as overturning class hierarchies. The power of such a threat reinforced the call to retain traditional gender roles. Positivists were important players in the elaboration of this discussion. The particularities of Mexican industrialization—foreign investment, rapid economic expansion, and new roles for women—informed the way that they placed this concern in relation to contemporary issues.

Mexican positivism provided fertile ground for construing women through the paradigm of paternalism. Gabino Barreda first introduced positivism in the field of educational reform in the 1860s, and by the 1880s Mexicans were adapting the ideas of August Comte and Herbert Spencer to the particularities of Mexican politics and national development. As a political philosophy, positivism emphasized reasoning that relied on science, and repudiated some elements of liberal theory. As a political movement within the liberal tradition, positivism was associated with an elite group of influential politicians during the Porfiriato. Historians have identified positivists as leaders of economic development. Yet some positivists held a critical view of development because they associated liberal-style development with materialism run amok. They defined progress as the development of order, as indicated by a favored phrase, "order and progress." Only by acknowledging the scientifically proven and biologically determined differences between the sexes could order be recognized and properly developed, they claimed. In fact, positivists argued that the maintenance of gendered separate spheres was necessary for progress. Industrialization that resulted in the entrance of women into the work force represented, for them, a clear lack of order and progress.

Horacio Barreda, the son of Gabino Barreda, was particularly interested in the topic of women and industrial development. His writings, viewed in conjunction with opinions expressed by journalists, men of letters, public officials, and criminologists, exemplify positivist thought on gender, industrialization, and class conflict. Horacio Barreda produced a series of articles titled "Studies on Feminism" published in *Revista Positiva* in 1909.[13] Barreda, like many positivists, considered competition essential for industrial development. This same quality, however, was seen as detrimental to women. For Barreda, the workplace stood in opposition to the home, not just physically but in associated gendered qualities as well. One journalist who frequently reported on labor issues reiterated the idea that the home and the workplace were physical and moral opposites: "In the former [the home] there is much ideality; in the latter there is much realism. This is the conflict inherent in the struggle which the obrera continually sustains within herself."[14] He feared that the obrera was being required "to remain steadfast in the middle of this tempest which surrounds her," thereby obliging her to a life of suffering. Barreda also saw this conflict within the individual writ large in society. Consistent with positivist thought, he argued that the value of women—with their feminine qualities of tenderness, love, and selflessness—could be measured in the equilibrium they brought to the naked materialism of progress. Individual behavior—women remaining in the home—would bring order and progress to the ills of modern society.[15]

Barreda's attack on feminism as overly concerned with industrial employment was not a response to efforts on the part of Mexican feminists for the right to work, and less so for the right to work in factories. In the first decade of the twentieth century most Mexican proponents of women's rights were focused on women's education and social value, not on work opportunities. As often as not, the scattered newspaper references to specifically suffragist activities that did appear referred to the United States and France.[16] Nevertheless, Barreda viewed the fact that women had entered the world of work and invaded public life as having been caused by feminist desires to work. Barreda wrote that the regenerated or liberated woman *(mujer regenerada)* was nothing more than a "true butch" *(verdadero mari-macho)*. He argued that feminists were completely misguided. They had mistakenly and irrationally focused only on "activities truly industrial." Barreda reminded feminists of their biological imperatives and exhorted them to seek the ordered functioning of society and the protection of female morality. Barreda attributed the actions of these misguided feminists to negative foreign influences, along with foreign monopolies and religions—that is, to Protestantism. He also attacked feminists for trying to "Americanize" Mexican women.[17]

Horacio Barreda offered his own definition of feminism. Barreda developed his thesis in an essay titled "Feminist Tendencies are the Necessary Result of Intellectual and Moral Disorder Which are Endemic to the Revolutionary Situation Through Which Societies Are Currently Passing." The "revolutionary situation" to which he referred was the changing aspect of work relations, not the Mexican Revolution that had yet to surface. In this essay Barreda charted the history of Mexico and of world civilization, arguing throughout that progress for women lay in the improvement of conditions that would allow her to remain in the home. He wrote, "The sense in which the emancipation of the female sex and the elevation of her social condition has progressed has consisted in the gradual liberation of women from all types of outside work and of all systematic meddling in questions of public life, to the end of better allowing her to concentrate on domestic functions in the interior life of the home, without the prejudicial need to extend this influence, exercised in the bosom of the family, to matters of social existence."[18] For Barreda, a true feminist fought to keep women at home.

Barreda also argued that women's entrance into industrial work caused more than a general disordering of society. It disrupted class relations. If positivists concerned themselves with order, that order was based on recognizing the reciprocal duties of superiors and inferiors. Hierarchy and reciprocity should inform both social and gender relations. For Barreda, the halcyon days were those of the feudal lords, who were obliged to provide for the man who could not support his family. To his mind, patron-client relations had served as a safety net for the working man, who now had to transfer the burden of survival—belonging properly to the male—onto the shoulders of his wife and children. In feudal times, the beneficent support of a lord had allowed men to carry out their function as breadwinners, and women theirs as mothers. Patron-client relations, "not a family wage," would right the wrongs of changing gender roles associated with industrialization.[19] Following this logic, the decline of patron-client relations and the emergence of class relations upset patriarchy and correct gender relations.

Barreda was not alone in his association of changing gender roles with disruptions in class relations, or in his belief that working women brought on class conflict. Statesman Francisco Bulnes deemed a feminist to be more dangerous than "a Barcelona anarchist," an epithet that implied feminists were as subversive as radical class conflict and indeed associated with it. In a similar vein, Ignacio Gamboa argued that work physically debilitated woman, necessarily leading to her incapacity to compete with men in the work force. Such failure, for Gamboa, would only lead women to the "bloody march of socialism, thus making woman the most powerful enemy of humanity."[20]

In 1906 the economic journal *El Progreso Latino* also reinforced the condemnation of women in factories by raising the specter of class conflict. A contributor to the journal questioned whether it was correct to solve the problem of a shortage of male laborers by employing women. This was to be avoided, he wrote, because employing women in factories would "end all distinctions between rich and poor, established by God in order that the rich give to the poor to eat and the poor work for the rich."[21] The article continued by presenting a fictitious conversation between two employers who were considering their options:

> —Well, forget about the Chinese, I'll take women.
> —It is better this way, *compadrito*. We must take advantage of the moment before women become proud and want wages and salaries commensurate with those of men and [as they say] charge us twenty-five centavos for a kilo of pears, or like our workers and artisans, go work for foreigners. Now that she is humble, like the Chinese, and willing to work anywhere and charge little . . . we must redeem her, giving her the opportunity to earn her meager yet honorable bread, freeing her from misery and prostitution.[22]

The author's ideas about race shaped the range of options he would consider and led him to consider hiring Mexican women. Arabs, Chinese, Japanese, American "Negroes," and Armenians were "not elements [suitable] for colonization" or for hire. Without explanation, he also dismissed the possibility of the repatriation of Mexican workers resident in the United States. "If our men be such traitors," he wrote, "abandoning us to throw themselves into the arms of foreigners, we will throw ourselves into the arms of women."[23]

The double-entendre of this last statement reveals that the author had proposed hiring women only as a foil against which to argue. His comments played on the association of women working outside of the home with compromised sexuality. In a highly sarcastic tone, he concluded by underlining how ridiculous it would be to employ women to work in factories. "As for going up and down the stairs . . . they [women] will have to dress like men. And we will have to dress like women so that women are not confused for men."[24] The entrance of women into the work force threatened either to reverse the sexes or to mix them in unnatural ways, making fools of men who would be forced to wear dresses so as not to be confused with women.

The unnatural mixing of gender roles in this *El Progreso Latino* article resulted from going against economic and biological laws:

—Well then, I was saying that this is nothing more than an economic phenomenon, and very economic at that; it is the law of competition; it is also the law of natural selection, which pertains to the field of biology; it is the struggle for survival, the supreme law of the universe; it is, finally, so that you understand me, woman throwing herself against man in the struggle for survival and disputing him in all his positions, one by one, until finally she ends up challenging his paternity. Are there not men with braids and women with whiskers? Don't you remember the "man-mother" [*hombre-madre*] attended to by Doctor Lavista? It is, in sum, the triumph of woman, more intelligent than man . . .

—More intelligent than you, doctor?

—More clever than the devil himself![25]

Within the logic of this discourse, when women took waged labor they put at risk their sexual morality. This author argued that mixing men and women in the workplace would lead to a devilish degree of gender confusion. The world was akimbo when men with braids and women with whiskers walked the earth. The very possibility that women could challenge male paternity precluded further discussion of employing women to work alongside men.

The Martyred Middle Class

By the mid-1880s public debate over women's entrance into the world of work was increasingly informed by efforts to define and delimit the middle class. Journalists and social commentators wrote of the "martyred, middle-class" woman who properly belonged at home but who had been forced to work. They reported on cigarrera strikes, the low wages of costureras, and the implications of work for women. This public conversation built upon conceptions of "mixing the sexes," so that women's entrance into the world of work was seen as posing a danger for female sexual morality. At the same time that this discourse defined normative female behavior, it also articulated middle-class identity. Discussions of the degradation of women also provided a forum for an implicit criticism of the pitfalls of industrialization and of the Díaz regime during a climate of restricted political protest.

In Mexico, a tradition of writing about middle groups had existed well before industrialization. However, it was not until the late nineteenth century that social commentators increasingly wrote about the middle *class*. Men of letters, criminologists, and observers of Mexican culture made distinctions between different sectors of society based on ethnicity, occupation, and cultural customs. They distinguished between different socioeconomic groups by the foods they ate, the clothes they wore, the homes they inhabited, and the sexual relations in which they engaged. By the late 1880s defenders of the middle class defined this class by concern over their declining socioeconomic position and the threat this posed to the propriety and culture that characterized its members. The social dislocation of working women epitomized that decline.[26]

A wide range of constituencies entered into debate over the activities and meaning of working women via the press. Throughout the course of the Porfiriato, more than one hundred newspapers were published in Mexico City, including papers that voiced the perspective of Catholics, Conservatives, Liberals, pro-government and opposition groups, and the working class.[27] While some independent newspapers did exist, the government subsidized most of the newspapers that had any significant run. For this reason, historians have questioned the representativeness of the working-class press as both voice and advocate. Such criticism is valid, and is the very reason why these papers give us insight into the portrayal of women found on their pages. The aspirations to middle-class status of representatives of the Congreso Obrero, which published *La Convención Radical Obrera*, suggest both sympathy for working women and a concern for distinguishing middle-class identity. *El Hijo del Trabajo* and *El Socialista* also directed themselves to the working class and expressed similar concern for the conditions in which women labored. Discussions regarding working women were not, however, limited to the working-class press. Two newspapers, in particular, stand out for the attention they paid to working women: the Catholic *El Tiempo*, edited by distinguished Mexican clerics and of considerable moral and political influence, and *El Imparcial*, edited for ten years by Doctor Luis Lara y Pardo.[28] That the public discourse that appeared within the pages of these newspapers was a shared conversation was evidenced by contributors' varyingly addressing themselves to employers, working women, and other newspapers.[29]

Within this public discussion, some understood the problem of working women to be one of female poverty, due to "an excess of women."[30] This explanation, based on conceptions of female dependency, relied upon purported demographic imbalance to explain the increasing number of women unable to support themselves. Simply put, too many women could not find a husband. Such an explanation was founded on the assumption that the primary "occupation" for women was wife. However, for many journalists the question of marriage partners was complicated by frustrated attempts to retain one's respectability. An article that appeared in 1897 in *La Convención Radical Obrera* discussed the topic of respectable marriage partners, while at the same time defining the position of the middle class. In "The Future of Woman," this journalist wrote:

> For poor women, the chance of marriage is slim, when she, due to her scientific education has climbed a ladder on the social scale: artisans flee from her because they judge her, and with reason, for she is their superior; and because she is of humble birth she is rejected by the rich due to their nasty pride. If they approach her, it is only to drown her in the abyss of degradation. Many do not dare join their future with hers for fear that they will then suffer the burden of the family of their wife . . . friends educated in the same school as she will mistreat her, be better dressed. After her time with them she has to return to her humble home, or if she is at a gathering and her mother comes for her, her friends might say the maid has come for her, and so embarrassed is she that she may not defend the woman who is the author of her days.[31]

The story of a woman who refused to recognize her mother due to social embarrassment rhetorically served to tell the tale of an entire social class. This class was superior to common artisans and yet rebuffed by the educated. It was a class that had all the cultural preparation it should and none of the opportunities it deserved.

Within the paradigm of the middle class, writers acknowledged that some women had to work. This acknowledgment was founded on conceptions of female dependency, and it followed that "respectable" work would save women from turning to prostitution in order to survive. However, the lack of respectable employment was precisely the problem, according to commentators. In 1897 *La Convención Radical Obrera* lamented the declining respectability of the occupations of cigarrera and costurera, and celebrated the opening of new, "respectable" occupations, including those in typography, counter service, and elementary school instruction.[32] Whereas dependent women were a scourge to society, the article claimed, in these new occupations women could find their "redemption." Writers for *La Convención Radical Obrera* used a limited vocabulary, centered on the verb "to redeem," when writing about women. Women would be redeemed by an education; working women would be redeemed by technical education; the poorest of women would be redeemed by work. "Respectable women" would be redeemed by the expansion of so-called middle-class occupations.[33] Repeated use of the word "redeem" indicates that sympathy for working women centered on safeguarding female sexual morality. It also suggests the centrality of virtue and gender to class distinction.

Journalists and social commentators understood the very organization of production as a threat to female sexual morality. The nature of that threat echoed conversations from earlier in the century that had construed women as antithetical to the types of interaction associated with the workplace. Language was one of the dangers posed to women who worked. The use in the workplace of the "tú" form of address suggested informality and a lack of respect that would have been offensive to ladies. Also, in the workplace women would be assaulted by dirty language, sarcastic tones, and aggressive indecencies.[34] The presence of male supervisors or co-workers also posed a danger. At times, these supervisors were further demonized by being described as "Spanish," or "from over the seas." Observers described respectable women who were brought into "promiscuous interaction" with men, an elaboration of the earlier idea of "mixing of the sexes." As an example of this, they wrote of women being forced to take lunch on the factory steps alongside men.[35] The danger to women was also posed as a physical one. Upon leaving one's shift an obrera could be searched, exposing women to actual physical contact. The idea of women being subjected to such searches before they could leave work communicated not only the supposed gravity of placing women in factories but also the abhorrence that artesanos cultos may have felt in having to submit to authority in the workplace.

However, it was not just men who posed a danger to women. Defenders of women workers also wrote about female overseers who abused their charge with harsh words and brusque manners. That both men and women could offend female workers belied as much concern for the social class of the person with whom "respectable" women were forced to interact at work as with either the type of treatment meted out or the gender of that person. In the tobacco factories, women were exposed to the hazards of mixing with "working-class types," for example.[36] Commentators assumed that their readers would agree that such conditions would disgrace any honorable woman. Women who worked in occupations no longer deemed respectable were themselves no longer considered respectable.

Stories of individual working women whose respectability had been threatened served not only as commentary on working women, but also as a means of explaining the degradation of the middle class. In the midst of economic decline, such women, who aspired to respectability, were being corrupted by the same forces affecting all the middle class—declining wages and an increasing cost of living. Thus, the compromised sexual morality of woman served as a metaphor for the immorality of denying opportunity to the middle class.

"She Has Moved Beyond Her Sphere:" Gender and Class Distinction, 1900–1910s

As the working woman became increasingly visible in public discourse, the *buscona, cruzadora*, and prostitute accompanied her. The word *buscona* comes from the Spanish verb *buscar*—"to look for"—in this case, implying a woman dedicated to seeking something not rightly hers: a petty thief, pilferer, or kept woman. *Cruzadora* comes from the verb *cruzar*—"to cross, cross over, or circulate within a given area." Within public discourse, both the cruzadora and the buscona were associated with the prostitute, and along with working women they represented women who had crossed the threshold into the world of work and public activity. In so doing, they had left behind their sexual morality. These turn-of-the-century Mexican social commentators seemed to draw upon the photographic and *costumbrista* literary genre that describes characters central to daily life—*tipos* (types)—and in the process creates social identities. From the colonial period to contemporary times, these tipos have depicted occupations, like street vendor, water-carrier, and public woman, that embodied ideas about class, ethnicity, gender, and social organization.[37]

In 1908 Doctor Luis Lara y Pardo, editor of *El Imparcial*, published *La Prostitución en México*, a study of the causes and circumstances of prostitution in Mexico City. In it, he dedicated considerable attention to the working woman. Lara y Pardo relied on scientific theory to draw his conclusions, but at the same time his analysis of working women was founded in the rhetoric of middle-class identity. His study drew on the work of

French criminologist Gabriel de Tarde and on that of evolutionary biologists Emile Vandervelde and Jean Massart, from whom he borrowed the concepts of parasitism, imitation, and contagion.[38] Using these concepts, Lara y Pardo explained the moral, social, and psychological inferiority of the women in question:

> In Paris, just as in Mexico, the majority of women who prostitute themselves were previously employed as domestic servant or factory worker, and just as French authors have attributed this phenomenon to low wages and the lack of work, it would not be out of the ordinary that someone among us raised their voice—in a magazine, newspaper or scientific assembly—denouncing the same causes of prostitution here in Mexico. Nothing, however, could be farther from the truth. Science has proven that prostitution is an inferior psychological and social condition, a degeneration, just as is vagrancy, mendicancy, criminality, just as with all other forms of social parasitism, from audacious predators to the indolent *rentier* class.[39]

Though Lara y Pardo stated that inferiority is learned, not biologically determined, his work implied that learned behavior is deeply ingrained in cultural practices, in this case, in the cultural practices of working women.

According to Lara y Pardo, if culture taught parasitic behavior, those lessons were distinguished by class and were learned in the workplace. He identified parasitism as characteristic of the "two extreme social classes": the working poor (predators) and elites (the indolent *rentier* class). Moral behavior resided in the middle. In the middle, people did not aspire to be more than they were; they did not attempt to live off of others. Following this line of reasoning, Lara y Pardo argued that female domestics were the consummate parasites. They produced nothing and lived off the wealth and beneficence of others. Such behavior easily led to prostitution. As with all parasites, prostitutes lost all the necessary aptitudes for sustaining a free life and so did not easily leave that lifestyle. Though domestics were more vulnerable to prostitution than obreras, Lara y Pardo found the latter made up the second largest category among prostitutes. The three industries that contributed the largest numbers to prostitutes, according to Lara y Pardo's research, were tobacco, textiles, and the needle trades.[40]

Lara y Pardo's interest in the influence of work on women's morality and comportment went hand in hand with his concern for women's behavior in public. For Lara y Pardo parasitism in all its forms, including prostitution, was caused by imitation. He defined imitation as the process whereby an organism inappropriately attempted to imitate the lifestyle of another. Lara y Pardo was not alone in arguing that the sight of women living "the easy life" would entice honest women into prostitution. Reports surfaced in city newspapers of prostitutes inhabiting certain corners of the city, spending their time enticing "innocent," "respectable" women into prostitution. That is to say, the poor example of some women had a proselytizing effect on others. This logic lay behind the fear that the public display of inappropriate behavior, and the mixing of "pure" and "modest" women with those who were not, were fundamental social problems.

Lara y Pardo's analysis of imitation contributed to class distinction, for it contained a critique of class aspirations and female desire. He claimed that women contributed to the ranks of prostitution depending upon the degree to which they imitated a social standing above the one provided by their employment. Women's desire for luxuries, a desire inherent to female nature, led them to enter into the public world of work, where they necessarily failed to succeed by honest means, and then turned to prostitution. Lara y Pardo provided a comparison of the seamstress and the obrera to elaborate his condemnation. Seamstresses, he argued, thought themselves superior in social class to factory women and domestics. Seamstresses were horrified by the idea of "mixing," in workshops, with a "forfeit mob of coarse women."[41] Obreras, on the other hand, though they supposedly earned less money, were more likely to be part of a family of workers whose lives were in consonance with their means. The seamstress "is generally the abandoned one, the down and out orphan, the older sister or the only daughter, who tries by her own labors . . . to maintain the decorum of an impoverished family."[42] In essence, Lara y Pardo praised recognition of class boundaries.

For Lara y Pardo poor people were accustomed to their situation. It was people in the middle who suffered:

> We can say the following, as a general rule, which can be proven at any time. The life of women in Mexico is that much easier the lower she is in the social classes: work opportunities are more numerous, and her needs are minimal. As one ascends to the semi-poor class, the difficulties increase. [It is with the] . . . middle class, somewhat cultured, decent but deprived of personal belongings, where the difficulties—in the form of irresolvable problems—pile up one upon the other. That is the place of true struggle, suffering, and vacilla-

tion, and all one's efforts are put into play so as not to fall, so as to maintain oneself within the parameters of dignified poverty.[43]

Lara y Pardo claimed that for the poor there was less of an imbalance between needs and means. The middle class, on the other hand, did not benefit from the increased opportunities for amassing a fortune, like the upper classes, or from the supposed rising wages of the working class. Rather, the middle class suffered the consequences of stagnant earnings and a rising cost of living. For Lara y Pardo, middle-class Mexican women at the turn of the century suffered "infamous seductions" and abandonment in silence.[44]

Lara y Pardo was not alone in his reasoning that class aspirations led to prostitution. Numerous newspaper articles expounded upon the proposition that "the fundamental origin of [prostitution] is love of luxury, and its constant fuel is the impossibility of obtaining this luxury by honest means."[45] Writing for *La Convención Radical Obrera*, one journalist assumed his readers would agree that desire for material goods above one's means was essential to female nature: "Luxury for the well to do woman is a jewel; luxury for a woman of the middle class is the possession of kid boots and a straw hat; luxury for a woman from 'el pueblo ínfamo' is the possession of a percale dress and a wool shawl. Then if you ask the first if her husband's income is sufficient to purchase jewels, the second if her father's salary is sufficient to buy boots and hat, and the third if her brother's wages are sufficient to obtain a percale dress and wool shawl, all three will answer you that no, they are not."[46] Once a woman got these things, as if diseased, she would only want more. "And once adorned with these objects, woman *has moved beyond her sphere*, contracted new needs, and she will prostitute herself in order to satisfy her desires before doing without" (emphasis in original). The author went on to argue that first a woman would buy these things and put the family in economic dire straits, and then she would buy them in exchange for her honor. The rhetorical force of this journalist's argument lay in presenting female desire as challenging male authority within each social class. The challenge to patriarchy also challenged class hierarchy, for the farther one moved away from the "well to do," the lesser the degree of male authority that was being challenged. While the well-to-do woman relied on her husband, the woman of "el pueblo ínfamo" relied on a brother. Female desire brought about a parallel breakdown of male authority and class hierarchy.

In fact, there was a special term for women who fed their greedy and lustful habits professionally. Known as busconas, these women were thought to aspire to a class status superior to the one they inhabited, living parasitically off of those with money. Lara y Pardo discussed this "type" in his work on prostitution, and journalists traced intricate myths of the buscona's activities. She was a woman who spent her day conniving, stealing, and compromising her sexual morality for overpriced luxuries. Some of these women "dared" to walk the streets during the day, leaving their homes in the morning without a cent in their pockets and returning in the afternoon loaded down with packages, small and large, containing fans, poplin dresses, and boxes of candy. Journalists often suggested that these frivolities had been purchased using the charge accounts of rich men, most likely Frenchmen or Spaniards, thus simultaneously criticizing the role of moneyed foreigners in Mexico.[47]

As night fell, the buscona would don her uniform consisting of sonorous-heeled shoes and copious quantities of perfume, which Lara y Pardo described as penetrating to "the final folds of the nasal passages." Only the cunning observer, he wrote, would be able to recognize the lack of culture of these women, who could make themselves attractive only by great effort. For the buscona, the "most propitious hour is the one when, like awakened pupils, the streetlights have just been lit." Just as she inhabited the hours of dusk, when the boundary between night and day blurred, as the street lamps were lit, she slipped into the crowd, blurring the boundary between respectable and immoral women. She mingled with the crowds of respectable people out for a promenade, invaded the sidewalks, bumped into people, and knowingly searched for those men who sought out the adventure she offered. In so doing, the buscona disrupted established public interaction. She customarily followed the same route, and could often be found blocking traffic, stopping to chat with others at specific street corners. Social commentators characterized her, not as an accidental floozy but as a person who utilized great skill in plying her trade. Like the obrera, she entered into the world of economic competition only to lose her better part: sexual morality.[48]

The cruzadora, like the buscona and the obrera, also entered into the struggle for survival, and so also compromised her sexual morality. While, as a type, she began appearing in public discussion as early as the 1890s,[49] by 1914 cruzadoras seemed to be so widespread on Mexico City's streets that *El Demócrata* issued a call for a public campaign against her.

This class of woman, intimately related to pickpockets and other thieves, appears in clothing shops dressed in ostentatious elegance, occupying rented carriages—unmarked—and given that they all are of average attractiveness, the shop attendants, fascinated by the studied gazes of these lovers of that which does not pertain to them, are distracted, and it is then that these women take the opportunity to grab the best of the merchandise they have perused; they leave, having bought nothing, and beneath their clothes are the best goods they could get their hands on.[50]

Several characteristics typified the cruzadora. She was a woman who used her sexuality in her work. She traveled in an unmarked carriage and so not only lacked family affiliation but a place in society. She kept company with pickpockets and thieves. The very nature of her work exhibited parasitism and imitation, as discussed by Doctor Lara y Pardo. The cruzadora, like the buscona and the prostitute, was willing to compromise herself for luxury.

While the prostitute, cruzadora, and buscona were not identified as working women, the appearance of these types at the peak of debates over female employment served to delegitimize behavior also identified as typical of working women. The supposed difficulty in distinguishing between respectable and questionable women reinforced the association made between each of these types inhabiting the public sphere, whether in a factory, a shop, or on a street corner. All four types symbolized women who, because of characteristics associated with female nature—a desire for luxury or for a class status superior to that which men could provide—had entered the world of work and the public sphere. The logic was, once women had sold their labor in the workplace, what could stop them from selling their bodies in dark alleyways? Women were incapable of independent survival without compromising their sexual morality. Foreigners aided them in their fall, whether as investors in Mexico City factories that hired women or as men willing to pay for a woman's virtue.

Obreras

And yet the obrera was not a prostitute. The discursive construction of the buscona and the cruzadora may have perpetuated the idea of female weakness, both material and moral; however, the Mexican Revolution served to transform the ways of speaking about working women. Adherents of the Revolution spoke in favor of the popular classes, and this restricted the space within which one could discredit workers, whether male or female. Furthermore, women's presence in factories alongside men was becoming less and less of a novelty. Questions about female sexual morality and domesticity largely fell out of public discussions of working women, though women of all social classes would still be forced to contend with these issues through the 1920s.

During the 1920s working women took to the streets in large numbers. Newspaper coverage of their demonstrations expressed sympathy for working women, the demands they made, and even for their presence on the streets. In May 1922 workers protested abuses committed at La Abeja textile and knitwear factory. The protest included women from La Carolina and La Fama Montañesa textile factories, cigarreras from El Buen Tono, women from the embroiderers' union, and, as *El Demó-crata* put it, "who knows how many men."[51] The journalist used ambiguous language to describe the women, who made "awkward, but sincere speeches," as if to suggest that women were unaccustomed to making speeches in public.[52] *El Demócrata* also reported that onlookers stood on the rooftops and ridiculed the women. During the conflict, a truck full of gendarmes from the city government arrived and attempted to block the demonstration. Standing in the truck, the gendarmes yelled insults at one group of obreras, "calling into question their morality."[53] In the blink of an eye, the newspaper reported, the women were joined by other workers, who toppled over the truck. When an inspector arrived on the scene and learned what had happened, it was the gendarmes, not the workers, who were detained.

The appearance of another group of women also changed the way Mexicans thought about obreras. By the late 1920s, a generation of women with graduate degrees were entering the workforce as journalists, social workers, and feminist activists. These women reconfigured public discussions about working women. Their access to media and government offices brought the condition of working women into the public eye. The activism of Mexican feminists in the 1920s and 1930s has been documented by historians Gabriela Cano, Esperanza Tuñón Pablos, Shirlene Soto, Ana Macías, and others.[54] Mexican women formed feminist organizations, held conferences, and struggled to include feminist issues in the Revolution. Integral to this struggle were feminists' efforts to shape public discussions regarding women and work. In the early 1930s newspapers began carrying columns on the conditions under which women labored.

Alicia Alva, Paula Alegría, Ana Salado Alvarez, Ana María Hernández, and Elvira Vargas were a few among the many who wrote on women in the workplace, in labor organizations, and in the domestic sphere. Women interested in female labor also conducted studies on the subject. Dozens of master's and doctoral students wrote their theses on the position of women in organized labor, the effects of labor on the female organism, and the legal status of married women in the workplace. They contributed sorely needed information on the condition of women's labor and added a feminist voice to sociological literature in Mexico for the first time.[55]

While making significant strides in education, employment, and organizational activities, feminists had to contend with the legacy of the past. In their writings on working women, they refuted traditional understandings of women as antithetical to the workplace and industrialization. In an article published in *El Nacional*, Alicia Alva wrote:

> The working woman not only has accepted the new impositions of the modern era, not only does she work with modern machinery, earn a salary, and in an infinite number of instances support her family, but in Mexican women there has persisted a spirit of continuity, respect for old things, and a deeply ingrained commitment to religion. So that, when ignorance is destroyed in her we have to see that her emotions have grown in precision and intensity, no longer stimulated by fanaticism, rather by a more ample idea, the desire for integral betterment. The increased cultural levels of the actual situation [of working women] and her generous manner of being, will without a doubt make of the working woman the most serious sector of the work force, now that—as we say—they are the partners of men in the highest sense.[56]

Alva's words addressed issues that had been raised as far back as the 1830s by men like Esteban Antuñano. She began her commentary by countering, as Antuñano had done, concerns that women could not work with modern machinery. She praised those women who earned a wage and supported a family. By seeing women as partners with men, Alva also countered fears that had been brought about by having men and women working in the same space, the "mixing the sexes." Moreover, Alva addressed concerns that Antuñano did not have to face in the 1830s. She had to contend with the negative connotations which associated women with religious practice and its political implications. For Alva, Mexican women had progressed beyond emotional and conservative religious sentiments, in part because of their participation in modern life, including the workplace. The Revolution, she argued, had improved the cultural attainments of working women, making them worthy of partnership in receiving its benefits. While Mexican women continued to struggle with the public portrayal of the obrera as antithetical to industry and the somewhat more amorphous concept of modernity, the "angel of the home" could now enter the workforce without necessarily being associated with the prostitute.

Conclusion

In the mid–nineteenth century public discourse construed men and women as occupying separate spheres and "mixing the sexes" as posing a moral danger to women. The public discourse that accompanied women as they went to work in the 1880s was grounded in this idea and was increasingly informed by changing conceptions of class. This chapter has examined two paradigms of socioeconomic relations that coexisted in the late nineteenth and early twentieth centuries. Those who understood the world in terms of patron-client relations argued that right gender roles were the keystone to social hierarchy. It followed, then, that threats to right gender relations threatened class hierarchy. Thus, when Francisco Bulnes decried that a feminist was more dangerous than a Barcelona anarchist, he was expressing the fear that the entrance of women into the workforce would bring about class conflict. Middle-class discourse, too, was premised on the idea of female weakness; however, it allowed for a middle space wherein "respectable" employment would save women from the weakness inherent in their sex.

Discussions of working women also served as a means of criticizing the ills associated with industrialization, in terms both moral and material. During a time of limited political protest, the middle class decried its own precarious financial and cultural status. In construing the cigarrera and costurera as caught between the rising cost of living and restricted economic opportunities, this woman of the "martyred middle class" suffered what all the middle class suffered. Such discourse also served as a means of class distinction, especially in distancing the middle class from identification with the working class. Within both paradigms, the corruption of Mexican women by foreigners served to criticize the role of foreigners in Mexican industrialization.

Following the lead of Joan Scott, historians have argued that gender as a discursive category has served to reinforce categories of class.[57] While gender functioned in this manner in Mexico, the opposite was also true. In Mexico, the discourse of class served to delineate the boundaries of gender. For Horacio Barreda, "activities truly industrial" turned a woman into a mari-macho. Within the discourse of middle-class respectability, a woman who entered a factory with other members of the working class endangered her morality. The desire for class mobility also circumscribed female respectability. In 1908 Doctor Lara y Pardo could reinforce class distinction by arguing that inappropriate desire for luxury led to the corruption of female sexual morality.

Beginning in the 1880s the obrera served as the repository of the contradictions of class and gender relations. These contradictions existed not only within the realm of discourse, but were manifest in the worlds of women's work. They informed women's everyday lives, in the factory and in their organizational efforts to shape the conditions under which they labored.

CHAPTER 3

"Moral and Material Suffering"

Protest and Power, 1880–1911

The position of women in the workforce laid the foundation for how they would organize. Chapter 1 documented the concentration of women in tobacco processing and sewing, as well as their entrance into new industrial occupations beginning in the 1880s. Female-dominated industries contributed to a strong, work-centered, organizational culture for women. Mexican working women also acted within the context of discursive constructions of working women. Chapter 2 showed how upper- and middle-class observers construed women as vulnerable participants in the work place, and honor and sexual morality as central to working women's identity. As working women organized, negotiated, sought alliances, protested, and went on strike, they utilized both this discourse of female vulnerability and sexual morality, as well as their own definition of the morality of working women, to voice their demands.

This chapter focuses on women's mutual aid societies, and in particular on the labor activism of cigarreras and costureras. These women drew upon prevalent modes of organizing mutual aid societies and female-specific forms of sociability. With increasing employer pressure on these workers in the 1880s and 1890s, women who had relied upon employer-sponsored organizations sought new methods of achieving their goals. Cigarreras and costureras differed in the paths they would follow. Cigarreras turned increasingly to other workers, petitioned the public, and went on strike. Costureras broke from employer-sponsored organizations and sought the patronage of upper-class women, but did not go on strike before 1911. Both cigarreras and costureras used the press and the language of morality as an organizational strategy. Newspapers representing a wide range of constituencies engaged in a public discussion regarding the morality of employers, workers, and the government. Within this public conversation working women utilized conceptions of female morality and weakness to buttress their claims for rights as workers.

In recognition of the multiple responsibilities of women and the historical presence of many women in the domestic sphere, Mexican labor historians have emphasized women's activities in consumer-based protest and in supporting the strike activities of men, arguing thereby that women saw their prerogative in protecting family and community.[1] By focusing on their work-related activism, this chapter contributes another facet to our understanding of Mexican women. In turning our focus to workplace protest, we see that in many regards women's labor organizing did not differ significantly from that of men. And their concerns, which remained roughly the same throughout the period, were also similar: production quotas, wages, the enforcement of regulations, the quality of the raw materials used by piece-rate workers, recognition of the right to negotiate, and worker solidarity. Women's organizational methods, however, did differ from those of men in that they were shaped by women's unique position in the workforce and by public discussions of working women.

"Because They Are Not Capable of Performing Miracles": Women and Mutual Aid Societies, 1880–1910

In Mexico, as throughout Latin America, the first postcolonial collective attempts by artisans and early industrial workers to protect their interests took the form of mutual aid societies. Economic development and Bourbon reforms had undermined the power of guilds, the means by which artisans had protected their trades. Artisans subsequently built upon the social cohesiveness of the guilds and the culture of confraternities to form mutual aid societies. Municipal ordinances regulated mutual aid societies, granting them little formal, recognized power. In the 1870s power brokers from artisanal backgrounds worked with the city and federal government to obtain resources for society members. The Porfirian government had little tolerance for other forms of labor organization, and so mutual aid societies, which had become increasingly active in the 1860s and 1870s, flourished in the last quarter of the nineteenth century. Both due to government support of such organizations and "because they [were] not capable of performing miracles," the activities of women within mutual aid societies strengthened in the 1880s.[2]

Workers formed mutual aid societies according to trade or as members of the same place of work, and according to gender. The separate organizations for men and women reflected both their separation in the workforce (although this was not always uniformly the case) and patterns of sociability of the mid–nineteenth century. "Women with women," as one observer objected when a man took over the leadership of the women's society Luz y Constancia.[3] Women's mutual aid societies were either female affiliates of men's societies, such as the wives of bakers and other workers who were members of the Mutua de Señoras Union y Amistad María de Jesus, or they were occupation-based societies for working women, like the Fraternal de Costureras.[4]

The creation of a female work-centered culture began in the workplace and is evident in the names women chose for their societies. Mutual aid society names generally described members' occupations, communicated a goal or orientation, or honored a noteworthy woman. Caners allied with women machinists in the shoe industry, for example, and named their society the Female Caners and Shoemaker Machinists' Hope for the Future (Esperanza del Porvenir de Señoras Empalmaderas y Maquinistas del Ramo de Zapatería), suggesting their cross-occupational interests as well as their optimistic outlook. Women at La Carolina named their society for their place of work, suggesting a strong workplace orientation. Two mutual aid societies named their organizations after two heroines of the war for Mexican independence: Leona Vicario and Josefa de Domínguez. Leona Vicario, whose name was adopted by a group of costureras, came from a royalist family but gave much of her wealth and support to the rebel cause. Adopted by another group of working women, Josefa Ortíz de Domínguez, La Corregidora, had been the wife of the *corregidor* of Querétaro but had nevertheless sent the message that sparked the call to arms in September 1810. Still another society celebrated the very culture of female societies by naming itself after Maria de Jesus Huerta; Huerta had been an active promoter of mutual aid societies in the mid–nineteenth century.[5]

Though men and women organized in distinct societies, in many regards they engaged in similar activities. Society members made regular monetary contributions in exchange for benefits in case of accident, sickness, death, or other catastrophic events. However, working women's societies also addressed women's specific needs, which ranged from issues particular to working mothers, such as education and childcare, to demands more directly related to women's role as wage earners. Some women sought a shorter workday because they needed to shop in markets before closing time. Others sought to be able to collect their paychecks during safe hours.[6] The Mutua de Señoras El Fénix (established in 1893) mediated labor conflicts with their employer, José Abdó, the owner of El Carmen knitwear factory. After the Revolution the women changed the name of their organization to Fraternal El Fénix and the society remained active as late as 1914.[7] Working women also joined Catholic mutual aid societies. Two such organizations were the Obreras Guadalupanas and the Asociación de Sirvientas Católicas de Santa Zita, the latter organized by the upper-class women's church group Damas Católicas and emphasizing evangelical rather than economic issues.[8]

Mutual aid societies helped their members in time of need while at the same time promoting cultural activities, friendship, and political support networks. Some societies held *tandas*, a weekly redistribution of group savings.[9] Many sponsored dances, dinners, and *kermess* (outdoor fairs, often charitable events, and feast-day celebrations for patron saints). These events were especially common when work was scarce or when larger than usual numbers of members had fallen ill and needed financial support. Some gatherings allowed for fundraising and the opportunity to establish links with middle- and upper-class sympathizers. Both male and female mutual aid societies depended upon the contributions of their members and also upon the patronage of prominent citizens and government representatives.[10] Patrons of women's societies included Manuel Romero Rubio, father-in-law of President Díaz; engineer and philanthropist Gabriel Mancera; and Eduardo Orrín, the owner of a popular circus.[11] Women also gathered for patriotic and political reasons, as when the seamstresses of the Leona Vicario society threw down their work and rushed to join in a commemoration of the death of Benito Juárez on 18 July 1887.[12]

By and large, in the early nineteenth century mutual aid societies aided each other in the struggle for survival without making demands on employers; however, this attitude changed in the last two decades of the century as society members increasingly began confronting their employers by the strike. During the Porfiriato there were at least 250 strikes in Mexico, especially in the years 1881, 1884, 1889–1891, 1895, and 1905–1907. More than half of these strikes occurred in Mexico City. Textile workers and cigar and cigarette makers staged the largest number of strikes, both in Mexico City and nationally. In Mexico City women were a significant percentage of the textile workforce (approximately 25 percent), and they dominated cigarette production, so their participation in

these strikes was central in the history of labor organizing during the Porfiriato. At the national level, after textile workers and cigarette makers,
bakers, miners, and transportation workers, primarily male occupations,
followed in the frequency of strikes.[13]

Cigarreras

Among all the mutual aid societies, the cigarreras were unique in their
strength, the unity of their action, and the support they lent to other working women in Mexico City. Cigarreras had a long history of collective
activity dating back at least to the 1780s, when they had taken up collec-
tions for widowed or ill co-workers and their children. During the North
American invasion (1847) cigarreras collected money in support of the
Mexican troops, indicating their interest in issues beyond the immediate
walls of the factory.[14] By the 1880s cigarreras utilized a wide range of resources to promote their interests, including the support of elite patrons,
members of other mutual aid societies, and the Mexico City press. Cigarreras also worked closely with the Congreso Obrero, though not always
without contention. Cigarreras and their advocates were able to establish
the legitimacy of the society's voice in the public sphere both by making
public the conditions of cigarette work and by relying on the language of
female virtue.

The Congreso Obrero played a key role in mediating relations between industrialists and cigarreras — as well as other groups of workers.[15]
Established in 1879 by a splinter group of former anarchists, the Congreso
came to play a more conciliatory role in labor conflicts than its origins
would have suggested. Pedro Ordóñez, the Congreso's president, served
on the Mexico City Council in the 1880s. El Congreso Obrero came to be
dominated by men in occupations that were marked by middling status:
a military commander, an artisan turned industrialist, and well-off artisans. Its leaders emphasized cooperation with government and industrialists, and nonviolence, especially for women. This emphasis contributed
to its survival. In 1889 the Congreso Obrero represented eighty mutual
aid societies, of which ten were presided over by women.[16] The newspaper
La Convención Radical Obrera served as the official voice of El Congreso
Obrero and as an important strategic tool for working women.[17] The death
of Pedro Ordóñez in 1903 marked the end of labor representation on the
city council and the rapid dissolution of the organization.

Cigarreras went on strike frequently throughout the 1880s and 1890s, as regional competition in the industry led employers to demand more of their workers.[18] Employers' demands varied. Some tobacco factory owners installed new machinery, using the occasion to increase production quotas without raising wages. Others fired workers or closed their doors definitively. In September 1881 the Moro Muzo cigar manufactory increased production quotas, from 2,185 to 2,700 cigars daily, for the same 4 reales a day wage. Cigarreras went on strike, but supported only by their own savings, hunger eventually forced them to return to their jobs having won no concessions from the factory. Similarly motivated strikes soon followed at other factories around the city, including El César, La Niña, El Borrego, and El Faro. With so many factories on strike, El Congreso Obrero stepped in to mediate between cigarreras and their employers. The Congreso negotiated a new quota of a 2,304 cigarettes for the workers' 4 reales daily wage.[19]

After the federal government imposed a new tax on the tobacco processing industry in 1884, a round of strikes broke out. Employers had attempted to pass the cost of the tax on to their workers by reducing the wages they paid per task. A group of cigarreras sent their formal complaint to the President of the Republic, and their letter was reproduced in a local newspaper. The recent imposition of taxes, the women argued, had led to a reduction of workers in some factories and to the closing of others. They asked the president, in his role as "father of the Mexican people," to do something about the problem.[20] Like the indigenous women from the same time period studied by Florencia Mallon, the working women of Mexico City associated justice with the actions of the "good patriarch." Mexico City working women did not derive this idea from indigenous communal organization based in concepts of obligation, however. Rather, as workers and as women, they invoked the language of patriarchy because they did not have access to the language of legal rights as workers or as women.[21]

No response to the women's letter appeared in the newspapers. However, three months later debate over the conflict revealed that more was at stake than the simple implementation of a tax. In some factories, owners had implemented a higher production quota, bringing in male convicts to do the same work as women for lower wages. At the behest of the Prison Commission, these factories had hired men from the Belém and Castillo de Tlatelolco prisons who would "voluntarily" work for less.[22] At this time, women had few other options for work; however, when the occupational captivity of female workers proved insufficient, employers turned to male captives for labor. Ironically, employers who frequently touted their protection of female morality did not express concern about employing male convicts to work alongside women. Although, they had been careful to create a separate department for male workers.

The questions of female poverty and the morality of work were of general public interest, and others stepped in to the debate that emerged. The newspaper *El Tiempo*, edited by influential Mexican clerics, carried considerable moral authority among the Mexican upper class.[23] The paper often reported on the situation of Mexican industry and on worker conflict. While *El Tiempo*'s editors might have lamented the loss of jobs for women, they were equally concerned with the effects of feminine labor on the convicts' masculinity. One article remarked that while *El Tiempo* did not believe in leaving prisoners in a state of inactivity, it did not see the virtue in giving men a "feminine occupation that is not even a masculine occupation, that would cover the needs of a father of a family."[24] The male prisoners' wages proved to be more of a concern than the already low wages of women.

In 1885 four factory-owners decided to break the 1881 agreement that had been negotiated by El Congreso Obrero, and they raised production quotas from 2,304 to 2,600 cigars daily, without raising wages. The cigarreras asked El Congreso Obrero to intervene on their behalf once again. When the factory owners refused to negotiate, the women went on strike. In order to help them sustain the strike, the cigarreras relied on assistance from other working women, both in and outside the tobacco processing industry.[25] The collection of funds by obreras from factories across the city allowed the cigarreras to remain on strike for nearly twenty days. With no resolution in sight, however, the cigarreras decided to write a letter to the editor of the women's newspaper, *El Correo de las Señoras*. By enlisting the support of society women, the cigarreras acted under the assumption that all women had shared interests, despite differences in social class; at the same time, they broadened their position within the public sphere.

In their letter, the cigarreras indicated the importance of the press in shaping moral opinion on several levels. First of all, the press served to give moral authority to working women. The cigarreras wrote, "If Mexican journalists deny their protection, enlightenment, and prestige to their miserable sisters, who prefer work over prostitution, then what hopes remain for the Mexican working woman?"[26] By raising the specter of prostitution women made use of the idea that exploitative working conditions threatened female morality. This cast their fight in moral terms, arguing strongly that low wages led to female dishonor. They also named the specific factories that had failed to adhere to the earlier agreement mediated by El Congreso Obrero, adding that the owners were Spanish. With this nationalist argument, the women were suggesting that foreign capital had corrupted the honor of virtuous Mexican women, women who should be defended by their fellow Mexicans. Thus, in this and other letters, the women were able to voice their side of the conflict, their ideas about themselves as workers, and their ideas about the moral economy of industrial relations.

The cigarreras took more drastic measures than writing to *El Correo de las Señoras*. In an unusual move, they placed signs on street corners around Mexico City explaining their situation. The signs read:

Oppression by the Capitalist!

Until October 2, 1881, we used to make 2,185 cigars for four reales, and now they have increased the number of cigars and lowered our salary. On October 3, 1881, through the mediation of El Congreso Obrero, we agreed to make 2,304 cigars for four reales. It is not possible for us to make more. We have to work from six in the morning until nine at night. . . . We don't have one hour left to take care of our domestic chores, and not a minute for education. The capitalists are suffocating us. In spite of such hard work, we still live in great poverty. What are our brother-workers going to do? What are the representatives of the Mexican press going to do? We need protection, protection for working women! [27]

In describing the conditions they faced, the cigarreras were indicating who they thought should come to their aid. While recognizing the work of El Congreso Obrero, they now argued that the new quota was untenable. They appealed to working men, the Mexican press, and all passersby who might read their signs. While appealing to male authority for protection, the cigarreras also expressed themselves in a class-conscious language by using the term "capitalists" and by referring to their "brother-workers." Cigarreras also communicated a sense of their own history, of a continuous struggle since 1881.

El Tiempo again weighed in on the conflict, supporting the cigarreras but deploring some of their tactics. Its contributors responded to the signs posted by the cigarreras by condemning the depths of misery to which the cigarreras had fallen. However, the paper also made veiled references to the women's picketing as a shameful practice that discredited the cigarreras. With women out of work, signs displayed across town, and newspapers heatedly exchanging opinions, the Governor of the Federal District was forced to intervene. A few weeks after the appearance of the signs, he brokered a settlement of 2,400 cigarettes at 4 reales (50 centavos).[28]

When the government imposed a stamp tax on tobacco products in July 1887, some factory owners, already squeezed by the competition posed by mechanization, again raised production quotas without raising wages. This time, employers sought a 2,700 quota for the same 4 reales.[29] In an effort to remedy the situation, the cigarreras wrote another letter to President Díaz, once again published in *El Tiempo*.[30] Apparently they received no response, because ten days later women from six factories went on strike.

The striking women wrote a letter to El Congreso Obrero, once again asking for intervention. In their letter justifying their cause, published in *La Convención Radical Obrera*, the women expressed both deference to conceptions of female debility and reference to their position as workers: "Given our situation, our humble condition, the weakness corresponding to our sex, our sentiments as women counsel us to seek assistance from the noble sons of labor, the only ones that can best understand our misfortune, we place before those whom it may concern, the sad future that awaits us."[31] In response to the cigarreras' request, El Congreso Obrero drew up a petition to the Ministro de Hacienda, Manuel Dublán, that the stamp tax be rescinded.[32] Dublán did not eliminate the tax, but he agreed to alter it. Dublán's reply was published in *El Tiempo*, signaling the importance of public opinion. In his answer Dublán stated that the tax had not been intended to place a burden on the cigarreras, implying rather that the choice to effectively pass the tax on to them had been made by their employers.[33]

Despite the cigarreras' success in pressuring the government to alter the stamp tax, working conditions did not greatly improve. Now, the women decided to appeal to elite women. In September 1887, 1,207 cigarreras signed a letter to the president's wife, Señora Carmen Romero Rubio de Díaz, that was printed in the newspaper *La Paz Pública*.[34] Then, in early December, the cigarreras formed the Sociedad Mutualista Hijas del Trabajo (Mutual Aid Society Daughters of Labor).[35] The officers of the society included Dolores Hernández, president; Paula Santa María, (who had been an active participant in the recent conflicts), vice-president; and Fermina Barajas, secretary. As was customary, the cigarreras also named an Honorary President and Patroness, Doña Manuela Arango de Carrillo, who was the wife of General Hermenegildo Carillo, Military Commander of the Federal District and honorary president of La Convención Radical. Las Hijas del Trabajo also sought sponsorship *(apadrinado)* from the Buena Madre and Alma de María societies.[36] On an equally practical note, the cigarreras named two men to serve as consulting lawyers: Juan A. Mateos (a Porfirian historian) and Gabriel María Islas. An Honorary Board included the wives of prominent politicians and representatives of the press.[37]

As a means of collecting funds, encouraging morale, and garnering public support, Las Hijas del Trabajo organized a circus that was put on by the famous Señor Eduardo Orrín. The circus included a performance of Cinderella, after which the women staged a ceremonial parade and blessing of their banner by a priest. The banner was an important object of identity and pride, and was described at length in the newspaper. Mexican artisans had made the banner of the finest silk and gold threads. It depicted the tools of the tobacco processing trade and scenes of daily working life: the worktable, a distaff "emblem of women's work"; a book representing the law and/or the regulation of mutuality; and a pair of scissors, indicating the principal occupation of women upon leaving the factory. *La Paz Pública*, which was one of the group's sponsors, noted: "It is well known that the poor woman has to make her own clothing."[38] The symbols on the banner indicated that cigarreras thought of themselves as women and as workers. The inclusion of both the worktable and scissors suggested a tradition of work that did not end upon leaving the cigarette factory. If clothing was considered central to expressions of femaleness, then working women participated in this culture differently, because they made their own clothing. Also, the clothing industry was one of the principal employers of working women.

The blessing of the banner took place in front of the offices of *La Paz Pública* on Progress Alleyway. Adding to festivities, a military marching band played. The Honorary Board and other distinguished guests participated in support of the cigarreras. Both male and female worker associations joined in the procession accompanying Las Hijas del Trabajo to San Cosme Church, where the priest blessed the enterprise. At the conclusion of the blessing, the cigarreras went to the house of their Honorary President, Señora Arango de Carrillo, to sing her *Las Mañanitas*, since the day was, not coincidentally, her birthday. In the months following the festivities, cigarreras turned to the task of confronting their employer and demanded a quota reduction.[39]

By 1888 the cigarreras had won wide, though not unconditional, support. They had made some gains in the battle over quotas. Nevertheless, their strength could not match that of their employer. Initially, all but one factory had complied with the agreement mediated by El Congreso Obrero. However, over the subsequent months many factories left off compliance. Strikes in 1888 and again in 1889 revolved around similar issues of quota size, wages, stamp taxes, and mechanization.

One letter written by the cigarreras stands out from this period. Written as a public statement and sent to a newspaper, it describes in great detail the production process and how employers manipulated that process to the disadvantage of the cigarreras. The letter is like many others wherein working women argued their cause in terms grounded in their experience as workers. And yet the detail with which they described the process of production shows their efforts to place working conditions at the center of public discussion of their rights. Forty-four workers at El Ideal had declared a strike on 29 August 1888. In the letter, the cigarreras explained:

> In this factory there exists the habit of giving the women the tobacco, after having weighed it, and then demanding that, when they return it, the product weigh the same. This is, naturally, impossible. They are given the work when the tobacco is humid, which means that it weighs more than when it is already dry. Furthermore, to make the cigarettes it is necessary to pull off the stems that have remained on the veins of the tobacco, and other inevitable waste, which necessarily reduces the weight of the amount that is returned to the factory owner. It seems that because they are not capable of performing miracles, the proprietor punishes this natural decrease by imposing fines on the unfortunate cigarreras, and this, in any light, is unjust. The fines, which range from five to thirty centavos, greatly diminish the miserable wage with which the poor workers barely eke out an existence. Day before yesterday workers gathered in an attempt to make their reasons known to Señor Pugibet, but the proprietor of El Ideal did not even want to speak to them.[40]

Cigarreras explained the production process to make known to the public that while quotas may have remained stable, their wages continued to decline. They also made known that their efforts to negotiate peacefully were denied, thus justifying their strike.

When cigarreras went on strike again in 1895, they utilized similar tactics. This time, the owners of El Premio cigar factory had reduced wages from 4 to 3 reales a day. A group of cigarreras who attempted to approach their employer and were refused even the opportunity to speak with him decided to go on strike. The cigarreras turned to other cigarreras and maestras in factories across the city for support. While in some regards the maestras might be considered managers, they sympathized with the cigarreras because often they had worked their way up the ranks themselves. Maestras assisted striking workers by making cash donations or serving as representatives to employers. A group of maestras and administrators from across town joined together to come to the aid of the striking cigarreras by offering them work. These maestras included Señoritas Lina Vega and Rafaela Galindo from El Buen Tono, Señorita Bernarda Montiel from El Modelo, the maestras at Los Aztecas, and the administrator of El César.[41]

When the strike seemed to have no effect, women from outside the factory stepped in to help. The teachers Isabel Guerrero, Francisca Guerrero, and Julia Escobedo went to the owners of competing factories and convinced them to hire a number of the striking workers. Female teachers probably were not from backgrounds too distant, in economic terms, from women working in factories, and their salaries, like those of the cigarreras, did not support a middle-class lifestyle.[42] While all this was going on, those who remained on the strike line made sure that no new workers were hired at El Premio. Violence broke out when a group of striking workers entered the factory and attempted to remove women who had agreed to work for the miserably low wage of 37 centavos per quota. The press scolded the cigarreras for resorting to violence. Resorting to violence, though it was one of their few remaining options, alienated allies, not only because of prevailing opinion against worker violence, but also because it violated the basic premise of femininity. The El Premio factory owner accused the women of attacking private property and turned them over to the authorities. El Congreso Obrero also condemned the women's violent behavior, yet tried to prevent charges being brought against them. They were not successful.[43] The cigarreras had made polite appeals to the public and their employer, and then they had been forced to resort to violence, only to be rebuked by the justice system. What recourse were they left with?

La Unión Obrera organized a benefit dance. At the dance, an announcement was made that the son of cigarrera Cipriana Bobadella had died of hunger because his mother could not provide for him during the strike. Enraged by this news, over one hundred women from factories throughout the city stoned the El Premio factory. The police arrived and arrested thirteen women, who then faced sentences of either two months in prison or fines of 50 pesos each. Although the Fraternal Military Society (La Sociedad Fraternal Militar) and El Congreso Obrero paid the women's fines, they were still sent to Belém prison.[44] One wonders if they were incarcerated with the same men who had been hired to replace them at the factory.

After violence broke out, sympathy for the striking women diminished. The press withdrew its support, claiming to stand on the side of the law, in favor of morality, and out of concern for encouraging appropriate female behavior. El Congreso Obrero had also reached its limit with the threat to industry and the public peace. It ran an article in *La Convención Radical Obrera* which cast shame on the cigarreras by noting that "everyone knew about the violent incident." El Congreso Obrero arranged new jobs at the San Miguel textile factory in the state of Veracruz for the thirty-five women who were identified as organizers. El Congreso could thus claim to be helping the women, but the group also seemed interested in eliminating those people who might disrupt their dispute-resolution efforts. The newspaper report of the women's departure noted that Pedro Ordóñez himself, accompanied by a group of cigarreras and some other "distinguished individuals," warned the departing women "that they [should] act as was appropriate to the dignity of the Mexican woman."[45]

In October of the same year (1895), workers from El Premio and another, unspecified factory (perhaps El Ideal) established a cooperative manufactory, La Nueva Fábrica de Cigarros La Alianza Obrera. It was a new step for the cigarreras, although not so unusual given the tradition among mutual aid society members, dating back to the 1870s, of supporting production and consumption cooperatives.[46] The 119 cigarreras of the Working Woman Alliance (La Alianza Obrera) and La Union Obrera chose Señorita Isabel Guerrero as their representative, "despite the fact that she is teaching elementary school, because she has dedicated all her efforts to assisting the cigarreras."[47] Guerrero had been an active participant in the El Premio strike the previous April. The cigarreras placed an advertisement in the newspaper, which stated that they hoped the visibility and unity of their cause, as well as their good standing in public opinion, would persuade customers to buy their tobacco products, thus raising the wages they earned for their eleven- and twelve-hour days of strenuous work. The advertisement read:

> The Separatists and Striking women ask that the public purchase their EXCELLENT TOBACCOS, confident that the most demanding smoker will be satisfied. Fifty centavos is the wage this Company will pay for a 2,500-cigarette quota, to all of its shareholders as well as all those who work as simple workers. Don't forget "La Alianza Obrera." Good Taste, superior quality manufacture, and exquisite quality is offered by the owner-workers, who hope that the public favors them with the consumption of their product. 20 Cigarettes at 3 centavos — 18 Pegados at 3 centavos. On sale throughout the Republic.[48]

It is not clear how successful the cooperative was or how long it survived. However, it is testament to the solidarity and creative efforts of the cigarreras that they produced and advertised the sale of cooperative products. The way the women phrased their advertisement also shows that the women combined pride in the quality of their work with the moral authority they had cultivated with the public over the previous fifteen years of strife.

Labor agitation increased throughout the country, although workers became increasingly disillusioned with the limits of mutual aid societies. In August 1906 workers throughout the country formed a national tobacco workers congress. Many members of La Gran Liga de Torcedores de Tabacos de los Estados Unidos Mexicanos advocated more forceful action. Other members continued to curry favor with the federal government. This latter faction held sway and invited Minister of Education Justo Sierra to represent the Díaz government at their first congress. Concerned with the positions some members of La Gran Liga were taking, Sierra made an impromptu speech warning that the right to organize ended when it was done with the intention of fomenting class struggle or "seditious acts." He reminded his audience that in the case of such acts the government stood ready to respond with sixty thousand bayonets. One member of La Gran Liga pointed out in his response to Sierra's threats how inappropriate it was that instead of talking of books and learning, the Minister of Education had stood with bayonets pointed at the working class.[49]

Costureras

During the 1880s, as cigarreras sought ways to gain more control over the conditions in which they labored, costureras also shifted their methods of organizing. Although the unknown number of seamstresses interspersed throughout the city might not have been able to find a way to organize, those who worked in the production of military apparel for government contractors did. In the 1870s the working-class press ran articles on the difficulties faced by costureras because the lack of protective tariffs made it difficult for them to compete with the low prices of imported clothing. Furthermore, the arrival of new technology had created additional divisions among those seamstresses who worked for contractors and those who worked independently. However, it was the growing importance of contractors in the production of military apparel that lay at the root of the decreasing value of the costurera's wage in the 1880s. Costureras differed from cigarreras in one important regard. While cigarreras had over a century of experience within a work-centered culture, costureras de munición had only recently been brought together as workers. Furthermore, costureras de munición worked for employers who monopolized the market, giving those workers less power over their employer.

In 1885 several newspapers ran articles regarding the lowering of piece-rates for the production of military apparel.[50] It is unclear whether the articles appeared as a result of petitions by seamstresses or not. Regardless, *El Tiempo* denounced the fact that many contractors were foreigners who profited while Mexicans writhed in misery. Contractors countered that they would move production to the United States where, they rumored, they could hire workers for lower wages. *El Tiempo* responded that before supporting such a move, they would rather give up their nationality as Mexicans. The newspaper also made an argument for abiding by tariff agreements, not only because they were the law, but also in the interest of defending honorable work for women. Three years later, the seamstresses themselves took action.

In 1888 a group of seamstresses broke away from the organization sponsored by the munitions contractor Señor Llamedo. Llamedo had required that his employees belong to his organization in order to work for him. If they quit and then returned looking for work, he required them to pay him 75 centavos to be rehired. After a series of abusive incidents, in which Llamedo had paid women their wages by throwing their money on the floor, the women organized. In their first public statement, the new Sociedad Mexicana de Costureras explained that they had formed "to protect those whose wages are the bread of their families' existence." They described their society as bringing together women "as if of one family," and their mission was "to encourage each other, making [ourselves] worthy of the respect and affection of those of the same Society and of those already established."[51] The reference to other societies signaled the importance of alliances with other working women. That same year, another group of women established the La Sociedad de Costureras Sor Juana Inés de la Cruz.[52]

These independent organizations soon served as a means for costureras to confront their employers. A conflict over wages erupted in 1889. In this confrontation, the costureras, like the cigarreras, turned to El Congreso Obrero. When this proved unsuccessful, the Fraternal de Costureras petitioned their honorary member and patron, Señora Díaz, for assistance. As a result of their petition, the Secretary of War and Marine Manuel González Cosío agreed to negotiate a new tariff agreement.[53] In this instance, the society's alliance with a powerful patron allowed the costureras to push the government to act. However, how far the government might be willing to push the contractors was another question altogether.

In March 1893 contractors continued to pay wages below the tariff. In a change of strategy, the seamstresses, with the assistance of their new benefactor, Señora Felícitas Juárez de Sanchez, established a number of Sewing Agencies. The agencies provided a place for women to work, machines to sew on, and a clientele. The Society hoped to attract orders for work from people interested in supporting the seamstresses' cause. In the newspaper article announcing their creation, the agencies were construed as both a public service and a means of assisting "honorable women."[54] A front office staffed by "suitable" people took orders for underwear, lacework, and "all other labors appropriate for women." The following year, the Sociedad Filantrópica Mexicana established another sewing cooperative.[55] The sewing agencies usually had rules, one of which did not permit women to use the machines to sew on sturdy fabrics that might break the machines. This included *paño*, the cloth used by many to make workers' clothing. If a woman broke a needle for any reason, she was responsible for paying for its replacement. Women were also asked to work the machines at a moderate pace, and they were required to pay for their own thread, which they could purchase at the agencies at a below-market price. The agencies did not allow women to enter with food or alcoholic drinks, either.

La Convención Radical Obrera hailed the sewing agencies as a saving grace for mothers of the martyred middle-class. It described the women who availed themselves of the services of the agencies as "widows or orphans with large families to attend to, who belong to the suffering middle class, martyred for their education, their morality, and we will say it once and for all, their enlightenment, which does not allow them to descend to the lowest levels of society, [and who] without aspirations and almost without awareness of their dignity, live in the most regrettable misery and abandonment."[56] The workshops allowed some women the possibility of work disassociated from "the lowest levels of society"— that is, work in a factory.[57] Unfortunately, it seems the sewing agencies met with limited success. This led patrons of the Fraternal de Costureras to organize a raffle for its members, most of whom were out of work. An announcement for the raffle appeared in *La Convención Radical Obrera* and pointed out that Señora Díaz herself had donated items. Eduardo Orrín also put on a benefit circus for the seamstresses, for which the seamstresses gave public thanks by sending a letter to the newspaper for publication.[58]

Contractors continued to ignore the government-established tariff. In 1896 more than fifty seamstresses wrote a letter to President Díaz, which they sent to *El Periódico de las Señoras* for publication. The letter noted that the reduction in the seamstresses' wages had led to "moral and material" suffering. This coupling of moral and material suffering served to reinforce the power of their interpretation of the conflict, which the women identified as the discrepancy between the government tariff and the wages they actually received. They also justified their demands by invoking their status as single mothers. Seamstresses framed this petition by portraying themselves as the "children" of Porfirio Díaz. In the absence of the possibility of claiming specific legal rights as workers, this allowed the women to make demands based on conceptions of family obligations. Unable to claim the rights of citizens, women construed themselves as individuals who could not, morally, be abandoned. Despite the publicness of the letter and the rhetorical strategies they used, the seamstresses saw no improvement in their wages. In 1897 they again petitioned President Díaz via the press, this time in the pages of *La Convención Radical*

Obrera. Even as seamstresses were asking the president to eliminate the monopoly contracts, contract holders again threatened to move production to the United States. Meanwhile, El Congreso Obrero suggested that the women organize a collective savings bank *(caja de ahorros)* as a means of ameliorating the financial difficulties they faced.[59]

As competition in the clothing industry grew in the first years of the twentieth century, contractors increasingly came to rely on subcontractors, which greatly exacerbated the problem of wage reductions for costureras.[60] In March 1901 *La Convención Radical Obrera* commented that if the costureras were paid any less they would be reduced to the position of "tortilleras or scullery maids,"[61] which implied that women who relied on the needle trades should be protected against slipping into what was considered to be the lowliest of working-class occupations. Given such circumstances, the paper also published the 1889 tariff, which was still in effect, pointing out that noncompliance with the tariff was an abuse that should be remedied by the authorities. An abuse, they noted, that all the press denounced.[62] Again, El Congreso Obrero, however tenuously, sought to place the seamstresses struggle in the public eye and to cast a moral tenor on their struggle. In a subsequent article, *La Convención Radical Obrera* used the situation of the costureras and cigarreras as a means of denouncing the condition of the entire Mexican working class. Both occupations had formerly provided a decent standard of living, but now they provided women with little more than a pittance. The problem was not unemployment, the newspaper argued, but the decreasing value of wages. Workers could no longer feed themselves on what they earned.[63]

Obreras, 1907–1910

Beginning in the 1890s new factories had begun locating in Mexico City and more working women had been hired. Along with the women who already worked in cotton, woolen, and silk textile production, large numbers of women now began working in the manufacture of knitwear, processed foods, and other consumer goods. Las Hijas de Anahuac, formed in 1907, has been identified by chroniclers of women's labor organizing in Mexico as the first female union, distinct from mutual aid societies. Las Hijas de Anahuac was organized in the textile factories of the Federal District and its environs. Charter members included La Abeja knitwear factory workers María del Carmen, Catalina Frías, Justa Vega, Eligia Pérez, Leonila Aguilar, María Gomez, Carlota Lira, Concepción Espinosa, and

Josefa Ortega. Obreras also participated from La Magdalena and Santa Teresa in Contreras, and La Hormiga in Tizapán. Several teachers joined with the textile workers and together their principal objective was to fight against the reelection of Porfirio Díaz and to improve the status of women. As a part of their struggle, Las Hijas de Anahuac supported the Partido Liberal Mexicano (PLM), which, in addition to its call for the overthrow of Díaz, called for the general betterment of the position of women in Mexican society. The PLM stood for an eight-hour workday, a minimum wage based on a reasonable cost of living, the adoption of a means of enforcing a minimum wage, a maximum day for piecework, and regulation of domestic work and outwork. The PLM also supported equality under the law for all children of the same father, which would eliminate legal differences between legitimate and illegitimate children. This question of illegitimate children would become an important issue for women involved in the movement for women's rights in the 1920s and 1930s.[64]

Consisting mostly of textile workers, Las Hijas de Anahuac originally met on Sunday afternoons in the Frías sisters' home or in other private residences. When meeting at their place of work, the women often depended on the assistance of a factory administrator by the name of Gómez. Whenever the police came looking for the women, Gómez, a Spanish immigrant, would secretly signal the doorman to warn the women. In order to escape arrest, the Frías sisters and their co-workers would then jump the factory wall and head off into a nearby field to hide until it was safe to return to work. The leaders of the organization were subject to constant persecution. The women continued to meet in smaller groups in the fields near the factories and grew to be three hundred strong before the police forced them to suspend their activities. After the outbreak of the Revolution they threw their support behind Francisco Madero, because they saw in him hope for a change in working conditions and for social policy relevant to women.

Although the number of strikes decreased in the waning years of the Porfiriato, nine out of ten of the major strikes that occurred in 1909 were in the Federal District. Alarmed by the increase in labor agitation, and perhaps by the activism of women in organizations like Las Hijas de Anahuac, in 1909 the Partido Científico (Díaz's party) commissioned one of its most prominent members to establish a Catholic worker organization. Don Guillermo Landa y Escandón, governor of the Federal District, worked tirelessly to promote the founding of sympathetic Catholic mutual aid societies based in factories throughout the Federal District. The year

1909 was also an election year, and cynics accused Landa y Escandón of acting out of political motives rather than out of concern for either workers or industry. They accused him of organizing textile workers in order to counter the growing support for Francisco Madero among their ranks. The societies Landa y Escandón organized would come together as the Sociedad Mutualista y Moralizadora Landa y Escandón in 1910. By June 1910, the Sociedad Mutualista y Moralizadora could claim a membership of over five thousand workers.[65]

The year 1910 was the centennial of Mexican Independence, and the Partido Científico hoped to turn the celebration into a means of uniting workers, industrialists, and the government. The progress of the working class, reported *El Obrero Mexicano*, the official newspaper for Landa y Escandón's mutual aid societies (and originally published by the owners of La Tabacalera Mexicana), would come via moralizing acts. Just as Hidalgo had lifted the yoke of oppression from the Mexican people, Díaz would liberate the working man. "Díaz formed el pueblo, and Landa y Escandón will imbue it with morality."[66] In early 1910 Governor Landa y Escandón directed a letter to factory owners explaining his objectives. His project was one of protection and moralization of *el pueblo*, an act of private charity "for men as well as for women." He reminded factory owners that they knew the benefits of "guiding workers along the path of honor, morality, health, and work."[67] To this end, society members were prohibited from discussing religion, politics, or any subject that might place in danger the coherence of the group.[68]

Landa y Escandón showed specific concern for working women. He feared the disintegration of the Mexican family. Women who were forced to work outside of the home, he argued, suffered as individuals and caused harm to their families. Based on this concern, much of his organizing activity focused on factories that employed large numbers of women, including La Perfeccionada knitwear factory, the Chambón silk factory, several cigarette and clothing factories, and factories that made hats, ribbons, mattresses, and candles, as well as a lithography and typography business.[69] To assist these women, Landa y Escandón established La Sociedad Instructiva y Recreativa Guillermo Landa y Escandón and the Casa Protectora de Hijos de Obreras. The former organization was designed for those who did not have the means to educate their children, and the latter attempted to aid women who did not want to leave their children home alone while they were at work.[70] Such an approach to ameliorating the difficulties of working-class life neatly dovetailed with upper-class preoccupations with motherhood. Certainly, these organizations also responded to working women's concerns for the care and education of their children; female mutual aid societies had organized around similar issues. However, not all workers who would have supported education for their children agreed with Landa y Escandón's politics.

Governor Landa y Escandón's method of organizing women reveals the priorities and preconceptions of Partido Científico–sponsored worker organizations. *El Obrero Mexicano* was more likely to publish articles in flowery language celebrating women's domestic responsibilities, their superior capacity for love, and their morality than to publish articles on work-related issues. Not only did Landa y Escandón express the ideal of women as distinct from men, he shaped his organizations accordingly, separating and subordinating working women to working men. At each factory he visited, Landa y Escandón spent a few minutes speaking with the workers, and then he dined at champagne brunches with the factory owners, where he heard workers give laudatory speeches in favor of the mutual aid societies. In one of his factory visits, Landa y Escandón began his day listening to a speech given by a woman, in the name of her sisters in labor *(compañeras de trabajo)*, followed by a speech given by a man, in the name of his brothers in labor *(compañeros de trabajo)*. At the Chambón silk factory one man was designated to speak on behalf of all the workers, and he noted with humility that there were many women, "their hair grey from the years of working at the factories, who should rightly have been selected for the honor."[71] The separation of the sexes in individual member organizations resulted in the subordination of women in the larger organizational structure as well. Despite the fact that women constituted one-third of the membership, women were underrepresented at the first general assembly in 1910 (they made up only 36 of the 226 delegates).[72]

With the departure of Porfirio Díaz and his wife Carmen Romero Rubio de Díaz in 1911, the Sociedad Mutualista y Moralizadora and affiliated organizations took on new meaning. In the month following the former president's departure, Landa y Escandón made a farewell appearance to members shortly before he also left Mexico City in June.[73] His departure did not change the real need for working women and men to organize; however, the way they interacted with the larger movement of workers did change. No longer guided by Governor Landa y Escandón, the Sociedad Mutualista y Moralizadora and other mutual aid societies formed new alliances and began placing their demands before the public in new ways. The women had cultivated a wide array of tools in their struggles, some of which they would leave behind and others of which they would continue to utilize.

Conclusion

During the Porfiriato women in a wide range of occupations formed mutual aid societies. Within these societies women participated in activities that were in many ways similar to those of men, but which also reflected their status as working women. Their identification with their place of work, the demands of motherhood, and the history of working women all shaped their activities. The concentration of women in female-dominated industries lent itself to a particularly strong, work-centered culture, particularly among cigarreras and costureras. Beginning in the 1890s, increasing numbers of women worked in consumer-goods factories alongside men; these men and women organized both in sex-specific organizations such as Las Hijas de Anahuac, and in mixed-sex societies that continued to tend toward the separation of men and women, as was the case with the Sociedad Mutualista y Moralizadora.

Cigarreras and costureras, in their efforts to defend their capacity to earn a living, laid claim to a place in the public sphere. These working women entered into the public discussion regarding the morality of industrial relations. They did so by publishing public letters, protesting in the streets, and seeking alliances with representatives of labor, like El Congreso Obrero, other workers, women of elite status, and representatives of the state. In so doing, they sought to counter the private power of industrialists by using "reason" based on conceptions of morality. Employer compliance with negotiated agreements was voluntary, and many industrialists had intimate ties both to other industrialists and to the government. Cigarreras lacked the significant legal rights and the private power that was exercised by their employers. Their engagement of the public in a discussion of the morality of women's working conditions was thus an effort to counter legal, political, and economic weakness. They spoke of this weakness in a gendered language. In their public petitions, cigarreras and costureras framed their demands within the language of discursive constructions of working women. These discursive constructions included reference to "la debilidad de nuestro ser."

Working women's organizing reveals a constellation of strategies that included making alliances with women from different sectors of Mexican society. They made common cause with women beyond the walls of their particular places of employment, across the industry, and with women in other occupations. Working women allied themselves with teachers, who while ostensibly of a different socioeconomic status, found common cause in defending the rights of women. Working women's alliances with elite women, whether Carmen Díaz or the readers of women's newspapers, expressed the potential power of reliance on a female identity that they hoped would undercut their weak position as working-class women.

Women's labor activism in mutual aid societies between 1880 and 1910 (which signaled the outbreak of the Mexican Revolution) would serve as the basis for their participation in unions. The changing position of women in the workforce would shape that activism: because unions were organized within the workplace, women would increasingly participate in mixed-sex unions. The power of female morality that had developed through women's struggles would continue to inform the formulation of women's demands. However, the place of women's demands within the larger labor movement would shift.

CHAPTER 4

Inclusive Marginalization, 1911–1930

The strong work-centered culture that women formed in the late nineteenth century served as the basis from which they entered into unions during the Mexican Revolution. However, important shifts in women's workforce participation shaped the way they organized. While women continued to dominate the clothing industry, an increasing number of women worked in the knitwear, processed food, and other consumer-goods industries. This shift brought women into mixed-sex places of work. The political context within which women organized had changed as well. Working women's organizational efforts would continue to be shaped by conceptions of women as vulnerable, in both the material and moral sense of the word, and by the concept of women's honor as relevant to the legitimacy of their claims. However, with the Mexican Revolution women would also formulate their demands in terms more narrowly defined by the conditions of work. Working women's engagement with the public also shifted. Women were less likely to publish letters in the press and more likely to demonstrate in the streets. Their voices were simultaneously more muted by their lack of public letters, and louder as they joined with the larger working-class movement.

Within the context of shifting political alliances and new labor organizations that emerged after the departure of Señores Porfirio and Carmen Díaz, working women allied themselves in new ways. In the early years of the Revolution (1911–1913) large numbers of women took to the streets to protest working conditions. This activism led many of them to participate in the formation of the Casa del Obrero Mundial. After the suppression of the Casa in 1916, working women and men participated in competing and overlapping unions. Several incidences suggest that although initially and publicly the Confederación Regional de Obreros Mexicanos claimed to protect the rights of working women, by the early 1920s it was courting unskilled female workers while simultaneously marginalizing women from skilled occupations. The Federation of Worker's Unions of the Federal District (Federación de Sindicatos Obreros del Distrito Federal) and the Confederación General de Trabajadores proved to be more protective of the rights of working women, but these organizations were less successful in gaining concessions for their members more generally.

From Mutual Aid Societies to Unions: Costureras and Obreras, 1911–1916

In the first decade of the twentieth century Mexicans debated the relative value of different forms of labor organizing. Some workers questioned the effectiveness of mutual aid societies and instead supported the formation of unions. Women's prominence in mutual aid societies opened them to attacks by opponents of this form of organizing. Despite negative portrayals, women's means of organizing did not differ significantly from that of men. And, in fact, it was precisely women's earlier participation in mutual aid societies that prepared them for an active role in revolutionary activities. Between 1911 and 1914 women in the clothing, textile, and knitwear industries staged massive demonstrations and strikes. In seeking out the most effective strategies, many of these women allied themselves with the Casa del Obrero Mundial. However, their success varied by industry and greatly depended upon the capacity of workers to form national ties and on the relative strength of the industrialists they were opposing.

The debate between adherents of mutual aid societies and supporters of unions dated back several decades.[1] In the 1890s participants in these debates utilized gendered conceptions of politics in formulating their arguments. In 1895 an article in *La Patria* had described mutual aid societies' members as "lost in poetry [and] dances where they eat turkey mole, et cetera, and don't take the time to buy an oven so as to break the bread monopoly in their neighborhood, or a corn mill with which to destroy the tyranny of the metate, that heartless tyrant of national labor." *La Patria* identified female pastimes—cooking and poetry—with women's supposed blindness to effective solutions to their problems. *La Convención Radical Obrera* favored mutual aid organizations and countered such criticism, arguing that women got together "for noble causes, not reasons of religious fanaticism," and that such accusations were "only an effort to censor mutual aid societies, and to make fun of national customs." For, as *La Convención* assumed its audience would agree, "the only way to make a tortilla is on a metate."[2] While El Congreso Obrero defended women's mutual aid societies, it did not question traditional female labor obligations such as grinding corn on a metate.

The identification of women with ineffective organizational efforts continued in the early 1910s. An opponent of mutual aid societies, Juan Sarabia took the opportunity of the 1911 costurera strike and the publicity it received to promote the unionization of workers. Sarabia was a founding member of the Mexican Liberal Party, and later of the Liberal Party (Partido Liberal) established in August 1911, as well as a member of Congress. He was of the opinion that Mexican workers were wasting their time organizing in mutual aid societies, which, he stated, occasionally helped individuals but were completely ineffective in the improvement of "workers as a *class*."[3] On the occasion of the 1911 seamstress strike, he wrote that it, "like almost all Mexican strikes, has been the result, not of conscious planning, but rather of a momentary and desperate impulse, evidencing from its inception all the characteristics of failure." For Sarabia, and a growing number of labor organizers like him, unionization was the more effective means of increasing salaries and decreasing the workday. The money that workers contributed to their organizations should be put aside, against the day when members must go on strike, and such strikes should be planned for the most appropriate moment, when workers were strongest. Mutual aid societies, he argued, did not plan. They used their money for dances and showy evening parties, when what was needed was "the effective progress of workers as a class."[4]

The gendered nature of this conflict over the value of mutual aid societies is evident from the terms of the debate. Both sides identified mutual aid societies with the domestic sphere: food, religion, and social gatherings—activities associated with women, of limited political influence. Sarabia characterized mutual aid societies as lacking any coordination or planning and as acting defensively and spontaneously. Such accusations ignored the history of women's mutual aid societies. Women across the workforce had joined the societies as a means to socialize, but more importantly they had also joined to improve their living and working conditions. In this regard, women's goals differed little from those of male members of mutual aid societies. Ironically, the strike that Sarabia was criticizing—the 1911 costurera strike—actually marked the beginning of women's move out of mutual aid societies and into unions.

The 1911 strike occurred at La Sinaloense clothing factory, which was owned by Ricardo Otero, a Porfirian congressman and the holder of a government contract for the production of military clothing. In November, Otero had attempted to move production out of the factory and into seamstresses' homes. The women protested that their employer was attempting to place an increased financial burden on workers. The new policy would also enable Otero to play one group of seamstresses against another, thereby reducing piece-rates. Otero also sought to reduce wages by 5 centavos per piece. The wage reduction struck the women as particularly unjust because Otero was already known to pay well below the tariff established by the Ministry of War. Moreover, Otero was also requiring the women to obtain a bondsman who would vouchsafe for the women's use of Otero's sewing machines and would cover any damage to the materials with which the women worked. Many of the seamstresses were so poor that they did not have sewing machines at home on which to work, much less money to obtain a bondsman.[5] The costureras were also angered by the fact that the cloth Otero provided for them was inexpensive and of exceptionally poor quality, sometimes rotting, thus further reducing their wage-earning capacity.

The women organized a representative commission and sought to meet with their employer directly. Señor Otero refused. In response, Enrique Bordes Mangel and Don Camilo Arriaga of the Partido Liberal arranged for mediation. The women offered to work in the shop and to pay for the use of sewing machines if their employer would pay the government-established tariff. Otero refused the terms and the women went on strike. Otero was also reported to have beaten Maria Rodriguez, one of the women involved in the strike. The seamstresses, who had begun two hundred strong, marched to the National Palace and shouted to Madero, "If the president doesn't pay attention, it's to the revolution for us!"[6]

The "La Sin" strike came at an important juncture in Mexican history and so carried significant symbolic power for workers. Porfirio Díaz had just been forced out of office and was headed into exile in France, and Francisco Madero had assumed leadership of the government. Señor Otero was a close friend of the ex–vice president Ramón Corral, and there was some question as to how he would be dealt with by the new government. Both the workers themselves and sympathetic journalists invoked the 1907 strike at Rio Blanco as an identical situation, one in which they understood Díaz had unleashed the wrath of the government on workers, resulting in rivers of blood. On 26 December the Attorney General requested that Otero hand over all the money he had saved from the costureras' wages. Both the costureras, who defended their right to strike, and the Mexican public waited for Madero's response as an indicator of things to come.[7] On 30 December 1911, *Nueva Era* published a piece by Licenciado Eduardo Fuentes, who pointed out that the Secretary of War and Marine had acted inappropriately when he "threatened [the women] with grave consequences if they did not return to their work soon, accepting such iniquitous and illegal conditions."[8] Fuentes also questioned the sincerity of the Partido Liberal and Don Camilo Arriaga in their efforts to mediate the conflict.

In January 1912 the Mexican government allowed Señor Otero to retain his contract for the production of military clothing and to close his sweatshop. The Secretary of War and Marine resolved not to abrogate its contract with Señor Otero, stating that Otero had complied with the stipulations of said contract. Señor Otero was free to close "La Sin," which allowed him to circumvent all the difficulties "caused by the obreras."[9] As for the striking women, Otero would allow them to complete their work on any pending items. They would do this work at home, and he could still require that they pay a guarantee for the value of the goods. Thus, in one fell swoop Señor Otero terminated the strike and reinforced the new work conditions over which the strike had begun.

Unwilling to accept such a settlement, the seamstresses of La Sinaloense went to the factory and guarded their place of work day and night. They were not protecting the factory against the violence of revolutionaries, or against Zapatista incursions, but rather against its owner, Ricardo Otero. Otero planned to contract out the remaining work to women who were willing to break the strike and work in their homes. On the night of 16 January, Otero sent one of his administrators, the unfortunate Señor Agras, into the shop to fetch raw materials and unfinished garments. Señor Agras was able to enter the building, but then the women trapped him inside and locked the doors—threatening to pummel him if he tried to escape. Otero responded by calling the police. Initially, two gendarmes arrived on the scene, and they were soon backed up by twenty mounted police. This show of force enabled Señor Agras to leave the building, though the women demanded that he do so without the garments he had come for. Agras did not get away, however, without the seamstresses falling upon him in an angry attack. The two women identified as the principal instigators were taken to the police station.[10] Shortly thereafter the number of strikers dwindled to fewer than one hundred, and many of the former strikers eventually found work in other shops. The conclusion of the La Sin conflict did not signal the end of women's activism, however. In the midst of the La Sin conflict, other workers throughout the textile and knitwear industries had also gone on strike.

What would become a nationwide movement began in Mexico City on 26 December 1911 when workers at the San Antonio Abad textile factory went on strike in response to wage reductions. Management had installed smaller pinions on the factory's looms, which allowed the machines to produce a lighter weave cloth and effectively resulted in reduced wages for workers. The workers at San Antonio Abad allied themselves with workers in textile factories across town, and by early January thousands of workers were on strike. On 2 January 1912 five thousand women who worked in textile, knitwear, and clothing production in the Federal District went on strike at La Hormiga, San Antonio Abad, La Carolina, La Linera, and Contreras. Workers were fed up with the "false promises of leaders of the Revolution." They also stated they were angry with the press for its lack of support. Each day the number of strike participants grew, from nine thousand workers who closed down seven factories on 4 January, to eleven thousand more workers who closed six more factories a few days later. The number of strike participants eventually rose to over thirty thousand men, women, and children after workers' families joined in. Many of these families had been thrown out of their employee housing and were left with no place to live and no income.[11] On 6 January 1912 more than four thousand workers staged a march, beginning at the statue on Calle Primera/Avenida Juárez, and progressing down Avenida San Francisco to the esplanade in front of the Palacio de los Virreyes. Workers carried banners for each of the factory-based organizations. A delegation of workers from Río Blanco also participated. When the demonstrators reached the Palacio and called for Madero, he appeared on the balcony. The President then made a speech in which he promised a reduced workday and an end to child labor.[12] At that time, many textile workers still put in fourteen- to fifteen-hour days.

Days later, on 10 January 1912 the women responsible for checking the quality of cloth coming off the machines at La Perfeccionada knitwear factory also attempted a strike. The obreras announced their intentions to their fellow workers, asking them for their support, and went to speak to the administrator. The women demanded a 20 percent increase in wages for the workers in that department. Initially, the administrator agreed to their demands, but when two women from another department argued that all workers should benefit from the 20 percent wage increase, he balked.[13] The administrator claimed that the two women who seconded the 20 percent wage increase did not "have any life experience, and must not work out of necessity."[14] He played on the idea that many women worked only to pay for incidentals and therefore did not need a decent wage, or perhaps even to work. The next day, at the end of the noon shift, a small group of women gathered outside of the factory to convince their fellow workers to strike. Indeed, they threatened the rest of the women with a stoning if they returned for the afternoon shift. The administrator notified the police, who arrived twenty strong. He also identified those whom he referred to as the "rebellious ones" and they were taken to police headquarters, while the rest of the women were assisted in returning to work.[15]

In January 1912 Mexico City's streets were filled with workers. The success of the different constituencies of workers differed dramatically. The seamstresses who worked for Señor Otero had met with little success, for example. Their strike had garnered some public support, but the Madero government had upheld Otero's right to set the conditions of employment at his factory. The women had been forced to either work for Otero out of their homes or to find work elsewhere. And, despite the strike at La Perfeccionada and the other knitwear workers who joined in the January street demonstrations, no such convention was convened among knitwear industrialists at this time. In contrast, at about the same time, textile industrialists expressed interest in a national textile convention. Workers organized commissions, in which women participated.[16] The relative success of the textile convention that resulted from workers' strikes can be debated. Compliance was voluntary, and guidelines were sufficiently vague that individual employers had quite a bit of leeway in how they interpreted them. Furthermore, the outcome of the textile convention was ambiguous for working women, as it restricted women from night shifts.[17] Nevertheless, the 1912 textile convention served as the basis for workers' demands in the following years. It also led to a subsequent textile convention in 1925–27, when the conditions of the contract were updated.[18] Neither seamstresses nor knitwear workers had been able to sustain their strikes, nor to establish ties throughout the country, as had textile workers.

Despite, or perhaps because of, the limited impact of their activism, knitwear workers continued to strike and make demands on their employers throughout the Federal District during the remainder of 1912 and 1913. Many of these strikes were in response to work stoppages called by employers. Factory owners justified temporary closures as being due to disruptions in access to raw materials and fuel caused by the Revolution. They also sought to avoid paying workers to produce goods that were piling up in storage, due, they claimed, to interruptions in transportation. Factories also closed to clean machinery. Regardless of the reasons industrialist gave, workers protested the impact the closures had on their livelihoods.[19]

As was the case before the Revolution, organized women formed alliances across occupational lines. In early 1913 female knitwear workers belonging to the Sociedad Mutualista y Moralizadora filed complaints with the Department of Labor. In July of the same year over two hundred women who worked at El Carmen knitwear factory made their cause known to the press and went to the Department of Labor to present their case. Women from El Cisne and Maria knitwear factories accompanied them in solidarity. Mexico City knitwear factory owners claimed that because industrialists in the interior of the country were able to pay substantially lower wages, they would have to lower wages in their own factories. The Department of Labor sought to resolve the conflict, given that "these poor women go to such great efforts to earn a living for themselves, and for many of them, their large families as well."[20] The women were not successful. José Abdó, owner of El Carmen, refused to raise salaries and the women refused to return to work at such low wages. The factories Maria and El Cisne offered to relocate the women from El Carmen when its owners closed that factory's doors.

Although the El Carmen workers lost their jobs, the pressure that they and others throughout the industry had exerted led industrialists to react. Knitwear industrialists expressed their interest to the Department of Labor in convening a congress, similar to the one that had been convened by textile industrialists the previous year, so as to establish a minimum wage. In addition, the industrialists were also interested in the impositions of a national tariff that would level the competition posed by producers in other regions of Mexico who could pay lower wages. The creation of a national congress would also allow them to address what they felt were debilitating taxes.[21] Nevertheless, after the convention workers continued to negotiate contracts with employers on a factory-by-factory basis, rather than industrywide. This continued to be the case well into the 1930s.[22]

With no industrywide agreement forthcoming from the knitwear convention, workers continued to face considerable difficulties. Over two thousand women were threatened with a loss of work in mid-1914. In June, several factories closed down. At the Corsetería Francesa, the owner claimed that a lack of fuel had forced him to do so. Five hundred out-of-work women thought otherwise, reporting that the owner had closed the factory because his warehouses were overstocked.[23] Corsetería Francesa later reinitiated production, but reduced the workweek from six to four days, without providing a wage increase.

The struggles of the seamstresses, knitwear workers, and other working women led to their early participation in the Casa del Obrero Mundial. Between 1913 and 1916, the Casa played a crucial role in providing support for working people in general, and for women in particular. Workers with anarcho-syndicalist beliefs had formed the Casa late in 1912. During 1913–1914 the Casa moved from an educational to an organizational phase. By 1913 its membership rolls included several women's mutual aid societies: Sociedad Mutua de Señoras Tejedoras, Sociedad Mutualista de Auxilios, Amistad y Progreso, and Sociedad Instructive y Recreativa Guillermo Landa y Escandón.[24] Women whose organizational history lay in mutual aid societies and early unionization efforts participated in the Casa May Day parade in 1913, during the military dictatorship of General Victoriano Huerta. Despite claims to the contrary by detractors, the mutual aid societies had provided the organizational experience that enabled women to partake in the move toward unionization.[25] How this occurred is evident in the alliance formed between the Casa leadership and the seamstresses, who were once again on strike in August 1913. For this strike, however, the seamstresses allied themselves with the Casa del Obrero Mundial.

In August 1913 seamstresses working for Ricardo Otero had approached members of the Casa del Obrero Mundial. The women were looking for support as they petitioned the Secretary of War and Marine. Their primary demand was similar to that which had been repeated throughout the last two decades of the Porfiriato: that the government contract directly with women for the production of military clothing. Luis Méndez, a central figure in the Casa leadership and secretary of the Metropolitan Tailors Union, took particular interest in the conflict, as it would impact the work of tailors as well. The Casa convoked a special meeting to discuss the issue.[26]

At the same time, other contract holders stopped production, firing all their employees. Another group of seamstresses went to the Department of Labor seeking assistance in finding work. The Department of Labor reported that General Aurelio Blanquet, Minister of War, had acknowledged that the instability of the times had led contractors to cease production, but that the general intended to place orders for equipment with them soon, thus assisting the "honorable and suffering" needle-trade workers.[27] Seemingly, both petitions to the Department of Labor and the Casa met with little success. The Casa may have been unable to assist, as Huerta had closed it down in May 1914. However, by August the Constitutionalists had defeated Huerta and General Álvaro Obregón had taken control of the city. The Casa reopened, supported by Obregón. In October 1914 seamstress went on strike again in what came to be known as the Needle Strike (La Huelga de la Aguja).

When the Needle Strike broke out, journalists sympathetic to the seamstresses utilized conceptions of threatened female morality, which they associated with the Porfiriato, to legitimate the demands of the striking women. *El Demócrata* portrayed the seamstresses as being hunched over their machines in the sweatshop, not even allowed to chat, while under the vigilant eye of the overseer. "Temptation, tuberculosis, and prostitution" was the only future that awaited them.[28] This reference to threatened female morality and disease was accompanied by specific descriptions of the conditions under which women labored for Señor Otero, "the bloodsucking contractor." The journalist claimed that Otero forced seamstresses to purchase their own buttons and thread, and that they were paid only 37 centavos for a dozen shirts. Like other clothing contractors, Otero would delay paying a woman if he found defects in her work: the skip of a needle or a misplaced button, for example. Meanwhile, the contractor wore diamonds on his fingers and drove an automobile. The strike, said *El Demócrata*, represented "the first step toward the redemption of the working woman."[29] Regardless of such support, it was neither the first time seamstresses had organized, nor the first time observers had construed work as redemptive for women.

The same day as the women struck, the newspapers reported on a meeting that had been convened by the Casa, in which members had drawn up a general list of demands to be presented to First Chief Carranza, Mexico City Governor Jara, and the city council. The content of these demands reflected the influence of seamstresses within the Casa, and included an eight-hour workday and a minimum wage of one peso fifty. The list of demands also called for the elimination of piecework and outwork, two central concerns of the seamstresses. The petition clearly stated the workers' position that piecework and outwork divided them, to the advantage of employers.[30] In the following days, the seamstresses, who had been on strike repeatedly, and who had sought the assistance of the Department of Labor and of the Casa, formed a union and formally allied themselves with the Casa. *El Demócrata* called it the "first female union" and reported that the Casa had offered this "nascent trade union" its standard amount of startup funds, as well as its "unconditional support."[31]

One of the first acts the seamstresses took was to request that the Secretary of War and Marine circumvent the subcontractors and contract with them directly. Department of Labor women inspectors had vociferously supported this request, but the Secretary of War and Marine did not respond. Rather, the Department identified the twelve women they identified as instigators of the strike and informed them that disagreements should be discussed "moderately and courteously."[32] If they were unfortunate enough not to find new work, the Department's representative informed them, the Department might be able to help them. Although, the representative added, given the current economic situation, they should not expect much. When the Department of Labor sought to reinstate them, the women declined, voicing their wounded pride and their doubts that conditions would change. In a show of support, the director of the Industrial School for Orphans contracted with the seamstresses directly for the production of six hundred student uniforms.

As seamstresses continued their strike, on 26 October "working men and working women" at El Palacio de Hierro workshops also went on strike. Their complaints centered on the low wages they received. Justino Tron, their employer, reported to the newspapers that wages at his shops were better than at others of the same quality.[33] Workers met to draw up a list of their actual wages, which they hoped the paper would publish, in order to show to the public that this was not the case. The Department of Labor mediated a settlement that included a 10 percent wage increase.[34] The Palacio de Hierro workers thus began a union that would persist throughout the 1920s.

By 1914 Casa membership was flourishing, in part due to the increasing numbers of women who joined. President Obregón had provided the Casa with a new location to house its growing membership, which included the cigarreras of La Companía Mexicana, who joined that same year.[35] Early in 1915 the Casa took the vote that led to the formation of the Red Brigades. The women of the Casa formed the Ácrata sanitary brigades to contribute their part. Within the context of these developments, by 1915 working women in textiles, knitwear, sewing, shoes, perfume, cardboard boxes, and beer also allied themselves with the Casa.[36] Jovita Barriel served as "secretary for the obreras."[37] Some of these women became members of the Casa just at the moment they were going out on strike. Such was the case in the fall of 1915 when the Union of Working Men and Working Women in Baking went on strike, an action that *El Demócrata* described as including "a large quantity of women."[38] Also in 1915 the workers at Eriksson Telephone and Telegraph Company, which included female operators among their ranks, also went on strike.[39]

In early 1916 a group of new worker organizations came together under the Federation of Workers Unions of the Federal District (Federación de Sindicatos Obreros del Distrito Federal). A citywide organization, the Federation brought together self-governing unions organized along industry lines, but it focused on individual places of work. Because member unions organized by workplace and industry, not solely by occupation, men and women participated in the same unions, or formed female affiliates, not as wives but as co-workers. Male and female knitwear workers organized together, as the Knitwear Working Men and Working Women of the Federal District. The Union of Electricians included female telephone operators. The Printers Unions included women who worked as folders, binders, and packers, though they were organized in an affiliated women's group. María del Carmen Frías, a textile worker and founding member of Las Hijas de Anahuac and of the Casa del Obrero Mundial, joined with other textile workers to found the Federation of Thread and Cloth Workers of the Federal District (Federación de Hilados y Tejidos del Distrito Federal). Workers joined from La Abeja, San Antonio Abad, El Salvador, La Linera, and La Union. Women formed mixed-sex unions at the Santa Rita thread factory, La Perfeccionada knitwear factory, and at Santa Teresa, where women added "Constancy and Progress" to the name of their union. Women also joined from the female-dominated industries, as was the case with the seamstresses who joined under the leadership of Esther Torres.[40]

The Federation affiliated itself with the Casa del Obrero Mundial, so that by 1916 the membership of the two combined organizations included women button makers, knitwear workers, teachers, and coffee packers, as well as makers of ties, corsets, bottlecaps, beer, perfume, cardboard boxes, biscuits, candy, and flour. The claims of labor organizations have been disqualified as exaggerated in the name of politics. Nevertheless, they give some idea of relative membership. By late 1914 the Casa claimed to have some five thousand members, and in 1916 the Federation claimed ninety thousand.[41]

By the time of the General Strike of 1916 women were acting as full participants in the labor movement, including in leadership positions. While the demands of the strikers were presented in non-gendered terms, the response of General Carranza relied upon conceptions of working women as weak and morally compromised. The General Strike occurred within the context of such high levels of inflation that most currency in circulation in Mexico City was nearly worthless. On May Day the Federation of Worker Unions of the Federal District demanded that workers' wages be paid in gold or its equivalent in paper, as a means of protecting the working-class's standard of living. A first strike, which failed, was declared on 22 May. The second strike, on the eve of 30 July, was successful. Shortly after the outbreak of the strike, the police arrested members of the strike committee, including seamstresses Esther Torres and Angela Inclán.

President Carranza met with the strike committee, including Torres and Inclán. In their meeting, he exploded at the strike committee: "You have sold yourself like a bunch of whores!"[42] In addition to insulting the members of the strike committee, Carranza insulted Esther Torres and Angela Inclán specifically. He told the women that they were "mujeres complicadas," suggesting they had been the unaware victims of actions instigated by men. In response, Torres argued that she and all the women who participated in the strike were just as responsible as the men. "No Señor, we *are* conscious of our acts," she told Carranza.[43] Carranza sent all twelve strike-committee members to jail, where they remained for twenty-six days.[44] During their trial, Torres was asked if she loved her homeland, to which she answered, "Well . . . that is so vague . . . I can't say whether I do or do not love it, I hardly know it." This question was followed by one from her own lawyer, Ventura Zamorategui, who asked if she would fight to defend Mexico if it were invaded by foreigners. To this question, Torres answered with an emphatic "yes." "Then you love your homeland," her lawyer summed up in front of the judge.[45] Esther Torres was acquitted, but she was punished nonetheless: she was blacklisted from employment.

While the organizing efforts of the Casa del Obrero Mundial brought diverse sectors of the working-class together, its existence came to an abrupt end in 1916. After Constitutionalists eliminated the threat of the supporters of Emiliano Zapata and Francisco Villa in 1916, they turned their forces against the workers with whom they had previously been allied. Government treatment of the leaders of the General Strike of 1916 was but one example of this turn against the Casa and the workers it represented. The demise of the Casa was a loss to workers. It was a significant loss for the women who had been active in strikes and organizing throughout the period 1911–1916. Despite the criticism of men like Juan Sarabia and the partial support of the Partido Liberal Mexicano, costureras and obreras had moved effectively from mutual aid societies to unions, such as Las Hijas de Anáhuac, the La Carolina Factory Commission, and the Casa del Obrero Mundial. With the dissolution of the Casa del Obrero Mundial, women, like all workers, had to rethink their organizational strategies.

Inclusive Marginalization: 1916–1930

After the General Strike of 1916 and the subsequent repression of the Casa, working women and men sought new ways to organize. Two currents of organization emerged within the working class: the Confederación Regional Obrera Mexicana (CROM), founded in March 1918, and a group of competing unions that were more independent in their relationship with the federal government, which included new incarnations of the Federation of Workers Unions of the Federal District (mentioned above) and the Central General de Trabajadores (CGT). While the CROM included women in its ranks, and even stated that the active recruitment of women was one of its goals, in the workplace the CROM was less favorable to women. Incidences among cigarette workers, market vendors, and waiters reveal that the CROM sought to keep women out of skilled positions. While women joined the CROM, they also joined oppositional unions like the CGT, where they were more likely to serve in leadership positions. However, women did not rely solely on unions to express themselves. During public demonstrations, including May Day parades, women voiced concerns specifically as working women. Years of women's organizational experience coincided with the flourishing of feminism in Mexico City in the 1920s, and working women voiced their rights as workers and their opinions regarding the continuing association of women with sexual morality.[46]

After the General Strike, workers' unionization efforts remained dispersed but not dormant. In 1918 Gustavo Espinosa Mireles, in his campaign for Governor of Coahuila, courted the worker vote, especially that of miners. With the support of his mentor, Venustiano Carranza, Espinosa convened a meeting to form a national labor organization. Out of this labor convention emerged a national labor organization, the Confederación Regional de Obreros Mexicanos. Luis Morones was elected secretary general, and he and his followers would shape the future of the union. Article 9 of the document that resulted from the convention stated that the CROM and affiliated unions held the active recruitment of working women as one of its central principles. The CROM also claimed to support equal wages for equal work, regardless of sex.[47] The largest group of adherents came from the Mexican Miners Union; however, in June 1919 fifteen thousand new members joined, when the Federation of Federal District Workers' Unions incorporated itself into the CROM.[48] The integration of Federation-affiliated unions brought considerable numbers of women into the ranks of the CROM.[49] The direction of the CROM, however, would not be clear until Morones made an alliance with Álvaro Obregón in August 1919.

Álvaro Obregón sought the presidency, and in so doing he looked for the support of workers. His efforts ran from making speeches at factories, praising workers for their spirit of cooperation with "capital," to the alliance he made with the CROM.[50] Historians have described the CROM as a union that brought real benefits to workers, but at a cost. That cost was a hierarchical organizational structure and reformist gains for workers. How did this work at the factory level, and what was the impact on working women? The CROM takeover of El Buen Tono cigarette factory gives some insight into this process.[51] In January 1920 a group of mechanics at El Buen Tono cigarette factory initiated a conflict with management that led to the formation of a union that would eventually affiliate with the CROM. The mechanics came together to demand a 25 percent wage increase for themselves. Management granted them 3 percent. The mechanics considered this insufficient and formed the Union of Employees, Male and Female Workers. Soon thereafter the union led the factory in a strike. Management granted an across the board 50 percent increase but refused to recognize the union. A subsequent strike won the workers recognition of the union, at which time they affiliated with the CROM. CROM leaders portrayed the factory management as being part of the "old regime," which was characterized by poor working conditions and the domination of factory discipline with paternalistic practices associated with women. The union was able to bring 900 of the 1,029 workers in the factory into its ranks, enforce the eight-hour day, control the hiring of personnel, and it even changed the system of promotions. Union leadership, dominated by skilled male labor, celebrated the installation of new machinery as an example of the benefits of worker/management cooperation.[52] And, Señor Margaín, the union secretary, was offered a job with the government in the Department of Social Welfare.[53]

Many of the women employed at El Buen Tono had less reason to celebrate. When a Department of Labor inspector visited El Buen Tono regarding the mechanics' demands, he found that many of the women workers also had complaints. Not only had women with years of seniority been passed up for promotions, management had taken the installation of the new machinery as an opportunity to dismiss older female workers. Some of these women had worked for the company for ten, twenty, or more years. As the years passed, they had become less and less able to make a living doing piecework. Women who were not members of the CROM were slowly dismissed. In November 1921 a brief strike succeeded in removing two maestras from the "old regime." The two women had been members of a rival Catholic union affiliated with the Knights of Columbus. Still, cigarreras sympathetic to the Communist Party also struggled to retain a place in the organizational culture of El Buen Tono by attending all union meetings and working closely with the new workers' governing board.[54] As members of a CROM-affiliated union, the men succeeded in eliminating rival unions; they also succeeded in gaining the dismissal of women in overseer positions. Their gains were further consolidated when the union redefined certain occupations as "unhealthy," and thus disqualified women from those positions. Men also were able to take night jobs, which women were no longer allowed to perform.[55]

An important number of the rank-and-file within the CROM grew disgruntled with the increasingly close ties between the CROM leadership and the government. In 1921 a wide range of syndicalist organizations, galvanized by the strategic power and organizational strength of the city's streetcar workers, convened to form a left-oriented body of representation for workers, the Federación Comunista del Proletariado (FCP).[56] Women participated as members of the Federation of Thread and Textiles, the Union of Workers and Employees of Eriksson Telephone, the Union of Working Men and Working Women of El Palacio de Hierro, and the Union of Working Men and Working Women of El Buen Tono. Members of the old Casa del Obrero Mundial also participated, including María del Carmen Frías, who served as a delegate to the convention. The FCP was short lived and subsequently superceded by the General Confederation of Workers (Confederación General de Trabajadores, or CGT).[57] María del Carmen Frías also served on the Executive Committee of the CGT. In 1923 the CGT claimed 60,000 members (the CROM claimed 800,000 the same year). CGT member unions included textile workers (just under 9,000), streetcar workers (4,000), bakers (3,500), municipal workers (1,500), tobacco workers (900), Palacio de Hierro workers (560), printers (400), telephone operators (35), carters (200), soap workers (150), and ceramics workers (100).[58] The Federation also integrated workers with artisanal skills, who by coming together in large numbers could form their own organization. This included seamstresses who came together as Seamstresses and Related Workers of the Metropolis, as well as producers of sweets, pastries, and related goods, and tailors.[59]

Furthermore, throughout the 1920s, working-class feminist organizations formed and participated in strikes and demonstrations. While the content and purpose of these latter organizations is unclear, their presence does suggest that the years of women's organizing, in combination with increasing feminist activity, created a space for working-class, woman-centered organizing. In 1919, 1923, and 1925 feminists held conferences in Mexico City. Newspaper accounts and the memoirs of feminists claim that working women participated, but the nature of that participation is unclear. What is clear is that working women would come together to combine their interests both as workers and as women.

The strikes in which the CGT and affiliated unions participated often included demands that suggest that the interests of working women were being represented. In 1922 CGT member unions staged a series of strikes throughout the textile industry. Their demands included wage increases, an end to wages paid by piece-rates for textile workers in preparation and thread departments (many of whom would have been women), and the enforcement of limits on the length of the workday as stipulated in Article 123 of the Constitution.[60] Workers also protested abuses that had been committed against an obrera at La Abeja textile and knitwear factory. Protesters included women from La Carolina and La Fama Montañesa textile factories, cigarreras from El Buen Tono, women from the embroiderers' union, and, as *El Demócrata* put it, "who knows how many men."[61] While workers at La Abeja locked themselves in the factory for several days, other women made speeches in the street. And although the coming together of women from diverse industries suggests they had some shared interest in this particular incident, what that interest was is unclear, as the content of those speeches was not included in press reports.[62] By the following year the CGT also included the Union of Anarchist Women, suggesting that working women created a means of expressing their interests specifically as women within the union.[63]

Women distinguished themselves in their participation within the CGT as strife with the government intensified. The CROM, in alliance with industrialists, had resorted to threats, humiliation, and the firing of many members of the CGT. Negotiations between the Department of Labor, industrialists, and various worker organizations over the means of calculating indemnification for loss of employment stalemated and led to a strike, declared on 21 January 1923. Despite efforts on the part of the CROM to undermine CGT efforts, on 29 January a General Strike was declared by all "reds." On 1 February a meeting was convened on the third floor of a building at number 25 Uruguay Street in downtown Mexico City. The purpose of the meeting was to discuss the struggle with government-allied unions like the CROM. Among those participating were a good number of women from Ericsson Telephone Company, El Palacio de Hierro, and various factories. When news arrived at the meeting that a trolley car had been driven, precisely down Uruguay Street, despite the strike, people poured out of the building and into the street to stop the car. They built a barricade at Uruguay and Bolivar Streets. When the trolley stopped at the barricade, armed soldiers jumped from the trolley and shot several armed workers. In the fighting which ensued several women distinguished themselves. Flor Padilla fought side by side with her fellow workers. She and at least 12 other women were among the 140 or so people taken to prison, which gained her mention in Luis Araiza's memoir of the Mexican working class.[64]

By the mid-1920s tensions between the CGT and the CROM had intensified, in part due to the increased power of the CROM, as a result of its alliance with the Calles administration (1924–1928). Calles had named CROM leader Luis N. Morones as Secretary of Industry, Commerce, and Labor. The CGT could expect little support from the government. On the contrary, the Calles administration passed legislation enhancing the power of the CROM. The CROM also withdrew its support of a joint assembly it had convened in 1925, and the CGT was forced to hold its own assembly to address wages in the textile industry in 1926.[65] As ties between the CROM and the government increased, the number of women in union leadership positions declined. For example, in 1925 CROM tobacco workers were 40,000 strong, yet they were led by an executive committee made up of six men and only one woman.[66]

However, working women did not rely solely upon unions to express their demands. In 1925 women used the May Day parade to organize as women and to protest their exclusion from unions. Thousands of working women from across the city marched, expressing contradictory sentiments of rebellion, celebration, pleasure, and anger. Obreras, cigarreras, costureras, vendedoras, teachers, and women from the Casa del Obrero Mundial Centro Feminista (House of the World Worker, Feminist Center) all made a strong showing. Each factory or organization marched in a group headed by leaders carrying banners. Popular female artists Cecilia Padilla, Maria Luisa Infante, and Cecilia Montalván dressed themselves in national pride, with red, white, and green cloth sewn into full skirts and sequins catching the light and excitement of the day. Parading alongside them were women dressed in more somber attire. Waitresses and women from the printing industry dressed in black skirts and red shirts, attesting to their anarchist beliefs.

The women who participated in the 1925 May Day parade incorporated a refashioned paradigm of female morality, which pointed out the contradiction between demands for cheap female labor and condemnation of the morality of working women. By the hundreds, waitresses carried signs of protest, including some which read: "Bourgeois: Do not prostitute woman; love her, raise her up morally" and "Bourgeois: We proletariat are people too."[67] The waitresses redirected accusations of immorality from victim to exploiter, and from working women themselves to class relations, in which the bourgeoisie was revealed as the responsible party. They identified themselves as members of the proletariat and asserted that such an identity warranted honor. The juxtaposition of the two slogans also allowed the waitresses to demonstrate the importance for them of female morality. Being a member of the "proletariat" did not mean a lack of sexual morality or honor as personal virtue.

A similar demand had been expressed years earlier when a group of women had marched with a banner declaring, "We are on strike, because when we demand an increase in wages they insult us by pointing us toward the path of prostitution."[68] While prostitution may have been one means of survival for working-class women, the conflation of working woman with prostitute was profoundly offensive to these women. The women in this and the 1925 May Day parade spoke against the idea that it was the immoral choices of individual women that caused prostitution. Bound by gender distinctions that relegated them to low-wage employment and limited in their means of organizing, women struggled precisely for working conditions that would make prostitution an unlikely option.

The forward movement of the 1925 May Day parade was stopped by what became a symbolic event. A young woman sat waving to the crowd from a CROM car driving slowly along the parade route down Uruguay Street. The people perched on the balconies of buildings lining the parade route must have seen the young woman sitting triumphantly in the CROM car. Suddenly, a deep crimson flower appeared on the breast of the young woman's dress. The flower, it was soon revealed, was blood seeping from a gunshot wound to her neck. The newspaper described the scene in vivid terms, noting that suddenly her head toppled over "like a withered carnation."[69] In the struggle for power between government-allied and non-allied labor unions, gunshots fired into the crowd from both sides of the fight. Subsequent conflicts between the two unions continued to be marked by violence.[70] In what remained of the decade, women's participation in labor organizing languished, while male-dominated, government-allied and non-allied unions alike struggled to define the boundaries of the other's power. These struggles only compounded women's declining power in the workforce, as they went from a high of one-third of the Mexico City industrial work force in 1920 to just 24 percent in 1930.

However, this did not keep women from voicing their demands. The May Day parade bled into the succeeding days. On 5 May waitresses again demonstrated in the streets. More than one thousand waitresses met to protest low wages, long hours, and inappropriate and poor treatment by both employers and customers. They complained that the men for whom they worked and those they served frequently made suggestive comments, acted lewdly, and otherwise harassed them. In compensation for their tolerance and service, waitresses received only paltry tips. Waitresses also protested against the exclusionary practices of the CROM. They claimed that restaurant owners required that they obtain a CROM union card in order to gain or retain employment. But when the women sought out union membership, they were told by the CROM that only those who worked in "first-class" restaurants could join. Coincidentally, men worked in first-class restaurants, "where respectable families dine," and women in second-class restaurants.[71] In a distinct lack of class solidarity, the Waiters' Union accused the women of strikebreaking and blamed the Chinese for the exploitation of waitresses. The men depicted the Chinese as "nefarious" foreigners who took advantage of "poor Mexican women."[72] As the parade passed, other women marched on, carrying signs that expressed demands for respect. One banner read, "Upon women are imposed the laws of humanity; but she is not called to become a part of it."[73] The language of the rights of working women was now more closely associated with legal rights than with female weakness and sexual morality.

In mid-May over one thousand waitresses formed an independent union. They demanded an eight-hour day, a minimum wage of 1 peso, and respectful treatment by employers and customers.[74] The waitresses union sought affiliation with the Federation. Also in mid-May vendors who sold goods outside of municipal markets formed an alternative union to the one for vendors sponsored by the CROM. The Union of Vendors from Outside Markets established a cooperative bank and goods-distribution system. Whether or not women participated in this latter union is unclear, though the large number of women who worked outside of markets, as well as the fact that by the 1930s this organization would be led by a woman, suggests that this was the case.[75]

Some of the women who had participated in the establishment of the Casa and Federation-affiliated unions in the 1910s and 1920s continued to struggle to improve working conditions for women by taking leadership positions or working for the government. Textile worker Catalina Frías, sister of María Carmen Frías, was blacklisted from employment due to her activism. Francisco J. Múgica later gave Frías work when he became Secretary of Communications and Public Works.[76] Adelita Macías, who began her working career in the jute industry, was also a textile worker who played an active role in founding the Textile Workers Union November 20, and she served as the treasurer on the union's first Executive Committee. She also represented female jute workers at the Workers-Employers Convention, sponsored by the Department of Labor, and led the struggle to impose tariffs on Singer sewing machines. In the 1930s she served as editor of the magazine *Mujeres*, produced by the Union of Workers in Sewing and Related Industries and the Café and Restaurant Workers of the Federal District.[77]

These individual stories of female leadership would serve as important reference points for feminists and working women alike in the years to come. By and large, however, by the 1930s women rarely served in leadership positions in textile and related industries' unions. The significant exceptions were Maria del Carmen Frías of the Union of Progressive Workers Puente de Sierra at La Abeja thread and knitwear factory, and Elena Cepeda of the National Union of Textiles and Related Industries, one of many textile industry unions.[78] The union in the female-dominated knitwear industry was led by a man as well. Furthermore, in industries that remained female-dominated, like clothing, women's union membership remained low. A 1936 study by the Office for the Investigation of Working Women found that only 10 percent of seamstresses claimed union membership. This meant that only two out of every fifteen clothing shops were organized. The seamstresses who claimed union-affiliation belonged to the CROM or the Frente Regional de Obreros y Campesinos (FROC). Only 20 percent of seamstresses worked under a collective contract, and 77 percent held individual contracts. Individual contracts usually guaranteed more to the employer than to the worker. In addition to the CROM and the FROC, seamstresses belonged to the Male and Female Knitwear Workers Union, unions affiliated with the textile industry, employer-sponsored "white unions," and the Communist Party.[79]

Conclusion

With the political openings created by the Mexican Revolution, working women added new strategies to the organizing practices they had developed in the late nineteenth century and in the first decade of the twentieth century. Contrary to the accusations of detractors of mutual aid societies, it was precisely the existence of these work-centered organizations that allowed women to be among the first to protest against working conditions in the months after the departure of Porfirio Díaz in 1911. The success of women's activism was mixed. Working women's lack of nationwide labor networks limited their effectiveness in prevailing upon Francisco Madero and succeeding administrations to pressure industrialists. So, while strikes in the textile industry led to a national worker-employer convention, seamstresses and knitwear workers received no such support. Indeed, for seamstresses, the case was quite the contrary. The government had upheld the right of employers to reduce wages by hiring seamstresses to work at home.

By 1916 working women were influencing the direction of the larger working-class movement. The unions affiliated with the Casa and the Federation reflected shifts in the workforce toward an increasingly mixed-sex workplace. The inclusion of the terms "working men" and "working women" in union names signaled both the legacy of female labor activism and the continued importance of women within the working-class movement. The organized labor movement incorporated the demands of working women for an end to piece-rate wages, regulation of outwork production, and wage increases in female-dominated industries and occupations. The closing of the Casa in 1916 signaled an important transition in women's position in unions and the workforce. The CROM made general claims to support working women, while at the same time it marginalized at least some female workers from skilled work. In this regard, it was not unlike the American Federation of Labor (AFL), with which the CROM established ties in the 1920s. Mexican historians have explained the declining workforce participation of women as due to the attainment of a family wage by the late 1930s.[80] However, the history of women's relationship with unions suggests that the causes for women's decreased participation in the workforce may have been complicated by union exclusion of women from skilled occupations. Furthermore, the "family wage" would have meant little to the single and female heads of households, not to mention the wives of men who did not earn sufficient wages to allow them to remain at home.

Though some worker organizations formulated demands that clearly reflected the influence and interest of working women, women's work-related issues were not fully represented by unions. Because of this, women did not rely solely on unions and took to the streets to voice their demands. Demonstrating in the streets, women criticized their position in the workforce, their treatment by unions, and their unequal citizenship. In the 1920s their protests coincided with increasing feminist activism, but they also presented a continuity with the voice of working women expressed in nineteenth-century labor activism. Women no longer spoke of "female weakness" as an expression of their social weakness; rather, they directly questioned judgments on their morality, which they explained as due to their disadvantaged position in the workforce. Although the Mexico City press and working women who directed their words to the press were more likely to speak of workers' demands in gender-neutral terms, the discourse of female morality continued to frame women's interactions with employers, which is the subject of chapter 5.

CHAPTER 5

"Poor Yet Honorable People"

Worker Response to the Gendering of the Workplace

Public commentary on working women highlighted the threat posed to female honor and sexual morality in the factory. This discursive construction of the working woman shaped women's activism in the public sphere in the nineteenth century, and continued to play a small role in that activism after the outbreak of the Revolution. But how salient were notions of honor and sexual morality to women's experience in the factory itself? Chapter 1 began with the story of Ignacia Torres as she went in search of work. Almost as an aside, she characterized the man who hired her in this manner: "This man paid well and only hired poor yet honorable people."[1] Ignacia Torres's comment suggests that honor was important to women's work experience. However, her comment makes less clear what it meant to be honorable, and how, exactly, the concept of honor might have shaped women's work. Although the discursive constructions of the female factory worker that appeared in newspapers, promotional pamphlets, and essays were not fully played out in work relations, concepts of honor rooted in sexual morality structured women's work from the moment they entered the factory.

This chapter examines archival documents that show the ways Mexican working women negotiated gender ideology at work. In negotiating the power of gender at work, some women distinguished between the notion of the morally compromised female factory worker and their own experience as workers. Others accepted honor as legitimating their rights, but defined honor in their own terms. And some of the most politically self-aware female workers protested the connection made between normative femininity and workers rights, expressing their own gendered categories of worker dignity quite apart from the concept of honor. The variety of women's responses reveals that a blanket statement

FIGURE 5.1
Strike of working women over mistreatment of workers, circa 1920s.
Source: Fototeca Nacional, Mexico City.

about whether women questioned or shared dominant gender ideology is somewhat beside the point, and regardless, too difficult to make based on fragmentary evidence. What is clear is that women often relied upon, *and* resisted, conceptions of normative femininity as a means of addressing larger issues of workers rights; they distanced private morality from their public personas.[2] Furthermore, as women negotiated the gendering of work relations they participated in the formation of a unique working-class identity among women (see figure 5.1).[3]

Women's working conditions were structured by honor and sexual morality in at least two significant ways. First, employers, overseers, and co-workers invoked normative femininity, the differentiation between honorable and dishonorable women, to discipline workers. Second, employers, overseers, and co-workers, as men, could use assumptions about female workers' sexual availability or vulnerability as a means of controlling labor, or for personal gain. Men could simply threaten women and not actually carry out an act of physical aggression, which signals the way this coercion worked on an ideological level. Though this gendering of the workplace might function on the level of ideology, it still had material consequences for women. Power struggles informed by gender ideology shaped women's capacity to work and earn a living.

What Is Honor?

Historians of gender and labor have richly documented the importance of honor. Most scholars of Latin American gender history distinguish between two types of honor: honor as social precedence and honor as virtue. Honor as social precedence is defined by family and economic status. Honor as virtue is defined differently for men and women. Sexual chastity (virginity before marriage and fidelity in marriage) defined female honor. For men, honor was a willingness to defend one's reputation for reliability, loyalty, and male privilege over women.[4] Honor as social precedence has been defined as based upon lineage and status. Most scholars have not associated honor as social precedence with working-class women.[5] I argue, however, that working women in late-nineteenth- and early-twentieth-century Mexico asserted their honor both as virtue and as social precedence. They not only insisted that they were sexually moral, but they also claimed social precedence, with the dignity and rights that it conferred, as working women.

In this sense, the concept of honor is better understood as a web of associations rather than as component parts, as Anne Twinam has argued for colonial Spanish America.[6] The centrality and flexibility of honor is evidenced by its prevalence in Latin American historiography. Historians have found honor tied to cultural understandings of illegitimacy, kinship, sexuality, gender, nation, modernization, and worker discipline. Like recent scholars, I take sexual honor to stand for a set of gender norms that provided the logic for unequal power relations in public life.[7] The notion of honor was construed as being based upon private qualities that legitimated public rights. One site of these unequal power relations has been the workplace, mostly documented for male workers.[8]

Mexican labor historians have shown that workers' assertion of honor was integral to workplace struggle. The struggle to define honor and dignity occurred within the context of fluid factory discipline during the Porfiriato and into the 1920s. Custom rather than law governed many aspects of work relations in the factory. As customs of work took shape, employers and overseers sought to control workers' social customs and work habits. Employers prohibited the drinking of pulque in the factory and penalized workers for observing San Lunes. They fined workers for behavior thought to inhibit production, like talking or "looking at women."[9] And, employers' and overseers' expectations about what was required of workers differed from those of the workers themselves.

Workers, for their part, continued to drink pulque, balanced the demands of their employer with their own needs, and defined the terms of their employment. They also resisted physical punishment and affronts to their dignity as individuals.[10] Women's struggle against affronts to their dignity as workers fits unevenly within the history of workers' conceptions of honor. Like men, working women denounced beatings, unjustified firings, and obstacles to carrying out their job properly. Unlike men, women were also forced to negotiate the insertion of sexuality and female honor into work relations. In Mexican labor history it is generally held that female workers held affronts to their dignity as women above other work-related demands.[11] This chapter shows that female dignity was inseparable from women's work-related demands.

For Mexican working women honor was intimately intertwined with their identity as female workers. This identity was forged over time, through labor struggle, and by women of a diversity of occupations and work tenures. In part, women's sense of themselves was shaped by their position in the workforce. Women who worked in female-dominated industries of preindustrial origin referred to themselves by their occupations, as cigarreras and costureras, for example. They continued to use these titles throughout the period 1879–1931. As women entered an increasing diversity of occupations in modern industrial factories in the 1880s, more and more women were referred to, and referred to themselves, as obreras. *Obrera*, from the Spanish *obrar* (to labor), is a female laborer. The term *obrera* was not identified with a specific occupation, but rather with wage labor more generally. By the turn of the century a new word appeared which more closely identified women with the factory: *fabricanta*.

Women's work patterns also informed their sense of themselves. Cigarreras and knitwear obreras often remained in one factory for their entire working life, contributing to their strong sense of workplace identity. In contrast, costureras and tortilleras often changed their place of employment in search of better working conditions or to avoid abusive treatment by their employer.[12] Despite changing employers, many of these women remained in the same occupation, thus explaining their self-identification, for example, as costureras or tortilleras. Other women did not have a fixed work identity. Women often labored in various industries over a lifetime or combined occupations simultaneously. One woman became a street vendor when work-related injuries made her quit work as a seamstress, another when she was laid off from a hat factory.[13] Others turned to vending when old age prohibited them from doing factory work. Some women combined taking in laundry with sewing. One woman sewed clothing and sold sweets out of her home.[14] These women often thought of themselves as working people but did not refer to themselves by categories recognizable in industrial census categories.

Despite the different ways women self-identified as workers, labor disputes often brought them together across occupations and led them to collectively identify by the word obrera. Such was the case in a dispute over the use of an identification card *(libreta)*. Employers in textiles, sewing, and domestic work proposed the utilization of an identification card in the 1880s and again in the 1900s. The card would list an individual's name, place of residence, and work record, thus giving employers more control over their workers. For workers, the card threatened their capacity to organize by warning potential employers of previous activity. Workers also thought of the identification card as an invasion of their privacy and an affront to their individual liberty and dignity. In 1882 a protest against the libreta developed in which women played a central role. As labor leaders and journalists entered into the debate, they made the honor of working women relevant to defining those women's rights. The more conservative *El Monitor Republicano* defiled the name of working women, accusing them of lacking any morality. The paper sought to delegitimize the women's protest against the identification card by invoking the idea of working women as morally compromised. Two newspapers, *El Socialista* and *La Convención Radical Obrera*, defended the women, and in so doing accepted *El Monitor Republicano*'s use of honor and sexual morality as the criteria for obreras rights.[15]

Six hundred women from across occupational lines, including cigarreras, dressmakers, and ironers, united in opposition to the libreta. Collectively identifying themselves as obreras, they used the concept of honor to legitimate their political rights. The obreras' letter, published in *El Socialista*, read in part:

> The constant need of workers is discipline at work. . . . We have earned, through sacrifice and the nobility of the proletarian class, the grand title of obreras; so that, upon acquiring said title, we have already been made aware of our obligations and duties, and we know that upon us weighs the condemnation of the Almighty. But what a misfortune that, just when we begin to see the fruits of our labor, time has incapacitated our parents' ability to provide for themselves

and, as is just, we lend them our aid In the same way they lent it to us in our childhood. . . . Our obligations are greater than those of a representative of the people, for the simple reason that the latter is temporal and ours is eternal. . . . We, from the first rays of dawn until well into the night, are dedicated to our labors; we cannot tolerate remaining silent, nor stand by indifferent in the face of a cloud that threatens our future. Furthermore, the inherent dignity of our labor, and the support which the laws of our Motherland provide us, con- flict with our possibly accepting the introduction of a libreta. . . . In protesting against . . . *El Monitor Republicano* . . . we are in the right, and we defend ourselves energetically because it is an offense to our honor and our dignity as obreras.[16]

The women protested the libreta by asserting their honor and dignity as obreras. While *El Monitor Republicano* judged the women with the lan- guage of honor as virtue, the obreras justified their demands with the prin- ciple of honor as social precedence, as workers. Both viewed honor as legitimating rights; however, the obreras redefined the content of honor. The obreras fought against the portrayal of morally compromised work- ing women with the argument that it was precisely their own capacity to labor, "the only asset on earth which our dear parents are able to be- queath," which intrinsically bestowed dignity on their lives. Their self- identification as members of the "proletarian class" and the reference to "discipline in work"—despite occupational differences—identified them with all workers, male or female. At the same time, they did not hesitate to emphasize the burden they, as women, carried, due to their responsibility for the care of aging parents. These six hundred women did not choose to separate their identities as women or as workers; rather, they claimed the title of obrera, purged of negative moral implications. Moreover, by referring to the laws of their Motherland, they also used their status as obreras to claim their rights as citizens of Mexico. In the end, workers successfully blocked the imposition of the libreta. In the process, women of diverse occupations had given new meaning to their collective identity.

Reputation versus Experience

Working women's ability to stake such political claims and to challenge dominant gender ideology began with an awareness of the judgments passed on working women. Given this awareness, some women distinguished between the reputation of working women and individual experience. An interview with textile worker Doña Justa, conducted by Verena Radkau in the 1980s, suggests how women accommodated those judgments. Radkau's oral history shows one woman's fear of stereotypes about working women and how her experience as a worker in a textile factory led her to reconcile herself with those stereotypes.[17]

Justicia (later Doña Justa) lived in Tlalpan with her mother, father, and three little sisters in the first decade of the twentieth century.[18] As a girl she did not work outside of the home because her father would not allow it. "I didn't even dream of going out into the street," commented Doña Justa. She was still young when the army forced her father to join in the Revolution. He died in battle in 1913. When her father died, Justicia had to find a way to contribute to the household income. After a few years selling pulque and then working as a domestic, a friend of her mother got her a job at La Fama Montañesa textile factory in Tlalpan. Doña Justa recalled that she began her first day as a factory worker on 13 June 1916. On that day, she cried. She did not want to be a fabricanta. "Better I kill myself than be a fabricanta! They had a bad reputation. . . . They were drunks . . . the women were bad people."[19] Despite the fact that Doña Justa thought factory workers were a questionable lot and did not want to be associated with women who were "bad people," she needed the job.

Don Pepe, the owner of the factory, reinforced her idea that work in the factory was dangerous and a threat to a woman's sexual morality. Justicia's first job was cleaning machinery. The factory machinery had been temporarily shut down and required cleaning before production could be reinitiating. Don Pepe made sure that Justicia had another woman in the room with her while she cleaned. He did not consider it safe for a woman to be alone in a room with a bunch of men. Indeed, Justicia was intimidated by her male co-workers. Her employer also warned her about the other women who worked in the factory.[20] While Justicia initially felt unsure about working in a factory, her experience led her to change her opinion about the bad reputation of fabricantas. She later commented, "They weren't bad. There were women who were married and were there with their husbands and everything. So, were they bad? Only because of their reputation as fabricantas. Here women and men worked, but there was never anything bad. For example things they did to me, little things that were of no importance. They wanted one to stand such things, and I wouldn't stand for any of it! But see bad things, bad things—I never saw it!"[21] Doña Justa acknowledged the place of teasing at work, but she also distinguished between the reputation of fabricantas and the actual behavior she observed in the factory. Doña Justa was clearly aware of the public discourse on working women, and was herself concerned with sexual morality. But her personal experience as a fabricanta contradicted social stereotypes, and she formulated her own sense of herself and the women with whom she worked.

Employers, Overseers, and Mechanics

However chaste women workers may have been, their honor was perpetually at stake. Day-to-day interactions between women and the employers, overseers, and mechanics who determined the terms of their employment, were shaped by both the sexualization of female workers and the force of normative femininity. While the inclusion of mechanics in this group may seem odd, these men held considerable power, since they repaired the machines whose production determined women's pay. A broken machine meant workers who were paid piece-rate wages earned less. Employers, overseers, and mechanics used ideas of honor to control female workers. The entire experience of workers, from hiring, wage levels, and benefits, to dismissal, created a situation in which employers, overseers, and mechanics could use the concepts of honor and sexual morality to wield power over women's capacity to earn a living.

Some employers held honor as a condition of their hire. Ignacia Torres commented that her employer hired only honorable people. The perception of a place of work as honorable made it attractive to some women. In 1919 Department of Labor interviews, when asked to make any additional observations about the women who worked for them, employers described them as "honorable and hardworking," or "serious, responsible, and honorable."[22] Other employers threatened female honor by bringing the threat of sex into the hiring process. A Señorita Carmen Wilson made a rare protest to the Department of Labor regarding an incident that occurred in the process of her applying for a job. According to Wilson, the very process of hiring sexualized the female worker. The owner of a sewing shop had "asked her various improper questions, which included whether or not she was a señorita, or if she were sensitive, informing her that if the answer were affirmative he would not have any work for her in his office, because he needed complacent employees, in virtue of the fact that he, as well as his associate, let his hands wander, as they say."[23] The shop owner was not concerned with Wilson's civil status. Rather, he had used the word señorita as a means of ascertaining whether or not she was a virgin. He wanted to know how sexually accessible she was. Such unequal relations between worker and employer, based on gender, were reinforced by a restricted labor market for women, and in part upheld by the ineffectiveness of the Department of Labor. Of the reports of sexual harassment brought to the attention of the Department of Labor, there is no record of action taken.[24]

Some employers and overseers insinuated that sexual exchange influenced women's earning capacity, whether or not such an exchange took place. A group of women working at La Francia clothing factory voiced this complaint in their letter to the Department of Labor in 1914 when they wrote, "They don't treat us like obreras but like beggars, 'cause there are times when they have us sitting there for a day and a half, just sitting there wasting our time, while on the other hand there are those who are the favorites of the overseer who are given work . . . after keeping us sitting there during the day they have us there until nine at night just to earn not even 5 pesos for the week. That is all we have to say for now. Various obreras."[25] The seamstresses argued that at La Francia flirtation was a prerequisite for work. This prerequisite, they stated, was treatment more apt for beggars, not obreras.

Because most women earned their wages by piece-rate, they were vulnerable not only to employers but to mechanics. Mechanics had the power to break and fix machines, thus influencing a workers' capacity to produce and earn. The Department of Labor recorded several incidences where mechanics used sexual threats to impede a woman's capacity to work. At La Perfeccionada in 1920 an inspector found that mechanic Crescenciano Torres had committed a series of related abuses. Torres had forced women to lend and borrow money. While inspectors and journalists lamented the practice of forced loans as a common abuse in Mexican factories, for the women working at La Perfeccionada the loans were reinforced by the mechanic's sexual threats. The women told the Department of Labor inspector that Torres had made sexual advances and threatened to break their machines if they did not oblige him. In his report, the inspector noted that "when for any reason he has ill-will against a worker, or one of [the women] refuses his advances, he breaks the machine she works on and makes her waste as much time as he feels like. The Manager is already aware of this, and is only waiting for concrete evidence in order to act forcefully."[26] One wonders what additional evidence management was waiting for in order to act.

Rather than fire the mechanic, the overseer threatened to fire those women who dealt with Torres. Management's threat to fire the women, not the mechanic, and the Department of Labor inspector's acceptance of this as a solution to the situation, legitimated the place of female sexuality in women's work relations. The mechanics' sexual advances offered in exchange for the repair of the machine on which the woman worked brought sexual barter into labor relations. The mechanic made a woman's capacity to earn a living dependent upon her sexuality. And yet not just men could use gender ideology as a means of controlling women.

Both male and female overseers could invoke normative femininity as a means of controlling those under their charge. A conflict at El Buen Tono cigarette factory provides a telling example of how this worked. During the 1920s women lost jobs in the cigarette industry because of the encroachment of male workers affiliated with the CROM and the installation of new machinery that would replace women in the wrapping department of the factory. Maestras (female overseers) facilitated this process by pressuring cigarreras to increase their production or firing them. Maestras used the norms of femininity we have discussed to publicly shame women, so as to gain leverage in these struggles. One maestra suggested that a woman had had a child out of wedlock and therefore had brought shame on the entire factory, thus justifying her dismissal. The maestras also sought to fire women who did not attend Mass at the Church built by Señor Pugibet next to the factory. Who were these maestras?

In some ways maestras Señora Valeriana de la Longa, Jacobita Romero, and her sister were like other overseers in Mexican industry. They played an important role in maintaining production levels, enforcing work discipline, and resolving conflicts with workers. Because of this, a forceful personality was an important job qualification. This was true for many factories, not just El Buen Tono. One employer turned away a Mexican who applied for the position of overseer, stating that he only hired Spaniards because they knew "how to speak with garlic and onions" to workers.[27] Overseers maintained order in the factory, but they could also be the source of conflict when, for example, they forced workers to perform tasks workers did not consider part of their job. Overseers also used their authority over workers to make demands unrelated to work, such as forcing workers to take out high-interest loans from them.[28]

In other ways, cigarette maestras differed from other overseers, in part because of the work culture of cigarette factories like El Buen Tono. From the early nineteenth century, Señor Pugibet, the owner of El Buen

Tono, had cultivated a workplace discipline founded on the separation of male and female workers and proper femininity. Chapter 1 described the organization of work within the factory, based on separating male and female workers from the moment they took to their workstations, throughout the lunch period, and until their exit from the factory through separate doors to go home. Señor Pugibet also provided a church, a school, a doctor, and other facilities for his workers.[29] He supported his workers' cultural activities by sponsoring fêtes, cinema, and outings. Maestras played a central part in both the celebrations and factory discipline. Cigarette manufactory maestras stood apart from those in other industries because of their own occupational history. The word *maestra* suggests the carryover of the position of teacher in the apprentice system to that of overseer in factory production. In the early days of the tobacco-processing industry, many maestras had worked their way up to the position from jobs as cleaners, strippers, or cigar makers. Some maestras were extremely popular with their workers. Anthony Morgan reported that more than five hundred women filled the streets to accompany the funeral cortège of maestra Rita Castaño in 1897.[30] Yet, shared-work origins did not necessarily foster sympathies. Some maestras made voluntary and forced loans, and used flattery of women's physical appearance to coerce them into purchasing baubles and trinkets at exaggerated prices. In 1894 newspapers reported on two El Buen Tono maestras who did not allow women to leave the factory for lunch. They also forced some women to work through the night, unless they gave the maestras gifts or money. Maestras also levied fines "as a means of enforcing morality."[31]

When in January 1920 El Buen Tono's maestras sought to publicly shame cigarreras as a means of justifying firing them, the cigarreras resisted. They wrote a letter to then Secretary of Industry, Commerce and Labor General Don Plutarco Elías Calles, complaining specifically about the maestras' use of sexual morality and honor as criteria to threaten firing them. The letter read:

> The principal object of this letter is to bring to your honorable and superior attention the abuses and injustices which are committed against us in the "Fábrica de Cigarros de El Buen Tono," which, despite the enviable reputation said establishment enjoys, has among its overseers a couple of women who are in charge of the Wrapping Department who treat people in a most foul-mouthed and indecent manner. Given that they are enemies of the current Government and

are therefore sanctimonious to the marrow of their bones, [they] are capable of employing reprobate pretexts as a means of taking away our work, using means that are valid just because they say it is so. What concern is it of theirs if a woman has children or not, when the children are not even brought to the factory, and then they claim that for reasons of hygiene the woman brings dishonor on the factory?

Or they ask whether or not they [cigarreras] go to confession or if they frequently attend Church or not, or that for missing a day of work (even while having given previous notice), or if they just do not like the looks of them, as they commonly say, they take their job away.

Are these strong enough reasons to act in such a disagreeable manner with people who are helping them to increase their profits? . . .

Señor, if we bring these things to your attention it is because the case is such that said problems have taken up residence, and we hope that you will do us the favor of preventing such abuses, because with the arrival of the new rolling machines they are scheming diabolic plans against us and are not acting according to the law.

If we do not put down our names it is not for lack of civic valor but, as you will understand, because we do not wish to be the object of vengeance and lose our jobs.[32]

The overseer's mention of hygiene and honor was a thinly veiled reference to sexual morality. The cigarreras claimed that the maestras attributed the women's children to questionable sexual behavior. At El Buen Tono maestras utilized notions of proper femininity, defined by religious observance, separation of male and female workers, and honor as sexual morality to justify dismissal of workers. Thus, in effect, conceptions of female honor defined employment rights. The potential material consequences of this incident reinforced a specific meaning of femaleness: women who did not attend Mass or who had children out of wedlock did not deserve jobs. The letter also reveals that the maestras could invoke a female-dominated workspace as having a reputation that was necessary to defend. They claimed that the morality of an individual worker reflected on the honor of all of the women of the factory.

The cigarreras did not make the same sort of distinctions as Doña Justa had done. Doña Justa had differentiated between the stereotype of fabricanta immorality and the actual moral behavior of the women with whom she worked. The cigarreras, on the other hand, protested the place of sexual morality and personal behavior in work relations. They did not choose to speak to the issue of their own sexual morality or adherence to norms of respectable femininity. Aware of the power of the ideal of female sexual morality, the women who wrote to the head of the Department of Industry, Commerce, and Labor defied the place of normative femininity in labor relations. Indignant that their private lives could be used to affect their capacity to earn a living, they argued that gender norms should not define workers' rights. Rather, work performance, responsibility, and their part in generating profits for the company should define their rights. Accusations of illicit sexual relations, illegitimate children, and cleanliness—physical and moral—were, in the eyes of the cigarreras, a means by which management could manipulate them and avoid the law. If the government allowed this practice, the cigarreras implicitly argued, gender would become more powerful in the workplace than the rule of law. And while the women who wrote the letter did not claim that one sort of morality was more in tune with the ideals of the Revolution than another, they did point out that such imperiousness was characteristic of enemies of the government.

The 1920 El Buen Tono incident casts paternalistic employer benefits for workers in a new light. As the cigarreras pointed out, El Buen Tono had an enviable reputation. This reputation was in part due to the way Señor Pugibet sought to create a factory appropriate for women. Employers often touted the provision of a church, along with schools, outings, cinema, and employer-sponsored organizations as generous benefits for the worker. Yet this group of women did not feel that management's concern for the moral tenor of the workplace benefited them. Rather, they saw it as a means of enforcing a certain morality and control over their lives. Cigarrera resistance to the imposition of employer-sponsored practices of religion and morality in their lives may long have been the case. Maria de la Luz Parcero found that in the mid–nineteenth century cigarreras complained that their employer required them to make donations to the Catholic Church. Workers in other industries also made similar complaints about their employers.[33]

The El Buen Tono letter is unique. When women approached the Department of Labor, or were questioned by inspectors, they often expressed hesitancy and fear of retaliation on the part of their employers. The cigarreras also communicated this fear, in explaining the reason why they did not sign their letter. Government inspectors often responded to letters written by women complaining of similar abuses, only to find upon visiting the factory in question that no one would admit to having written the letter.[34] However, when they did come forward, women spoke of the very real power of sexual honor in the workplace.

Conclusion

Within public discussions about working women, the factory posed a moral danger to female honor. Within the paradigm of paternalism, this danger justified keeping women out of factories. Within the paradigm of middle-class identity, the factory represented a potentially threatening space within which employers, overseers, and workers might violate the norms of femininity. Both class paradigms played upon the idea of female vulnerability, the weakest point of that vulnerability being sexual morality. Mexican working women did indeed have to resist employers and co-workers who made sexuality one of the "skills" necessary for a woman to earn a living. But the discourse of female sexual morality was more than a description of possible working conditions, it was also a threat to women's wage-earning capacity in and of itself.

Women used different strategies to negotiate conceptions of female sexuality and honor while at work. Some women accepted honor as relevant to workers' rights, while at the same time they resisted the imposition of normative femininity in the factory. Their understanding of themselves as workers included their struggle to keep private behavior separate from their public identities. Furthermore, women articulated their own understanding of class as a sense of continuity with past traditions of working people. Put in a way that speaks to current historiography, they sought to separate honor as private virtue from honor as social precedence. While historians have associated honor as social precedence with elites, working women considered being a worker precedence enough to qualify as honorable.[35] It was as working women that they deserved respect, not as repositories of sexual morality.

This chapter examined normative femininity and the idea of the sexual vulnerability of women as an integral aspect of factory discipline. As the next chapter will show, industrialization included women who worked beyond the factory walls. Female vendors worked at the physical and symbolic forefront of the public sphere, as their sales literally put them in the street. As female workers they, too, had to contend with the power of gender ideology in shaping their efforts to earn a living.

CHAPTER 6

"And That It Is Custom Makes It Law"

Vendedoras in the Public Sphere

In May 1908 Juana Gutiérrez, with the assistance of a public scribe, wrote to the municipal government requesting a license allowing her to sell cooked corn on the streets of Mexico City. "It is with much embarrassment," she stated, "that I write to you, begging that you have the goodness to grant me a license to sell cooked corn, as I have done in years past, on the corner of Puente del Correo Mayor and Zaragoza Streets." When her request was denied on the basis that said location was too centrally located, Gutiérrez wrote again. In her second letter, Gutiérrez wrote that she hoped she would be given a license as she was "a poor woman with children who by selling corn struggles for an honorable life." The municipal government subsequently granted the license to Gutiérrez.[1]

Juana Gutiérrez shared a common predicament with many vendedoras (female vendors). Beginning in the 1880s government efforts to reorganize markets and street vending reduced the number of prepared-food vendors on the streets of Mexico City. Women, in particular, faced increasing difficulties in making a living. An important recourse for such women was to petition the Mexico City municipal government. In these pleas, men and women often provided an assessment of their position in Mexican society and economy. Like Juana Gutiérrez, women often understood their status as women to be relevant to such requests, and utilized conceptions of female sexual morality to frame their petitions.

Between 1880 and 1910 Mexico City underwent a profound reorganization of urban space. Historians have described in rich detail how this reorganization implied a tendency toward separation of social classes in housing and recreation, and class-informed regulation of behaviors ranging from dress to peeing.[2] But the gendered nature of this process has been little explored. The dynamics of class distinction often centered on practices of femininity, and more specifically on the role of women in public. This chapter examines the conflict between vendedoras and municipal authorities as a means of exploring the intersection of class conflict and gender ideology in the public sphere. Contests over public space reveal the efforts of vendedoras to constitute a place for themselves, both in that public space and within the public sphere. Vendedoras framed their demands for individual rights with issues of public concern, namely female morality.[3]

Porfirian contests over the use of public space had direct ramifications for definitions of femaleness in Mexico. The first half of this chapter begins with a brief discussion of markets as part of the public sphere in Porfirian Mexico City. It then examines the efforts of city officials to reform marketing in Mexico City. Municipal authorities built markets, passed laws, and enforced new regulations imbued with an implicit questioning of women's rights in public. The removal of *comideras* (female vendors of prepared food) from many streets, of *enchiladeras* (enchilada vendors) from pulquería entrances, and the reorganization of municipal markets to house large-scale commerce infringed upon women's ability to work. In denying these rights to women, the municipal government reinforced elite definitions of femaleness. Their actions paralleled the preoccupation with women's role in public voiced in media ranging from medical treatises to women's magazines. Journalists, doctors, and a new generation of female writers expressed in print the ideas about women's presence in public that informed municipal reforms of marketing.

Female vendors' response to impositions on their right to use public space makes up the second half of this chapter. Vendedora petitions emerged out of the collision of differing ideals of women's place in the family, the economy, and on the streets. Vendedoras explicitly countered the practice of using a woman's morality as a means of denying her rights. Vendedoras did this by asserting what they termed a traditional right to a legally and morally sanctioned place on city streets. Vendedoras constructed this "tradition" by selecting from and interpreting the circumstances of their daily existence. Aware of the way their rights to the public sphere were contingent upon gender, vendedoras asserted alternative categories of femaleness that resonated with their own quotidian material experience and the cultural meaning which developed surrounding those realities. In seeking to convince municipal authorities of their rights, vendedoras, like the working women described in the previous chapters, showed compelling self-awareness as workers with rights grounded in their collective and individual history, and in their frequently shared status as single heads of households, dependent only upon their own efforts and occasionally the assistance of God.

The Public Sphere and Public Space

For vendedoras like Juana Gutiérrez access to public space was contingent upon her rights as a woman to the public sphere. The physical space included municipal markets, unregulated provisional markets, city streets, plazas and parks, and the doorways of factories, private homes, and businesses. The public sphere, as a realm of engagement regarding issues of common concern, was constituted in vendor petitions and actions in public places. At the same time, Mexico City residents debated who had what kinds of rights to public space, a conversation in which vendors appeared as subjects and not participants. Within these various media the rights of individuals to public space were defined. Though some scholars define the public sphere as the realm of the literate, with the assistance of public scribes, illiterate vendors participated in literate culture and sought to define their rights.[4] But these remain abstract descriptions. Let us look in more detail at the municipal markets, city streets, and plazas where vendors worked.

La Merced was perhaps the most important municipal market, both in terms of the distribution of goods as well as its central place in city life. As the largest of more than fifteen markets administered by the municipality of Mexico City, La Merced was where most inhabitants of the city and even small vendors purchased foodstuffs. An Inspector Monteverde, in his 1903 survey of all government-regulated vending, noted that "[La Merced] is too small for the vendors and the public who gather daily in the market, and it is well-known that the market serves most inhabitants of the Federal District and many from outside of the area."[5] Vendors filled 363 stalls inside La Merced and sold mostly large quantities of foodstuffs, such as fruits and vegetables, cereals, meat and viscera, birds, fish, eggs, and milk products. There was no refrigeration for perishables. Foodstuffs not sold were kept in wooden boxes and remained in the market stalls until the following day. This, in addition to the low ceilings and poor ventilation, must have contributed to an overall atmosphere of market life in a particularly pungent manner. At the same time, more pleasant smells mingled in the air. Amber chips of copal burned to attract customers to the *hierbera* (herbalist), from whom women could buy large amounts of verdant rosemary to make infusions for inducing miscarriage, or a pinch of

this and that for what ailed her—maybe *té de tila* (linden blossoms), mari-
juana, or orange leaves. Hierberas could even help capture the heart of an
unrequited love by supplying dead hummingbirds to be placed under the
bed at night. In addition to shoppers, the aisles of municipal markets were
filled with peddlers in search of customers, thieves in search of pockets to
pick, and prostitutes in search of a trick.[6]

The exchange of goods and services was not contained solely within
the physical walls of municipal markets such as La Merced. The streets
outside of markets were filled with the smells, sights, and sounds of market life as well. Each year, more and more vendors filled stands all along
the outside perimeter of the building. Outside markets like the Mercado
San Juan, indigenous women sold avocados, tomatoes, and kitchen utensils made of clay. They laid out their goods on canvases or *petates* (woven
palm-leaf mats), violating a 1903 law which mandated that vendors utilize wooden tables, and a 1905 law which prohibited the use of *guacales*
(wooden carts) and *zacates* (woven mats).[7] While vendors at Mercado San
Juan sat exposed to the elements, those at La Lagunilla provided themselves with shade using makeshift covers made out of burlap sheets and
rags. Up in the northern reaches of the city, women selling *gorditas*, a common street fare made of corn meal, could always be found sitting, wrapped
in rebozos (Mexican shawls), on the ground underneath tripod parasols
(see figure 6.1). Not everyone was able to sit while they sold their wares.
At the Buenavista train station, women stood shoulder to shoulder with
baskets of eggs and prepared foods.

Such municipal and ad hoc markets were a central part of city life for
many inhabitants of Mexico City. Markets throughout the city served to
link producers and service providers with various groups of consumers.
While workers could grab a tamale and a cup of coffee before work, or
fried innards for an occasional taste of meat, those who could afford it
bought cooking utensils to prepare meals for their families at home. For
all Mexico City residents, every pulquería had its enchiladera stationed in
a nearby doorway preparing tidbits to warm the mouth and senses. While
some markets sold a wide variety of goods, in others vendors selling the
same goods gathered in specific locations. Seasonal flowers could be purchased on the Zócalo. There, women sold vibrant yellow marigolds and
hot-pink lion's paw in early November for Night of the Dead. Toy vendors put up their stands at the Portales de los Mercaderes, while women
selling prepared foods such as tortillas stationed themselves—day after
day—at the Buenavista train station or the Portales de Santo Domingo.

FIGURE 6.1
Buying and selling *gorditas*, circa 1900.
Source: Fototeca Nacional, Mexico City.

As street sales spread in Mexico City, vendors stationed themselves at the *portales* (arches) because it allowed them to be near fixed establishments and the clientele these shops attracted. Women *ambulantes* (itinerant peddlers) could be found in the streets surrounding La Merced market selling shoes from Nuevo León. Some of Mexico City's earliest textile shops depended upon sales of cloth at the Guerrero neighborhood market.[8] Markets were also fertile ground for scavengers, many of whom were women and children who gathered and stole items to be sold as scraps to various paper factories and metal works in the city. Scavenged items also found their way into people's homes, in the form of second-hand clothing, tools, and other assorted goods that circulated around the city and through the hands of the rich and then the poor. Women like Jacoba Hernandez sold the day's leftovers from Sylvain Restaurant in Tepito Plaza.[9] What was left behind by scavengers piled up as garbage in the middle of the streets just outside of markets and, until the 1920s, was infrequently removed by the garbage trucks.

As indicated by Juana Gutiérrez in her petition at the opening of this chapter, vendors who had sold on the streets for years, even decades, without any interference from the government, were, by around 1900, faced with the possibility that their source of livelihood might become an illegal activity. Though the federal government encroached upon the powers of municipal government during this time, as the municipal government endeavored to shape the public sphere it increased its presence on the streets and in the lives of vendors. Mexico City governmental efforts to modernize markets began around the year 1880 and increased significantly in the first decade of the twentieth century. By the 1900s the municipal government was in the throes of redefining its relationship with vendors. City streets, sidewalks, parks, and plazas were redefined in terms of who would use them and how. For the government, the regulation of vendors, particularly women, was concurrently an issue of governing the use of street life and of defining gender roles in the public sphere.[10]

Bienestar Público:
Municipal Market Reform and Gender Ideology

With the relative peace of the Porfiriato, government at the federal and municipal level was solidified and strengthened. In fact, Porfiristas liked to characterize the regime with the phrase *paz y buena administración* (peace and good administration), suggesting the centrality of administration to creating a Porfirian-defined peace. Local-level manifestations of this dictum were particularly relevant to vendedoras, for improved means of governance meant quantitative and qualitative changes in their lives. It meant new impositions of government authority and the increased presence of government on the streets. In 1879 there was a change in the personnel of the city council, which initiated stepped-up efforts of modernization and bureaucratization in the administration of markets. The 1903 Law of Municipal Organization further tightened the connection between national and city government and the political control of Porfiristas engaged in a concerted effort of urban reform. At the level of city governance, this meant the solidification of institutions, the division of duties, and the clarification of hierarchy. Municipal authorities also created new departments, such as the Department of Slaughterhouses and Markets, which oversaw street vending by ambulantes as well as sales at fixed stands in municipal markets and at slaughterhouses.[11] The Department's task was to improve the distribution of food, clothing, cooking utensils, and other sundry items, as well as generate income for city government. A corps of market inspectors was hired to enforce a system of licensing, and to remove those vendors who did not comply (see figure 6.2).[12]

FIGURE 6.2
La Lagunilla Market, circa 1922.
Source: Fototeca Nacional, Mexico City.

As municipal reformers increased the construction of new markets, they also increased regulation of street sales outside those markets. They focused considerable attention on vendors of prepared foods. Beginning with the completion of La Merced in 1880, market officials encouraged vendors who worked with large amounts of capital and sold bulk foods such as meat, fruits, and vegetables to secure locations inside of municipal markets.[13] In further efforts to clear the streets, inspectors then were instructed "to remove the vendors of enchiladas, fried and grilled foods, and *cecinas* [cured meat], coffee, *atole* [a non-alcoholic grain beverage], and sandwiches," the vast majority of whom were women.[14] Nevertheless, vendedoras often returned to their customary street corner or to municipal markets to sell in the aisles. Given the constant resistance of vendedoras, over the next thirty years the Mexico City municipal government passed a series of laws directed at vendors of prepared food. In June 1901, and again in February 1902, the city council declared that all comideras would be thrown out of municipal markets. The next year, the women were reported "to continue to abuse this law, occupying large sections [of certain municipal markets], interrupting the passage of pedestrians, and they were of a filthy and unhygienic appearance."[15] In 1903 a municipal law dating back to 1897 permitting the unregulated sale of items on the public thoroughfare was revoked. In 1904, and again during 1907 and 1908, police and market inspectors increased their regulation of sidewalk sales.[16]

In the process of regulating marketing, municipal officials made repeated efforts to shape cultural practices in public. Their efforts affected the place of food in daily life, hygiene, aesthetics, the use of time, and definitions of femaleness in public space. For example, following the 1907 law inspectors removed a group of vendors from their usual location because their simple presence was thought to threaten the cleanliness of consumers. The municipal government wanted to "move [the] vendedoras because their dirty clothes are ruining the clothes of señoritas who go to buy flowers."[17] In 1911 the municipal government sought to regulate vendors and prostitutes, both of whom city councilor Leopoldo Villarreal thought of in the same breath as causing the degeneration of the Zócalo.[18] Municipal authorities directed another series of regulations at women's participation in the cultural and economic life surrounding pulquerías. In 1904 the municipal council made it illegal to conduct sales in doorways and entrances, and especially outside of pulquerías and taverns, which until then had been a legal selling location for comideras.[19] By regulating comideras, the city authorities hoped to discourage women from being on the streets and from association with pulquería culture. This would be reinforced in 1919, when women were allowed to enter taverns only to eat or to purchase pulque "to go," but not to consume it on the premises. Municipal authorities explicitly associated not only women drinking in public but also women working on the streets with moral degeneracy.[20]

Two terms pervaded discussions of public space: el público (the public) and el pueblo (the people). El pueblo literally means "town" or "people of a town," and came to mean "the common people or popular classes," in distinction to el público. El público, also a general term for people, referred to citizens who would be included in modernization projects. These two terms belied a power struggle both economic and ideological in nature. Mexico City elites concerned themselves with shaping the city for "el público." Common phrases that revealed a fundamental frame of reference for elites were el bienestar público, las obras públicas, la salubridad pública, and la vía pública—public welfare, public works, public health, and the public thoroughfare. While the term el público suggests an unlimited number of people, it was in fact a phrase that imposed limits. Those not explicitly included in el público were considered part of the periphery, that is, el pueblo. Street vendors acted within the realm of, but were only accidentally beneficiaries of (or adversely affected by), legislation enacted for el público. Electrification is one example. While ostensibly for the benefit of the entire city, it was really meant to protect el público from el pueblo after the sun went down. Likewise, the municipal government fashioned markets to service elite and middle-class needs first and the needs of vendors only secondarily. *El público* was a term that avoided explicit recognition of the economic basis of class difference.

Discussion of the cultural differences between el público and el pueblo was particularly relevant to streetlife and vendors. Media as diverse as newspapers, government documents, and scientific journals printed articles construing economic issues in terms of cultural difference. For example, a contributor to the women's newspaper *La Mujer Mexicana* examined the eating habits of el pueblo and worked herself into a frenzy over what she deemed the horrific food sold on the street. She described in detail the smell and appearance of the food and the people surrounding the stands, arguing that such food encouraged people to drink alcohol. The alcoholism of el pueblo, she argued, had led to epidemic levels of intestinal problems and one of the world's highest death rates. The reference to death rates was a loaded comment, as this statistic was commonly cited as contributing to Mexico's relative lack of economic development vis-à-vis the United States and European nations.[21] The article's author perceived individual weaknesses to be the cause of societal ills, not societal weaknesses as the cause of individual ills. While such commentary was meant as a cultural critique of food and health, it contained the class-bound assumptions that working people had unlimited choices as to where they could eat and that they had the time to do so in the privacy of their homes. Such assumptions about what constituted appropriate public and private behavior put economic conflict in cultural terms, so that elites were able to disparage working-class life without politicizing the causes of those differences they hoped to emphasize.[22]

Municipal reform gave concrete meaning to these conceptions of el público and el pueblo. A conflict that emerged in 1902 shows how. A group of citizens complained that the town council was violating fundamental rights of citizens by limiting street vending. Legislation limiting "sidewalk sales," they argued, would be an attack on freedom of commerce. They went on to say that such an abuse was even more deplorable when it was inflicted upon the poor, who made their living in such a fashion. To this, the town council responded, "Freedom of commerce is not at variance with police proclamations or hygiene, and, as with all other freedoms, it ends where the rights of others begin."[23] For municipal authorities, vendors blocking the public thoroughfare were at variance with "el público"—that is to say, those people transiting the street. With this response, municipal authorities implied that vendors were not a part of the public and had no right to station themselves on the streets if in doing so they infringed upon the rights of those who were "el público." The municipal authorities argued that they were not depriving anyone of a right, but rather of a convenience. This argument was reinforced with a turgid description of the rotten garbage and filth that filled the streets as a result of such vendors, implicitly reinforcing the idea that those who did not partake of elite culture, those who lived in filth, were justly denied conveniences. The city official closed by reminding those who would object, "One of the first obligations of the municipality is to assure the cleanliness and elegance of the public thoroughfare, and the freedom of circulation for all."[24] This argument privileged elite concerns for appearances and access to the public thoroughfare, while discounting the concerns of those without sufficient capital to occupy established market stalls.[25]

Municipal officials recognized the problems that strict enforcement of new regulations could cause. In 1908 the Department of Slaughterhouses and Markets temporarily stopped removing vendors from outside of markets, noting that "to do so would result in serious complications not only due to the high income [which they generate], but the distribution of food, and social consequences as well."[26] This same correspondence also indicated that to ban those vendors from selling immediately outside of the public markets would mean a loss in vital municipal income amounting to 150 pesos a day, or 54,750 pesos a year. Furthermore, anywhere from four to five thousand vendors would be affected, potentially leading to social unrest, both on the part of vendors and consumers.[27] Despite the potential difficulties that would result from strict enforcement of regulations, municipal authorities viewed market administration as part of the imposition of governmental authority on the lives of the working poor within public spaces. The Mexico City governor frequently reminded market inspectors of the connection between respect for *buena administración* and the authority and well-being of the government.[28]

Cultural distinctions between el público and el pueblo were complicated by gender. Municipal authorities carried out market reform during a time when gender relations in Mexico were in flux, and regulations were informed by people's attempts to shape and control the new role of women in the public sphere.[29] But enter into the public sphere they did. Certainly, women had inhabited the streets before the late nine-teenth century; however, which women and how they did so was chang-ing. Women worked selling items on the streets throughout the colonial period, but women's habits of consumption had changed since the begin-ning of the century, bringing them out of the home and into shops, mar-kets, and streets. Whereas vendors had traveled through neighborhoods, calling their wares from house to house, by the 1880s middle-class con-sumers frequented the markets themselves. Nineteenth-century geogra-pher and historian Antonio García Cubas fondly recalled in his 1905 mem-oir *Recuerdos de mis tiempos* the cries of water carriers, bric-a-brac vendors, secondhand clothiers, and others. He depicted typical street characters *(tipos)* with photographs and descriptions of how they looked as well as their work habits, creating for his readers a folkloric image of the vend-ing occupations. For García Cubas these vendors signified a lost, familiar channel of interaction between the upper class and the people who sup-plied the goods they consumed. He lamented the loss of negotiation be-tween the mistress of the house and vendors. Implied in his lamentations was an awareness that social classes now interacted in new ways, with women going to market. The ideal of a woman remaining within the walls of the home as a sign of female respectability was disappearing. Other shopping habits changed as well. Elite women no longer pulled up to the curb outside of a textile shop so that the shopkeeper could bring bolts of silk to the carriage for her perusal. Now, middle- and upper-class women entered into shops and markets, hesitantly rubbing elbows with their fel-low shoppers.[30]

During the Porfiriato upper-class Mexicans expressed concern about the mingling of the social classes, and this concern was at times com-municated by focusing on the danger such mingling posed to women. In part, this was due to the widespread currency of belief regarding the spread of socially undesirable habits. Women, and in particular middle-class women, were considered to be particularly vulnerable to such con-tagion. Municipal authorities expressed their concerns in their planning of various public projects, including the creation of parks and tolerance zones, the regulation of plazas and streets, and market reform. They hoped markets could become places for "family outings," which implied middle-class family outings.[31] Separate parks designed specifically for workers would be most desirous, municipal authorities stated, because "workers need large spaces where they can recreate honestly and hygienically. They need economic options for diversion where, without being in contact with the social classes superior to their own condition, they may abstain from absolute idleness, so as to be distracted from crime and vice on holidays."[32]

Such a concern with the intermingling of different classes was not restricted to government officials and was merely a reflection of upper- and middle-class thinking of the time. The municipal government received letters, such as one from a group of neighbors south of Mercado San Juan, who requested that the city remove women who sold prepared meats on the street. The neighbors expressed concern for what they considered the filth of the women, justifying their petition by noting that "said market is frequented daily by a multitude of persons from all classes and categories of people."[33] In another petition city inhabitants demanded something be done about the "invasion" of certain "señoras" in the Alameda, a central park of Mexico City. The petition claimed that the women bothered families, and that respectable women had been confused for prostitutes.[34] Another petition expressed fear regarding "a filthy room open to the street, where day and night an infamous old woman seduces poor young middle-class women, who remain forever dishonored."[35] Such petitions were in part a reaction to the increasing presence of middle-class women in public and reflected the realignment of the gendered aspects of class relations. As women of varied class backgrounds shopped in municipal markets or promenaded on foot instead of in carriages, a premium was placed on creating boundaries between so-called respectable and disreputable women. These boundaries were marked by one's clothing, activities, and actual presence on the street.

Whether a perceived or a real problem, the presence of women on the streets and how they behaved there became a topic of public discussion. Journalists, social commentators, and government officials often viewed women in the streets with ambivalence. In an article titled "Rules of Society in the Street," a journalist begrudgingly accepted that single women might go out into the streets, but married women, he counseled, should be free to go into the streets only if they donned simple and modest dress, so as not to attract attention or turn heads. Women should know where they were going to shop, he suggested, what they were to buy, and how much they were to spend, so as not to lose time in useless conversation. Women should not speak in loud tones, or exhibit extemporaneous laughter. Obviously annoyed, he begged women not to stop where they would block other people walking on the sidewalk. Women were also urged to travel into the streets alone rather than with their domestics, "who for the most part were daughters of el pueblo, completely lacking in tact due to their scant education, which impedes them from discerning between that which is correct and that which is not."[36] Another journalist irritatingly commented on women who brought children into stores, he thought, solely to be entertained. These journalists construed women's publicness as uninformed and somewhat undeserved.

Discussions of how women should act contributed to an atmosphere wherein being female mitigated one's rights in public. On 15 December 1913, just three days after the Day of the Virgen of Guadalupe, a soldier named Vicente Sanchez attempted to flirt with a young enchiladera named María Jimenez who sold her goods on the Zócalo, the central plaza of Mexico City. At one point, Sanchez threw himself on Jimenez, trying to kiss her. When she showed no interest in his sexual advances, not even smiling, he left in a rage. Later that day he returned to find Jimenez, grabbed her, and poured a can of gasoline on her. The soldier then set a match to her, turning the woman into an immense burning torch that lit up the late afternoon shadows of the Zócalo. Sanchez's actions were not condoned, but the ambiguity in newspaper reports meant to denounce the act simultaneously revealed the discomfort people felt about the rights of women working on the streets. The *Nueva Era* newspaper reporter noted Jimenez's name as "María, the most vulgar of names," and described her as "one of these women who, beneath a mask of innocence reveals a sort of budding perversity."[37] In explaining that the enchiladera had had to "stand the impertinence of customers, among whom one could find all sorts, from the *pelao*, dirty and bad smelling, to the neighborhood dandy, a Mexican character of the most interesting stripe, due to his manners and clothing," he managed at the same time to impugn her morality.[38] Rather than suggesting a sympathetic tone, the journalist created an argument for María Jimenez's guilt based merely on her presence in public. Besides, he remarked, "What woman that is attractive does not know it?" A woman of questionable morality had a questionable claim to civil rights. While such violence was by no means the common response to women on the streets, both the act of lighting the woman afire and the response of the journalist indicated a cultural climate where rights to the public sphere were only marginally extended to women.

The Marginalization of Vendedoras

The cultural construction of women's rights in the public sphere had a concrete effect in the daily life of vendedoras. Working-class women have a long history of participating in street sales in cities throughout the Americas, including Mexico City.[39] In colonial Mexico City women dominated the sale of prepared foods, such as tortillas, sandwiches, gorditas, stewed meats, enchiladas, and atole. This "tradition" had its origins in a restricted employment market and in women's domestic roles.[40] Women had owned more established forms of businesses as well. Since the colonial era they had commonly run the smaller *almuercerías* (lunchrooms), whereas men had owned bodegas, which required more capital and brought in greater earnings.[41] To determine women's precise participation in vending is difficult because they resisted talking to census takers and tax collectors. Additionally, corruption and understaffing put into question the validity of the census data that do exist.[42] With these caveats in mind, municipal records suggest there were two general trends between 1880 and 1910. First, the number of women selling in municipal markets declined. And second, large numbers of women worked legally or illegally selling outside of municipal markets, in ad hoc markets, and independently on the streets.

Vendedoras figured centrally in the socioeconomic changes wrought by industrialization. Though industrialists hired increasing numbers of women, occupational segregation by sex meant many women could not find factory work, and they turned to street vending as either a part- or full-time source of income. So, for example, Antonia Barreiro from Guadalajara was not unique in her journey to the city in search of a wage. Neither was her experience unique when in 1907, after finding no other source of employment, Barreiro petitioned for permission to set up a small stand, in her case to sell ice cream, which recently had become popular with consumers.[43] Municipal reform affected where Barreiro, and vendors of other products, might establish a stand and under what conditions.

As government agencies became more efficient at regulating street vending, they effectively pushed women out of legal municipal markets and into the streets as illegal vendors or as marginalized ambulantes. Women had been a small percentage of municipal market vendors until the 1890s, at which time their participation in municipal market sales decreased to even lower levels. Furthermore, men dominated as vendors inside of the majority of municipal markets, including San Juan, Iturbide, La Merced, and El Baratillo. In the markets of San Cosme, Plaza Misioneros, and Santa Ana there was relative parity between male and female vendors until about 1895 or 1903. Then men came to dominate in these markets as well. The few women who owned stands inside the municipal markets worked with significantly smaller amounts of capital than men in the same markets. In 1885, before stepped-up government regulation, women made up half of the vendors at Mercado Iturbide, which had the largest percentage of women vendors of all the municipal markets. By 1893, they represented one-third of the established vendors. Iturbide's location on the outskirts of the city where more men would have been working the land, may explain the larger percentage of women vendors selling there.[44]

City and federal censuses also indicate a trend of marginalization of women as legal street vendors. The 1900 census of the Federal District found women to be 20 percent of the total work force, with 167 female and 158 male registered ambulantes. In the 1910 census, women were 310 of the 1,078 registered ambulantes. By contrast, a sample of 454 license requests received by the municipal government in 1908 for street sales of prepared food, firewood, tiles, ice cream, and other items included requests from 326 women and 128 men, indicating the predominance of women selling goods outside of markets without the legal right to do so. Women tended to sell their goods in areas such as the Alameda, Primera Cuadra, the Plaza de la Constitución, and near the Basilica in Guadalupe Hidalgo, all places which became regulated selling locations and the object of aggressive removal campaigns in the year 1904, and again in the period 1907–1908. Nevertheless, the restrictions on women's capacity to sell on the streets contradicted the central role they played in Mexico City marketing and in filling city government coffers. Nor did their illegal status prevent vendedoras from figuring centrally in discussions of women's place in the public sphere.[45]

Vendedora Conceptions of Public Space

In response to the increased regulation of marketing, both men and women used gendered conceptions of rights in the public sphere. Market inspectors, vendors—both male and female—police, and journalists all could attempt to exercise power over a vendedora by questioning her morality. How did vendors—women, in particular—respond? Vendedoras responded vigorously to any infringement on their livelihood but also on their way of life, including their conceptions of the appropriate use of public space. Where women worked, what they sold, their legal status, their contribution to the economy, and how government officials defined their rights, all combined with their own sense of history to shape the words they used to describe their struggles. Vendedoras laid claim to the public sphere by defining morality in their own terms, and by disassociating class-bound definitions of morality from what they considered their rights in public. In this regard, vendedoras relied on a language of morality and publicness, despite their disregard for practices of female seclusion, just as historians have found to be the case for men and women of the working or popular classes in other places and times.[46]

In their petitions, vendedoras presented an understanding of public space that often differed from that of municipal authorities. These differences resonated with their reasons for having undertaken vending as a livelihood and with the way that occupation had shaped their daily lives. For vendors, the street was a place to work, but it was also where a person might sleep, eat, socialize, make love, raise children, and fight. Housing was limited and expensive; services such as water were of limited availability to the poor. In preparation for the 1910 centennial celebration, for example, the government attempted to clear the streets of many of the vendors in the center of the city. In one roundup of vendors, at El Baratillo market in Plaza San Bartolomé de las Casas in Tepito, seventy people of both sexes were arrested for sleeping in their stands. A market inspector scolded the two watchmen who were responsible for ensuring that vendors did not live in their stands. He had found the two watchmen "committing carnal acts" in a vendor's stall at two in the morning with Julia Lopez, a well-known prostitute.[47] The watchmen were informed that that was not the job for which the government paid them. The city government considered vending stands as places of business, to be used as businesses during regulated business hours, while for the vendors themselves there was no such clear distinction. When police questioned people as to why they were in the Plaza at night, they told police they were relatives of the vendors. They believed vendors and their families had a right to occupy public places where stands were located, at any hour. Stands were shelter when night came and places of work and diversion at all hours of the day and night. In contrast, the market inspector characterized them as "people of el pueblo, servants and well-known thieves."[48] Economic imperatives often lay behind vendors' seeing the street as a place to live. A thirty-four-year-old woman living in her stand with her five children explained to a market inspector that the street was where she could afford to live. Her husband had abandoned her five years earlier, and since then she had dedicated herself to buying and selling secondhand goods. She earned between 1.50 and 1.75 pesos a day, enough to cover the 7 pesos a week rent she paid for the right to the space where she had established her stand.[49]

These social relations were essential to life on the streets. Within this community of city dwellers, life was shared with a wide variety of people. When a vendor defended her right to sell in a specific location, she was also defending her right to live on the streets as well as the social connections which supported that lifestyle. These social relations included people who provided lines of credit (in cash or barter), those who provided insurance against the vagaries of life, and the friendships made based on daily interaction. Such social relations formed on the street also aided vendors in staking out territory. Vendors knew which corners made the best sales, and they depended on that information to place themselves in physical relation to other vendors in order to maximize earnings. Sometimes this meant securing distance from other vendors, and at other times it meant sticking together to attract customers. It was precisely these social relations that vendors depended upon at times of resistance to government impositions in their lives.[50] These social relations were essential to vendor conceptions of the public sphere.

While a vendedora's own sense of respectability may not have mirrored upper-class concerns with publicness, she nevertheless had to contend with the association of women in public with immorality. Male market inspectors, vendors, and customers all could potentially wield power over a woman in public. The way this power was wielded served to reinforce the fact that women's rights were contingent upon gender. For example, when a market inspector could not get a group of vendedoras to pay a bribe, he resorted to this type of power by questioning their morality. He acted haughtily, made lewd suggestions, and claimed the women were "of questionable notoriety."[51] In 1910 Angela Fuentes, a fruit vendor in the Alameda, was arrested for allegedly not paying required taxes. However, a policeman testified on her behalf that the market inspector, one Señor Villa, had refused to accept her payment when she offered it. "Said woman states that she is married to Pedro Hernández, and that the tax collector in question wants something with her ('anda requeriendo amores'), and she has not accepted, so he intends to revenge himself in this manner."[52] A position of power provided the privilege to attempt to take sex from women who worked on the street, regardless of their desires or marital status. In the eyes of some, a woman working on the street was part of the public domain in more ways than one.

Male vendors also used morality to question women's presence on the streets. In 1907, at the Portal de Mercaderes, the employees of a printed-goods business came into conflict with a group of women selling *aguas* (flavored water). The men working at the printed-goods stand distinguished themselves from the women by stressing that they had in no way contributed to the "lack of respect to morality and to the public that is committed there. . . . We do not have employees who, with suggestive coquetry, attract the kind of public which lends itself to scandals and obscenities. We all have formed our homes and we support them honestly with our limited earnings."[53] The men further emphasized the contrast between themselves, as male heads of households, and the women, as women, on the street. They referred to the "scandals motivated by the presence of the women who dispense the aguas, and who are visited and courted by wild youth of indecorous offers and actions."[54]

In defending themselves against such accusations and municipal regulations, vendedoras resorted to a variety of means of resistance and legitimation. Most vendors resisted by the elegantly simple and powerful act of ignoring municipal regulations and continuing to conduct their business in their customary locations. In addition, both men and women worked to persuade other vendors not to pay taxes or purchase licenses—and were blacklisted as agitators as a result. Groups of vendors occasionally resorted to spontaneous rioting, organized refusal to pay fines, and street fighting. Many vendors went to a public scribe, who would most likely be found sitting at a small wooden folding table placed along the perimeter of Plaza de Santo Domingo. There, the vendors would have the scribe write a letter for them and send it to the city government. Of three hundred petitioners in this archive, approximately 70 percent were women. They wrote as groups and as individuals.[55]

In their petitions, women spoke directly to the questioning of their morality due to their presence on the streets. Furthermore, they refuted the qualification of their rights based on this questioning of their morality. In so doing, they walked the rhetorical tightrope between accepting a restricted public sphere for women and asserting their rights. When a group of seventy-three women were told to move two blocks away from where they were used to selling at the Buenavista train station, they all signed a letter which began, "We the undersigned, neighbors of this City and dedicated from a very young age to the small-scale sale of tortillas, with no other means than this from which to subsist, and from which our families subsist, no matter how much they speak ill of us, denigrating and slandering us because we are weak and defenseless women . . . [protest] that the

Prefect of Guadalupe Hidalgo [has declared] that we clear out of from in front of the Portal de Hidalgo at Morelos and Pozito streets."[56] In pointing out what they knew was being said about the connection between the categorization of their morality and its relationship to their rights, these vendors discredited such modes of thought, precisely by accepting their identity as women in a vulnerable position in society. In this and countless cases, women fought the tie made between the questioning of their morality, due to their presence on the streets, and their rights to the use of that same public space.[57]

Some petitions more implicitly questioned the premise of certain laws. Such was the case with the 1907 law against comideras and enchiladeras stationing themselves outside of taverns and pulquerías. When Petra Carrillo was fined for selling sandwiches outside of a pulquería, she went to a public scribe, who wrote the following for her: "She the undersigned, respectfully puts forth: that I am a poor widow, with various children and among them three young women to whose families I have to attend, not only for their food but for their instruction as well . . . [I had been located] for eight years at Portal de Santo Domingo selling sandwiches without ever being fined, though was recently just for being near a cantina and a pulquería. Save a family from indigence. Petra Carrillo."[58] As with many vendor conflicts, the written record does not allow us to know the outcome of Carrillo's petition. What we can know is how vendors like Carrillo portrayed themselves. As was the case with Muñoz Viuda de Trejo, discussed at the opening of this chapter, Carrillo emphasized her practice of street sales as having predated municipal concern for women's threat to public morality.

Even if a woman's morality was not explicitly brought into question in the process of denying her rights, in their petitions vendedoras indicated their efforts to strive for an honorable life. In some petitions, women promised that if their petitions were granted they would "by all means possible strive to maintain morality and order among their clients."[59] They protested being moved because, as they pointed out, no reports of immorality had been filed against them. Eight women selling food in front of a Tepito neighborhood pulquería made their case by reminding the municipal government that they had been in "quiet and pacific" possession of their business for several years. They requested "for reasons of equity and justice, and as a truly humanitarian act, that you concede the continuance our small business."[60]

Vendedoras shifted the focus on their morality to alternative means of legitimating their claims. They defined their use of public space as "traditional" when making claims on the public sphere. So, a battle over space was fought with different weapons. Elites enacted laws. The popular classes invoked "tradition" as a tool to defend their interests. The battle over what the government defined as law and what the vendors on the street defined as tradition was very explicit in government documentation and in the words of the vendors themselves. One group of vendors argued:

> It is a long-standing custom, and that it is custom makes it law, that the stands selling sweets and other goods appropriate for children establish themselves in the Plaza de la Constitución, on certain civic and religious festivals, as the most central location in the city. In virtue of this custom, the undersigned, all compañeros, have already undertaken expenditures of more or less substantial amounts, some more, some less than others, according to his resources, in order to put up their stands during the Christmas holiday. . . . One could say that we should relocate ourselves, but the custom is such that there would be no sales for us, and this has been proven by experience, because when we have been moved to any other locale, our losses have been inescapable.[61]

Tradition was not some amorphous idea of taste, or conservative or inherited behavior. As anthropologist William Roseberry argues, tradition is "socially constructed meanings that inform action. . . . It [is] a reflection upon and selecting from a people's history. The process of selection is political and is tied to relations of domination and subordination."[62] As a selection from and interpretation of a people's history, tradition emerges out of the daily lives of the dominant and dominated alike. Tradition in turn-of-the-century Mexico was, in part, the passing down of certain rituals and values; it was also the practice of these rituals day after day. It was activity firmly rooted in quotidian practices, intertwined with ascertaining a livelihood, and so made essential to one's existence. Vendors resisted selling in new locations such as the Mercado de San Cosme because *desde tiempo inmemorial* (since time immemorial) — an expression of tradition — vendors sold to customers at La Merced and Mercado Iturbide. Tradition was good business sense, exemplified in the practice of selling in the same place everyday so that customers could find you. At these markets, and other street locations, customers knew that they could find the best prices and certain items they desired. These markets had established reputations for variety and quality goods. Certain neighborhoods were known for the sale of specific items. Lag time in developing the reputation of a market, in addition to higher licensing fees, could mean times of serious hardship for vendors with smaller amounts of capital, like women and Indians — precisely the groups in Mexican society commonly labeled "traditional."[63]

In their petitions vendors used words and phrases such as "customary location," "since time immemorial," and other expressions of long-established and to them legitimate practices.[64] A group of eleven women and two men responded to a directive that they move from their location in La Villa de Guadalupe by referring to themselves as "*vecinas* . . . who have sold the traditional gorditas of La Villa since time immemorial."[65] The word *vecinas* is the plural feminine form of neighbor. It was also the term used to denote citizenship, legally defined in terms that only men could fulfill, including the exercise of the vote and eligibility for military service.[66] The vendors combined this reference to the rights of citizens with the legitimating force of tradition. As a part of this reliance on — and re-creation of—tradition, women commonly specified the time they had worked in the same occupation, often in the same location. Juana Gutiérrez had sold cooked corn for over ten years on the same street corner. At the time of her petition against removal, Antonia Garcías had been selling sweets in the same location for nineteen years, when "just the other day [they] took her license . . . [with which she] supports family, pays rent and buys clothing with money from the sales."[67]

Vendors marked time and tradition by local and national politics as well. The letters that vendors sent to the city government revealed a detailed awareness of politics and a knowledge of government priorities. While elites knew little about the world of vendors, vendors knew much about the world of the elites. Ignorance was a privilege of power. In her petition written in 1908, Señora Muñoz Viuda de Trejo marked time by the succession of presidents since Benito Juárez. Other vendors marked time by the passage of laws affecting their work, citing specific laws which they might be accused of violating, such as those regarding blocking pedestrians in the public thoroughfare, hygiene, and competition with established businesses. Vendors were also aware of the fact that elites were prejudiced against working-class expressions of culture, such as language and cleanliness. In attempts to sway authorities in their favor, vendors claimed to have cleaned up their language, their appearance, and even to have filled holes in the pavement so as to improve the public hygiene. For women, this meant awareness of conceptions of female morality in the public sphere.[68]

When vendedoras utilized the language of tradition, they laid claims to the rights of working women to the public sphere. Because women were increasingly limited to street sales, they were more adversely affected than men by campaigns in the 1900s to remove street vendors, especially vendors of prepared food. And while men also spoke of tradition as a means of defending their rights, women tended to have more cause to utilize this manner of speaking. So we cannot argue that an affinity for tradition was particularly female. Nor was a vendedora's defense of marketing rights an expression of a narrowly defined "female consciousness" emanating from particularly female prerogatives. Rather, vendedoras resorted to arguments of tradition and female honor in the face of a sex-segmented labor market and the need to counter municipal authorities' efforts to question their rights to sell on the streets. Roseberry's argument regarding the construction of "tradition" can also help us understand how femaleness was defined in the process of women selecting from aspects of their life and interactions.

One of the identities women selected was that of sole breadwinner of their household. In 1907 one woman described her situation: "Given that I am a single woman I have to work in order to gain a living for my children and [because] I don't have anyone with whom to leave them I always have to have them within sight."[69] A group of five women wrote in 1901 to protest their proposed removal from their usual location, supporting their argument by noting that "the majority of us are exceedingly poor and burdened by large family, and as you will understand it is not possible to make expenditures of any kind. Not doubting that you will attend to this request, which we believe to be just. We thank you most respectfully in advance."[70] Male vendors occasionally mentioned the families they supported; however, women pointed out that they were the *only* support of their families. For example, in 1901 a group of women sent a letter to the municipal government pointing out that after the Volador market burned down they had been left to wander the streets, able to sell only that which they could carry in their hands. They referred to their meager sales as that "from which we, as single women provide the sole sustenance for our families."[71]

Protection of the morality of mothers resonated with elite concepts of motherhood. Another group of itinerant vendors requested permission to continue selling on the streets because "otherwise it is our children who will suffer."[72] Vendedoras discussed the challenges they faced as women on their own, sometimes gladly, other times with a feeling of the weight of the world. One woman revealed the bitter edges of the responsibilities of motherhood when she wrote that upon her husband's death she had "inherited nothing more than two small children."[73] One woman framed her petition by requesting "government support in the pursuit of an honorable means of making a living," noting that conceding her petition would help her in "setting a good example for my children."[74] While upper- and middle-class families upheld mothers in the home as the image of ideal motherhood, many vendedoras raised their children in the homes they formed on the street.

As sole providers for their families, women asserted themselves as workers. Sometimes this class-consciousness was explicit, while at other times it was suggested in the range of issues raised by petitioners. Vendors tended to mention previous or second occupations as a means of identifying themselves. Vendedoras worked in a wide variety of occupations, including seamstress, factory worker, and laundress. Women might turn to vending when work-related injuries kept them from other forms of work, as was the case for Natalia Lopez. In 1908 Lopez wrote, "I beg of you, Señor Governor, in the name of justice and as a tribute to your good name, that you attend to my petitions. I am a single woman and I suffer a painful infirmity due to so much work on a sewing machine, and having nothing else I opted for sales."[75] Women also voiced concerns regarding the availability of jobs. Several female petitioners evaluated their situation within the labor market, expressing an awareness of the sex-segregation of the work force. Petra Carrillo not only pointed to the limited job opportunities she had as a woman, but provided her own race-based analysis. In February 1909 she petitioned to continue selling sandwiches near the Portal de Santo Domingo. She hoped to establish a small business and justified her petition by describing herself as "a widowed woman with small children, and not being able to work due to the babies; before I was a laundress, but the Chinese have taken this work from us."[76]

Vendedoras participated in a collective sense of history which extended to other workers and to generations past. This sense of inheritance was an expression of class-consciousness and of continuity with the past traditions of working people, just as it had been for the obreras. One woman reminded those she petitioned that she was "a widowed woman with a large family, not having any other patrimony with which to sus-

tain myself."[77] A group of women concluded their petition by saying, "because we count on no other patrimony, nor resources with which to sustain our families than our labor."[78] The vendedoras emphasized that this
was a concrete, physical inheritance with references to labor and their
hands. Their patrimony stood in direct contrast to the increasing wealth of
Mexico City elites, suggesting their right at least to work despite the unequal distribution of wealth. Vendedoras held that their capacity to work,
in the face of no other resources, was the basis of the legitimacy of their
vending practices. Furthermore, the capacity to work implied the rights
of citizens. In this regard, Alejandra Sanchez stated, "It is regarding my
four small children that I write to you, because the wage that my *Madre
Patria* (motherland) assigns me does not suffice for their sustenance or for
their education."[79]

Thus, as a group, vendedoras invoked both their roles as heads of
households and as disadvantaged participants in the workforce. In so
doing, they countered elite discussions of working women in the public
as immoral. The social and economic disadvantage to which women referred was combined when a woman described herself as *desvalida*.[80] The
word *desvalida* means both "destitute" and "unprotected," and thus con-
notes both economic status and a lack of social power. In describing themselves as desvalidas, vendedoras spoke to prevalent notions of women as
lacking socioeconomic power while presenting that fact as legitimating
their petitions. In essence, they argued that it was precisely due to their
vulnerability that they merited protection, including the right to work on
the street.

Vendedoras did not limit themselves to words to express their sense
of history and tradition, or their feelings about their rights to occupy
the public spaces of Mexico City. Women occasionally found themselves
physically fighting with other vendors, police, and market inspectors. In
1922 a specific effort was made to remove food vendors from their customary sales areas in and along the Alameda. An Inspector Castro went every
day over a period of at least four months to remove these vendors, all of
them women selling atole, enchiladas, coffee, and other prepared foods.
There were also a few men selling bread. One day in mid-November Inspector Castro went again to remove the vendedoras; he did not go alone,
and for good reason. Inspector Castro and the police who accompanied
him were greeted with a volley of oranges, scrap-metal, and obscenities.
A few days later Castro reported another incident, in which he had got-

ten into a tiff with the vendedora Josefina Buchá, who "offended those of us who were present, those of the guard of this Honorable Superiority, and at the same time offending my person, giving me a kick in the testicles, and this in the presence of Commander Apolinar Gil Herrera and the guards."[81] Inspector Castro's reports concerning his efforts to remove the women from the street and the vendedoras' repeated efforts to resist by returning continued for several months after this incident. Then, the records end abruptly, leaving us without knowing whether Josefina Buchá continued to sell in her customary location.

Conclusion

The regulation of public space in Mexico City was mediated by practices of class distinction, in part based on norms of femininity. Within the context of industrialization, the growth of Mexico City, and shifting class relations, upper- and middle-class Mexicans emphasized the distinctions between the classes in cultural terms. Municipal authorities and social commentators frequently expressed their concerns regarding the interaction of people of different classes in the public sphere by focusing on the behavior of women. Commentary disapproving of the public activities of women like the enchiladera María Jimenez who was set afire was also commentary distinguishing between working- and non-working-class culture. Commentary regarding the difficulty in distinguishing between prostitutes and respectable women expressed anxiety over not being able to make class distinctions. At the same time, elites expressed disdain for the working class in writing about the latter's use of the street for eating, food preparation, leisure, and certain types of work. Such distinctions in the realm of culture had an impact on material realities and power relations between social classes.

In their own defense, vendedoras wrote their own petitions or asked that their words be written down by public scribes and sent to the municipal government. They fashioned an identity articulating women's place in the history and public sphere of Mexico City. Vendedoras understood the power of upper- and middle-class gender ideology that questioned a woman's right to work and to be in a public space. They felt it every time they were removed from the doorway of a pulquería, banned from selling prepared food on the street, or compelled to justify their claims for a vending license with discussions of their own morality. And they addressed the place of morality, honor, and one's presence in public places in their petitions. In so doing, vendedoras participated in common public conversations regarding gender in the public sphere.

From working women in factories and sweatshops to vendedoras on the street, conceptions of female nature defined by sexual morality, honor, and weakness shaped working conditions and labor activism. While such conceptions could be used against working women, women themselves also utilized this language to defend their rights. Vendedoras did not have the same access to the public sphere as working women in the late nineteenth and early twentieth century who published petitions in the press, made alliances with middle- and upper-class women, and created alliances across the workforce. However, vendedoras did speak to the question of the right to public space, and of el público as a social grouping of political consequence. In some respects, vendor participation in the public sphere declined after the Revolution: vendor petitions to municipal government decline significantly in the late 1910s, and vendors did not write to the Department of Labor.

Despite these differences in access to the public sphere, like working women, vendedoras' petitions addressed the association of morality with their rights in at least two ways. First, they redefined female morality as belonging to those who would work and therefore inclusive of publicness. Vendedoras emphasized their roles as mothers, as the sole support of their families, and referred to their socioeconomic debility with words like *desvalida* as a means of legitimating their demands. Second, they denied the link made by municipal authorities between a supposed lack of morality and vendedora rights by asserting their own conception of legitimate claims to the public sphere. Their petitions referred to the quotidian realities of their lives: work on the streets, limited employment alternatives, and a tradition—both personal and collective—of street sales. As single heads of household, working women, mothers, and long-time participants in street sales, vendedoras forged their own definitions of femaleness.

The power of discursive constructions of working women also manifested itself in women's relationship with the federal government, the subject of chapter 7.

CHAPTER 7

Working Women and the State, 1879–1931

Over the course of the period between 1879 and 1931 discursive constructions of working women shifted in emphasis from a focus on female weakness in the realm of work, and the threat to morality which that implied, to a recognition of the rights of working women based in working conditions. Despite this shift in emphasis, a concern for female weakness, both moral and physical, persisted. This chapter examines the changing relationship between working women, employers, and the Mexican state. As Mexican government representatives sought to promote industrialization and mediate between workers and employers, they had to contend with the close identification of working women with morality and female weakness; this identification continued to mediate the rights of working women even after the Mexican Revolution.[1]

During the Porfiriato the government attempted to ameliorate the impact of industrialization on working women via support for charitable institutions, mutual aid societies, and vocational training. These activities were often premised on concerns for protecting women's morality and maternity. With the Mexican Revolution, successive administrations sought to assert power over organized labor and promote industrialization. Despite important differences in how they dealt with workers, Francisco I. Madero, Victoriano Huerta, Venustiano Carranza, Plutarco Elías Calles, and Álvaro Obregón each oversaw a Department of Labor that manifested important continuities: the identification of the rights of working women with morality and maternity. The Constitution of 1917 legislated important distinctions between male and female workers, although widespread enforcement did not begin until the 1920s. Even in their efforts to support the Constitutional rights of workers, Department of Labor officials still had to contend with how sexual morality mediated the rights of working women. The Federal Labor Code (1931) marks the close of this period, and the beginning of increased legal recognition of the specific conditions of working women—as workers, not as repositories of sexual morality and reproduction.

This chapter brings together the insights of several strands of historiography. Historians have shown that at least to some degree the Mexican Revolution opened a space for increased assertiveness on the part of workers, which led to the establishment of the Department of Labor (1911), the 1917 Constitution, and the Federal Labor Code (1931).[2] This chapter argues that for women the rights derived from these laws and institutions were mitigated by conceptions of female morality in ways similar to those found by historians of Mexican social reform.[3] This chapter expands the definition of the state implicitly used by labor historians to include the wives of Mexican presidents as integral to labor policy directed at women. It then traces Mexican labor policy from the Porfiriato through the Revolution, showing how the identification of working women with compromised sexual morality mitigated the rights of working women.

Law and Charity:
Working Women during the Porfiriato

During the Porfiriato the law did not distinguish between male and female workers. However, "labor policy" during this period was more broadly defined than by the rights founded in the Constitution of 1857 and the Federal District penal code. Government-supported mutual aid societies, vocational training, and charitable institutions formed an integral part of how the government addressed the question of the working woman. Although President Díaz transferred charitable activities to private interests, the men and women who ran these institutions functioned de facto as a part of the state. Faced with repeated demands for assistance from women like the costureras and cigarreras described in chapter 3, Porfirio Díaz, Carmen Romero Rubio de Díaz, and others sought to mediate between prescribed gender norms and the impact of industrialization. Their efforts were based on the idea of threatened female sexuality and a concern for women in their role as mothers.

The Federal Constitution of 1857 served as the legal basis of worker-state relations during the Porfiriato. Under the Constitution, Mexican law granted workers the right to organize and strike. These rights were founded in Article 4, which guaranteed workers and employers the freedom to negotiate; Article 5, which allowed any party to withdraw from a labor contract; and Article 9, which guaranteed the right to form associations. However, in day-to-day labor relations, the interpretation of these articles did not necessarily support workers' rights to organize or to strike. The Díaz government's efforts to promote economic growth shaped its interpretation of the 1857 Constitution and often led it to thwart and sometimes repress organized workers and strikes. This, combined with a tension between federal law and states rights, meant employers and supporters of capital in the Federal District were more likely to invoke Article 925 of the 1871 Federal District penal code than the Constitution. The Federal District penal code stipulated fines and incarceration for those found to be exercising "physical or moral violence" in an attempt to alter wage levels, employment status, or working conditions. "Moral violence" could be used to describe workers who acted collectively to strike, as they did during the cigarrera conflicts in the 1890s.[4]

In the absence of strong legal rights, workers relied upon interpersonal relations to protect their interests. Their negotiations tied workers not only to employers, but to benefactors of labor as well, especially through mutual aid societies. President Díaz routinely interacted with working women, thus complementing his more well-known and dramatic actions surrounding the events at Cananea (1905) and Rio Blanco (1907) and his behind-the-scenes negotiating with industrialists and state representatives. In all regards, Díaz cultivated his role as the individual in whom power rested. One example shows the symbolic nature of this relationship, which was described in more detail in chapter 3.

A fête put on by a group of working women to celebrate Porfirio Díaz's birthday can be seen as a ritual enactment of the paternalistic relationship between the president and working women. At the reception, the women asked Díaz to step inside a replica of a cage, at which point the women made a speech. In their speech the women congratulated the president on the occasion of his birthday, thanked him for his patronage, and lauded him as the eternal "prisoner" of the people. Journalists reported on the event, highlighting the president's good humor and support of working women. The humor of seeing the President of the Republic as the prisoner of working women communicated his actual power over them, while the birthday celebration for the "man" Porfirio Díaz (not the President) tacitly named him as the individual embodiment of state authority vis-a-vis working women. This position allowed him to epitomize a paternalistic benefactor while remaining above any legal obligations to laboring women.[5]

Complementing the activities of mutual aid societies, the Porfirian government relied upon charitable institutions to address problems of female poverty. The transfer of charity from the Catholic Church to the Mexican state during the Reform period, and then to private interests in the late nineteenth century, implied a partial transfer of responsibility for, and authority over, female poverty. President Porfirio Díaz expanded the government reliance upon private charities that had been encouraged by President Juárez. Although President Manuel González (1880–1884) had placed public charity under the direction of the Secretaría de Gobernación in 1881, when Díaz returned to the presidency he began the process of transferring charitable activity to the private sector.[6] In 1885, 1899, and 1904 Diaz passed a series of laws meant to protect and encourage private charities. He expressed the official position of the Mexican government when he wrote, in a circular dated 10 September 1885, that Mexicans believed "private charity, [is] recognized in all civilized countries as the most natural and effective means of responding to the pain and misery of humanity."[7] By encouraging private charity, the Mexican government distanced itself from the responsibility of public assistance. Charity as a private and voluntary endeavor was a gift and as such denied obligation on the part of the giver. It was conceived of as giving in a situation in which one was not obliged to give — and gifts cannot be demanded by those who would receive them. Charity thus filled a need to address poverty without legitimating that need in political terms.

Private charity complemented industrialization in creating the *pax porfiriana*. In 1887 a writer for *La Convención Radical Obrera* confirmed the gendered nature of the relationship between statesmanship and charity in an article about the growing need for shelter, showers, and daycare for workers and their children. These services would be provided via private charitable acts, charity soon to be provided, the journalist happily announced, by the wife of the president, Señora Carmen Romero Rubio de Díaz. The writer also stated that it was the charitable heart of the president himself that allowed for the charitable works of his wife, and added: "Fortunately we don't have at the head of our government a man whose life has been golden from birth, rather, we have a republican soldier, of generous and tender heart . . . although armored with a harsh military outward appearance, and whose existence has slipped between dangers and combat, and situations of extraordinary vicissitude."[8] The statesmanship of men, consisting of facing danger and fighting for peace — implicitly understood as the foundation of economic development — stood hand in hand with women's private charitable work, just as Señora Carmen and Don Porfirio Díaz stood hand in hand as a couple.

This symbolic relationship between the statesmanship of men and the charitable activities of women played itself out in practice. Government encouragement of private charity built upon the mid-nineteenth-century activities of distinguished ladies and wives of socially prominent men. In this capacity, elite women and men functioned at the blurred boundary between private acts and the collection of institutions that made up the state. Indeed, historians have found that in Latin America it was often the government that was responsible for establishing charities subsequently run by women as private citizens.[9] This afforded women a means of so-cial activity construed as within the realm of the private but which prof-fered social privilege, public participation, and civic power. Furthermore, with the decline of Church-sponsored charity, elite women filled an im-portant national need by providing assistance to working-class and indi-gent women.

Much of the charity directed at working women sought to assist them in their role as mother. Asunción Lavrín tells us that beginning with the turn of the century there was a growing movement to protect working mothers in the Southern Cone of the Americas. In response to both inter-national trends and the pressure exerted by working women themselves (as described in chapter 3), Mexicans pursued a variety of activities to protect working women as mothers, and their children. In 1908 Mexico would hold a national congress for the foundation of maternal clubs to ad-dress child education, truancy, and home economics for women.[10] Señora Díaz had served as the patron of mutual aid societies and had lent her name and resources to the establishment of the Sewing Agencies. Diaz also founded the Casa Amiga de la Obrera (Friend of the Working Woman House), inaugurated on 1 December 1887. Though working women had not included daycare in their labor demands, Señora Díaz sought to ame-liorate conflict and hardship in this manner. The Casa Amiga was the first long-standing charitable lay institution directed specifically at the needs of working women. First housed at number 11 Moras Street, the Casa Amiga welcomed the children of factory workers and street vendors. There, the children received education, food, and medical attention. Se-ñora Díaz, known as a devout Catholic, also made sure the children re-ceived religious instruction. The Casa Amiga was meant to address the anomalous, not the routine, and therefore offered assistance only to chil-dren without a father and to those whose mothers had to work in order to survive. Preference was given to young mothers under thirty years of age.[11]

Casa Amiga administrators sought to inculcate in working women a series of qualities, with female morality as integral to the rights and responsibilities of its clients. Based on this priority, the Casa Amiga made several requirements of the women who sought its assistance. Prospective clients had to provide a passbook with a photograph, their place of residence, and the signature of their employer. Rules demanded that children arrive in good health, clean, and kempt (and if under the age of three they were required to have a change of clothing). Women who did not come for their children at the end of the day were disqualified from assistance. If a woman failed to bring her child to the Casa for more than a week, she was disqualified from receiving further benefits.[12] Above all, the Casa Amiga required that the recipient of assistance must work to improve her own situation in life. These requirements were meant to teach working women lessons of hygiene, punctuality, and responsibility. If employers imposed new rhythms of work on the newly proletarianized, as historians have argued, administrators of charities also sought to teach similar qualities to the women who received their assistance.[13]

The concern for women's capacity to fulfill their domestic responsibilities and for protecting female morality also led the Mexican Philanthropic Society to establish the Asylum for Infancy and the Regeneration of Woman. The Asylum founders hoped to serve young women, preferably under thirty years of age, who had "enter[ed] into a life of vice . . . and who wish[ed] to leave behind their degenerate lives and reform themselves [regenerarse] by means of moral uplift and hard work."[14] The criteria for admitting women to the Asylum were similar to those of Casa Amiga and reinforced paternalistic relations between working women and the upper class. The potential client had to submit a written application to the Board, and her application had to be accompanied by a letter of support from a respectable person of society. Like the passbook required of Casa Amiga clients, Asylum assistance was contingent upon the support of either an employer or another "respectable" individual. The applicant was also made to promise to stay in the asylum the time necessary to learn to live an honorable life with the work required to sustain it. The women paid dues and learned a trade, enabling them to earn an "honorable" living. Those who already had a trade skill would teach others. Women's earnings were divided between a fund for the individual women and an Asylum fund. The Society claimed to find work for clients upon their departure. Women dismissed for bad conduct were not eligible for readmittance for one year, and those who left without Asylum approval would not be readmitted. The Asylum allowed visits from family only, and then only during visiting hours. Thus, the rights of clients were premised on sexual morality, which was intimately tied to the capacity to work, save money, and to obedience to authority.[15]

Charitable institutions such as the Asylum and the Casa Amiga served a limited number of women compared to the growing number of working mothers with children. At the beginning of the twentieth century, the Casa Amiga received 107 boys and girls. As the state became more effective in keeping children out of factories, the need for childcare became more pressing for working women and a more visible problem to society at large. Señora Romero Rubio de Diaz constructed a second Casa Amiga, which was up and running in April 1904.[16] During the height of the revolutionary upheaval, between 1914 and 1916, the Casa Amiga of Mexico City remained closed due to a lack of resources. However, in 1916 Venustiano Carranza ordered it reopened. *El Demócrata* newspaper reported that more than six hundred children received meals at the various Casas Amiga that year.[17] The Casa Amiga continued to exist well into the 1940s, when eight hundred children were cared for in two separate facilities. In the late 1940s the Casa Amiga came under government control and, as Irma Betanzos found, continued to influence female morality by encouraging the legalization of free unions of the parents of children it served.[18]

In efforts to promote economic growth and gender-appropriate occupations, the Mexican government established trade schools for women in the late 1880s. Benito Juárez mandated the first Escuelas de Artes y Oficios for men in Mexico City in 1856; however, it was not until some twenty years later, in 1887, that a school for women was opened in Mexico City.[19] The Mexican government also built night schools *(escuelas nocturnas)* for both men and women. Both systems of schooling for women reflected not only the growth in federal budgets and in the number of women employed in nondomestic work, but also a growing acceptance of women's education. Female economic independence, while not necessarily desirable in and of itself, would prevent corruption of female sexual morality. To insure a trade would keep women from prostitution, school curriculum integrated lessons in moral improvement. In 1904 administrators stated that the official objectives of the schools were "to give women an education in the manual arts and the necessary preparation in a trade or lucrative occupation which would enable her to provide for herself in an independent and decorous fashion, and to encourage her self-improvement by means of intellectual development and moral uplift."[20] School administrators thus linked female independence and morality. A woman who had to support herself but did not have the proper skills to do so might turn to immoral means of survival.

School administrators defined "decorous" occupations with an eye to employment and conceptions of middle-class culture, overlapping though not analogous concerns. The curriculum included training in bookbinding, sewing, cigarette manufacture, and perfume production. An article in *La Convención Radical Obrera* described the schools as providing a measure against the corruption of female morality. The women attending classes were described as "a sympathetic group of pretty young women, revealed to belong to the martyred middle-class. . . . We understand that because of their inherent education and the instruction that they receive, they must suffer horribly in finding themselves in so humble a social condition, and their dignity must be offended when a boss or overseer, ignorant and ordinary, of those who come from beyond the seas to establish industries in our country, speak to them informally [using *tú*] and treat them with arrogance. But this is destiny, and to fight against it the obrera needs abnegation and virtue."[21] Vocational training, self-denial, and virtue would save women from a disgraceful fate.

The school curricula prepared women for occupations associated with domesticity. Between 1887 and the 1910s, the school offered classes in sewing, machine embroidery, and the production of artificial flowers and hats.[22] Enrollments reached nearly 1,200 in 1913.[23] As the employment market changed, so did the curriculum. In the 1920s women could also take classes in sausage making, fish and meat preservation, baking, and confectionery, all skills tied to the industrial occupations opening up to women. Government-sponsored vocational education also encouraged women to combine domestic duties and income-earning activities, thus contributing to the development of home economics in Mexico. This coincided with newspapers that carried columns that instructed women in canning, packaging, and food preparation. Administrators of the escuelas hoped that with such skills lower-middle-class women could stretch what little income they had at their disposal. Indeed, throughout the labor unrest of the 1910s and 1920s the Mexican government encouraged similar programs of thrift and savings for workers, and home management for working women in particular. By the 1930s, the School of Arts and Vocations for Women offered classes in beauty salon training, fashion, languages, geography, and civics. Ana María Hernandez, an ardent supporter of working women, urged them to cook for their families, attend school, engage in home industry, and keep a clean house and kitchen, all in addition to joining unions.[24]

With the Mexican Revolution, vocational training and charity continued to play an important role in addressing questions of female poverty. Alan Knight argues that political instability, the persistent power of the Porfiristas, and competing demand on federal resources meant that Maderistas achieved relatively little of the educational and moral reform they championed.[25] Much of what reform they did accomplish was similar to the combined Porfirian goals of self-help and philanthropy. Throughout the country, governors and military commanders enforced ad hoc laws to restrict pulque consumption, build a limited number of schools, and distribute food and clothing to the poor. Nonetheless, the demands of working women forced some sort of response on the part of the government. In late 1911 and throughout the year 1912, while women struck for better working conditions in the clothing, textile, and knitwear industries, and President Madero attempted to mediate in these conflicts, his wife, mother, and other female family members contributed their part.

The Madero women focused their efforts on working women. Sara Perez de Madero and a group of her associates visited factories employing large numbers of women. They visited La Tabacalera Mexicana, El Negrito, La Fabrica de Sombreros de la Antigua Casa Zolly, and a ribbon and cardboard box factory. During these visits they encouraged working women to attend the schools recently established by Sara Madero with the aid of the White Cross. Perez de Madero hoped, with these schools, to achieve the "redemption" of workers.[26] At El Buen Tono, on 29 January 1912, Perez de Madero attended the inauguration of the El Buen Tono Church on Plaza San Juan.[27] Archbishop Monsignor Mora performed the blessing of the chapel. Perez de Madero then entered the shops and, according to the Maderista newspaper *Nueva Era*, the cigarreras cheered and applauded. Señora Mercedes Gutiérrez de Madero, Francisco Madero's mother, also made efforts to support working women. In February, Señora Gutiérrez de Madero visited various clothing factories, including one owned by a Mister Goodman on Camelia Street. Señora Gutiérrez de Madero noted her pleasure with the modern organization and cleanliness of the factory. At a meal celebrating the visit, Mister Goodman's daughters presented the president's mother with a bouquet of violets. During dessert a group of seamstresses requested that she and

Señora Prudencia Madero de González Treviño sponsor the construction of a dining hall for the workers. Señora Gutiérrez de Madero gladly accepted.[28] The Madero women's factory visits and charitable acts continued the Porfirian practice of elite women serving as surrogates for the state in ameliorating the effects of industrialization on women.

During the height of the revolutionary conflict, 1913–1916, industrialists and other citizens of means continued to support a wide range of charitable activities. For example, in 1913, industrialist Carlos B. Zetina built the Casa de Beneficencia Carlota Mena de Zetina for his workers' children. The home included sewing rooms for the women and a school and bathrooms for their children. Industrialists also worked in conjunction with the Mexican Red Cross and White Cross to provide a wide range of health-related services. Throughout the 1910s, when asked if they provided health benefits for their workers, employers pointed to contributions they made to the Red or White Cross for the benefit of workers. Such was the case with El Buen Tono, where in February 1914 the White Cross installed a dental and medical clinic. The White Cross also established various sewing workshops, the profits from which went to aid working women. In 1911, Francisco León de la Barra began efforts to regularize public charity. In 1915, Alvaro Obregón formed the Revolutionary Junta of Popular Assistance, presided over by Alberto Pani. This was accompanied by ad hoc policies such as the opening of government-sponsored sewing workshops like those founded by women's private charities during the Porfiriato. Following these ad hoc efforts on the part of Presidents Madero, Huerta, and Carranza, in 1920 President Obregón placed a large portion of Federal District charities under the responsibility of the government. By 1924, the Ministry of Government was managing public charity.[29]

The Department of Labor, 1911–1931

While public and private charity continued, the mobilization of the widespread social forces of the Revolution altered the relationship between the Mexican government and working women. Following continentwide trends, in early 1911, during the interim presidency of Francisco León de la Barra, an initiative to establish the Department of Labor was introduced to the Mexican Congress. The Department of Labor, which would reside under the jurisdiction of the Ministry of Industry and Commerce, came into being under Francisco Madero. Señor Licenciado Querido Moheno, Minister of Industry and Commerce, and Señor Molina Enríquez, director of the same department, proposed a government office dedicated to the protection of working women and children, which they included as Article 13, chapter 3, of the Department of Labor By-Laws, dated 13 December 1911. However, it was not Madero, but General Victoriano Huerta who opened the Department for the Protection of Working Women and Children (DPWWC) in 1914.[30]

The activities of these two offices contained tensions reflected in historiographical debates. Historians have debated whether Huerta represented a throwback to Porfirian times, or whether he was a progressive in disguise.[31] Regarding working women, Huerta was both. Some Huerta administration initiatives did not help working women, as was the case with the Labor Exchange (Bolsa de Trabajo). Charged with finding employment for hundreds of workers a month, the Exchange found jobs for mechanics, carpenters, machinists, and day laborers. In a sample of 380 placements, women did not make up even 1 percent of those assisted.[32] At the same time, it was during the Huerta administration that the Department of Labor opened DPWWC, which though short-lived, exemplified the transition from programs narrowly focused on protecting female morality to ones that also recognized the political and economic needs of working women.

Inspectors carried out investigations in factories identified as major employers of women. The resultant studies examined the sorts of work performed by women, the hours they worked, the wages they received, the sanitary conditions of their places of employment, and how employers treated them. Based on these studies, the DPWWC was charged with proposing protective labor legislation, and took as its premise that women should be subject to different working conditions than men. A press release announced "the decided intention of the government to achieve the strengthening of our race by means of morality and the physical strength of mothers."[33] The press release went on to specify how some of these objectives would be accomplished, including the provision of well-ventilated and comfortable work spaces, bathrooms, free or subsidized pharmacies, and facilities for women who found themselves sick or in need of "assistance in raising their young children."[34] Separate housing and recreational spaces would be provided for the young women, so that they could go about "freely and honestly," showing continued concern for women interacting with men.[35] Thus, the Department defined benefits for women as based in both physical and moral considerations.

All of the inspectors, nine in total, were women These *inspectoras* (female inspectors) stepped into a new space for Mexican women, along with a generation of women entering into public administration and the professions in the first two decades of the century.[36] Their actions were informed by the relationship that had been established between working women and upper-class women during the labor strife of the 1880s. The class position of these inspectors granted them access to government posts, but industrialists questioned their authority as representatives of the state precisely because they were women. In their reports the inspectoras described how their work was both facilitated and undermined by their status as women.

The inspectoras' work began in June 1914 when seamstresses made an anonymous complaint that French workers were being paid more than Mexicans at El Puerto de Veracruz sewing shops. Several inspectoras went to interview the two Frenchmen who owned the store, Señor Honorat Signoret and Señor Donnadieu. Señor Donnadieu, who received the inspectoras, would not answer any of their questions. In fact, he kept them from even speaking. When one of the inspectoras showed Señor Donnadieu her credentials and a form he was to sign, acknowledging that the inspection had been made, Donnadieu shouted that he would not sign any paper and threw it down on the table. At this point, the inspectoras left Donnedieu's office, and archival documents do not tell us if the issue was taken up again. The workers did, however, go on strike the following month. As women, inspectoras were subject to the same kinds of intimidation as obreras, though it was less violent. Often, female inspectors were not allowed to speak to workers or even enter the place of work. While employers were sometimes unwilling to cooperate with male government representatives, the refusal to allow male inspectors access to a factory was not as common as with female inspectors, nor was it as all-encompassing a denial, since the women inspectors were often denied access even to information.[37]

While their gender limited their power to deal with employers, inspectoras argued that it was precisely because they were women that they were qualified for their charge. Female workers, they argued, were more likely to speak in confidence to female inspectors. The validity of this argument is debatable. Despite the confidence of the inspectoras, many workers were suspicious of government representative—female or not. Nevertheless, because inspectoras made an extra effort to speak with female workers, they would end up speaking with some who, upon leaving the workplace, would more openly relate their conditions of work. Furthermore, Department of Labor standard-of-living studies made no distinction between men and women or different household configurations; the DPWWC based their studies on several models, reflecting the particular conditions of Mexican working women. One series of interviews conducted in 1914 included households made up solely of women and their children. Inspectoras also created models of mixed-sex households dependent upon the income of its female members. When calculating cost of living, inspectoras defined basic necessities in women's terms. In addition to pulque, coffee, beans, chile, tortillas, and simple bedding, inspectoras accounted for the cost of women's clothing like undergarments, shoes, and a rebozo. They also included the cost of the needles and thread with which women made and mended their own clothing or plied their trade. Their investigations of women's work reflected knowledge of where women worked and the issues they faced. Inspectoras interviewed obreras, artisans, home workers, and street vendors. The industries they inspected included clothing, hats, ties, shoes, cushions, paper, bakeries, and commercial houses. Inspectoras often mentioned that the most prevalent problem they saw was the extremely poor pay women received as a group and the abuse of apprenticeships.[38]

As a group, inspectoras represented a transitional moment in understanding the place of education, vocational training, and female sexual morality in the lives of working women. As individuals, the inspectoras differed in how they defined working women's needs and how they hoped to address those needs. All inspectoras argued that education was essential, both for its moral and for its practical benefits. Inspectoras themselves were of a recent generation of educated women, and their writings reflected the growing belief that education was important for women, not only as mothers of future citizens, but also because the women might have to support themselves economically (a topic perhaps particularly on the minds of the five inspectoras who were widows). All wrote of education as essential to preserving the sexual morality of working women, which they considered to be at risk.

Inspectora L. Folsa Viuda de Menocal argued that a Catholic education provided the foundation of a healthy home and society and would best serve women. She and other inspectoras did not consider a healthy religious upbringing as repressive, either for themselves or other women, but rather as a useful source of guidance and strength. At one level, Catholicism would provide individual benefits. Widow Menocal wrote, "The basis of happiness is in morality and religion. Religion is the most pure blossom to which, in the garden of life, we must avail ourselves in order to find protection, and without which we will find the road we travel arid and full of thistles [abrojos]." The role of religion in softening individual suffering was reinforced by her mention of abrojos, the term used to refer to a thistle-shaped device used in the whip of a flagellant. Señora Folsa Viuda de Menocal argued that a Catholic education enabled women to fulfill their superior social potential as well. In fact, she considered Catholic education a means of elevating women's social status, which men should support. She closed one letter, "And so I repeat, a woman should be given infinite means to support herself on her own. And to men, we ought to say, your obligation is to help women, not put her down and humiliate her as if you believed you were a titan, because women are your equal if they know how to take advantage of the situation, and more . . . they are your superior."[39]

Education would teach working women respect for the norms of sexual morality and authority in the workplace, which, they wrote, were intimately related. While some of the inspectoras felt that women did not need "an abundance of knowledge," they agreed that "religious education, provided by teachers of irreproachable morals," would instill "virtue [which] is the foundation of morality." This, in the minds of the inspectoras, would teach girls to respect their parents, steer clear of vice, and make themselves useful in the home and therefore to society. One inspectora wrote, "In general, the women of our pueblo do not know their duties. I believe it would be possible, in the factories where they work or some other given place, to impart some simple, but clear principles, making them understand their obligations and the mission they must fulfill as wives and mothers, as well as teach them the respect which they owe to their superiors." Mothers would learn, and pass on "healthy moral principles and a fondness of work." Inspectoras thus closely identified female sexual morality with workplace discipline, echoing mid-nineteenth-century conceptions of the role of mothers in the formation of citizens, now workers.

Other inspectoras were more inclined to promote vocational education. A combined curriculum of moral and vocational training would, they argued, keep women from begging and prostitution. While the inspectoras feared for the morality of working women, they also argued that Mexican women were model workers, "innately docile and self-sacrificing, and to a certain extent kind and virtuous."[40] These qualities served them well, one inspectora wrote, because Mexican women were also the heart of the domestic sphere. Technical training would also educate women in home economics. Inspectoras believed that women of humble origins needed to be taught how, if a household were run "with order," they could extend their earnings to cover basic needs. In turn, this would aid in the primary goal of forming a solid family foundation, "a place from which the husband would not stray or fall into disgrace." For inspectoras, this would prevent domestic violence and alcoholism among working-class men.

Though the inspectoras are important for what their work reveals about the continued association of moral and material conditions, the DPWWC was short-lived. One week after Victoriano Huerta resigned on 15 July 1914, the interim administration of Francisco S. Cabrajal ordered the closing of the DPWWC for budgetary reasons.[41] The activities of the DPWWC were to be subsumed by the Department of Labor. Inspectoras wrote letters complaining about the closure, noting that the exploitation of women, which they argued would surely persist without their efforts, would lead women to see business owners not as partners in work but as the enemy. Women would, they argued, raise children who would grow up to hate the government that had not protected them.[42] One inspectora exclaimed it was a crime that "the Revolution would allow women and children dressed in rags to go begging for charity on the streets while foreign entrepreneurs received special privileges in exchange for bringing capital into the country."[43] Their protests were to no avail and the DPWWC was shut down. Anger at such contradictions would continue to fuel the women's suffrage movement in the subsequent decades.

Between 1913 and 1916 the Department of Labor generated little documentation on women. The violence and political instability that marked the period, beginning in February 1913 with the assassination of Francisco Madero and José Pino Suarez, limited the capacity of the newly formed government office to function. The Mexican economy suffered the most during this period, and federal funds decreased accordingly. Furthermore, the Department of Labor had not fully established its authority. Major labor conflicts during this period (for example, the 1914 Palacio de Hierro strike, 1915 Telephone and Telegraph Company strike, and the General Strike of 1916) were dealt with, or not, by revolutionary generals and presidents, as each tenuously took his turn at controlling Mexico City. This lack of control by the Department of Labor contributed to confusion among workers as to the purpose of the Department, so much so that occasional articles appeared in the newspaper announcing the purpose of the Department.[44]

The Constitution of 1917

The Constitution of 1917 laid much of the foundation upon which the Department of Labor would function during the 1920s. Among the rights accorded to workers, either by the Constitution or by subsequent legislation, two were of particular importance to women. First were the ostensibly gender-neutral rights that actually prejudiced women in certain segments of the workforce. This was most obviously the case with minimum wage laws and Sunday rest laws. Second were the laws that defined working women as distinct from working men. These included restrictions on women's working at night and in dangerous occupations, and maternity benefits, and they were quite similar to the protective labor legislation that was being promulgated at the same time in the United States.[45]

Historians have noted the degree to which the Constitution was, more than the result of workers' demands, the product of mediation between Carranza and members of the Congress, few of whom were representatives of labor.[46] This also holds true for working women. Nevertheless, the final version of Article 123 shows some signs of Department of Labor input, as well as input from Venustiano Carranza, who always showed an avid interest in regulating the public morality.[47] The committee that formulated the original draft of Article 123 was headed by Pastor Rouaix, a Carrancista and former governor of Durango, and included both José Inocente Lugo, the one-time Maderista governor of Guerrero and now chief of the Department of Labor, and José Natividad Macías, a Carrancista who exhibited wariness of organized labor.[48] Between 1911 and 1917, the Department of Labor had collected information on a wide array of issues, ranging from minimum wage laws to protective labor legislation. Inspectors had conducted studies on workers' standards of living, wages, and the sanitary conditions in factories.[49] They had also assembled information on protective labor legislation and maternity benefits from Argentina, Italy, and the United States. The *Boletín del Trabajo* published some of this material in its early editions in 1913.[50] The Rouaix committee introduced their draft of Article 123 into Congress late on the evening of 23 January; no changes were made and it was approved unanimously.

The Mexican Constitution of 1917 guaranteed a minimum wage. Article 123, section VI, established that "the minimum wage which the worker should enjoy and which will be considered sufficient, will be based on regional differences in cost of living, meet normal subsistence needs of a working man, his education, and honest forms of diversion, considering him as head of household."[51] So, while women were ostensibly granted a minimum wage, this definition, which would inform future minimum wage laws, excluded female heads of households and other working women. Rather than considering equal pay for equal work, Congress was more interested in discussing protective labor legislation.[52]

One such law restricted women from working at night. The question of night shifts had been one of some conflict over the previous several years. Some workers had demanded such restrictions, while others protested the harm it caused women. Employers, perhaps somewhat self-interestedly, also pleaded the cause of widowed and married women, who depended upon night shifts to earn their living and support their families.[53] In congressional debates the subject of women working at night seemed to be particularly titillating for some senators. When Senator C. Martí spoke in favor of allowing women to work at night, he provoked considerable laughter:

> For any individual who loves Liberty, it does not sit well to see a woman and a child working at night: however, we have thousands of women who if we were to take away their opportunity to work at night, would, one day to the next, all find themselves without anything to eat, thanks to the idea of Liberty. (Here, here!) Señores, you may not share my opinion, but there are thousands of women who work at night. (Laughter.) Señores, just a minute ago a delegate called to my attention the fact that I was not taking this debate seriously, and now it seems that it is you who lack seriousness. In cafés, candy factories, and thousands of other locales women work the night shift; the day after this law is put into effect, these women will find that they can no longer work.[54]

The laughter was provoked by Senator Martí's reference to "women who work at night," which brought to mind prostitutes as much as it did working women.

Assumptions about the immoral effects of the night shift on women prevailed in Mexican political circles. The Constitution of 1917 stipulated that "[t]he night shift . . . will be absolutely prohibited, from ten at night until six in the morning, for women in general and those minors under the age of sixteen in particular, to work in factories, industrial workshops, or commercial establishments."[55] In subsequent years, Congress would pass legislation to reinforce these standards. In 1923 the government proposed the Plan for Regulation of the Work of Women in Commercial Establishments, which defined night work as work conducted from six in the evening to seven in the morning, extending by five hours the time during which women could not work in commercial establishments, compared to those in factories. A maximum eight-hour day and seven-hour night shift was established for "mixed[-sex] establishments, cantinas, restaurants, etcetera"[56]; and shifts that overlapped day and night shifts could legally last seven and a half hours. Thus, concern for "mixing the sexes" continued to manifest itself in the discourse surrounding women's work nearly a century after its appearance in Esteban Antuñano's 1840 pamphlet.

Following continentwide trends, the Mexican Constitution provided for maternity benefits for working women. As early as 1912 a proposal had circulated in Congress that would have required employers of more than twenty-five female workers to provide daycare. With the Constitution of 1917, the protection of working mothers and their children now became law. Section V of Article 123 stipulated, among other things, that three months before giving birth a pregnant woman would not be allowed to perform heavy work. She was also obligated to rest for one month after the birth of her child, during which time she should receive her full salary and benefits, as provided by her contract. Women were to receive these benefits without threat of losing their job. Upon returning to work and during the time she was nursing, employers were to provide women with two extra half-hour breaks per day and a place apart from other workers where they could nurse their newborns.[57]

Legislating Morality, Moralizing Legislation, 1918–1928

The Constitution of 1917 laid out basic rights, but the fulfillment of those rights was a slow and uneven process. It was not until the administrations of Álvaro Obregón (1920–1924) and Plutarco Elías Calles (1924–1928) that Department of Labor personnel actively sought to enforce maternity benefits, a day of rest, the minimum wage, and limits on women's night work. Historians describe the 1920s as a period of institutionalization; in this period, the power of the federal government to mediate labor conflict expanded, especially through the new incarnation of the Department of Labor, the Ministry of Industry, Commerce, and Labor (created 1917).[58] Business interests, however, resisted the increasing involvement of the state in labor relations. Demonstrating the point, scholars point to the resistance by private interests to textile convention tariffs, the recognition of worker organizations, and federal labor legislation.[59] The Department of Labor archives reveal yet another level of resistance to the rights of workers on the part of employers. This resistance was often informed by an employer's understanding of the rights of working women as being based on female sexual morality. Female morality was invoked in a wide range of discussions and was tied to conceptions of hygiene, both industrial and individual, of women's health and reproduction, and of factory discipline. The distinction between male and female workers was reinforced by differences established by law in wages, and by the support of government for unequal labor contracts for working men and working women.

Between 1918 and 1920 the Department of Labor sporadically investigated the conditions of women in the workplace. In 1919 the Department of Labor developed a survey which was meant to identify what kind of problems women faced. The following questions were included: "Have there been any strikes by women?" "How many times a month are women absent from work?" "What does the owner think of women as workers?" The 1919 questionnaires also noted workers' ages, their civil status, how many children they had, and their literacy, reflecting an attempt to understand the relationship between women's work and domestic responsibilities, as well as employer's evaluation of female workers. Such investigations into the specific conditions of working women had largely disappeared by 1920; however, the enforcement of labor legislation once again brought women to the fore of Department of Labor activities.

In the process of inspecting factories for the 1921 industrial census, inspectors frequently noted the hygiene of either the workplace or the workers therein. Both male and female workers suffered physically at work. Inspectors noted that workers in *nixtamal* mills (processors of corn for making tortillas) labored in extremes of hot and cold, which was only exacerbated by the fact that few of them wore shoes. Tortilleras and nixtamal workers were often required to sleep on bags of grain or on the cold cement floor of the shop in order to protect the goods overnight. Women who worked on the polishing machines at La Union ribbon factory were blasted by strong currents of air, which inspectors suspected caused pneumonia and sometimes death. In textile and mattress factories workers suffered from pulmonary diseases due to dust in the air and wind currents created by the machinery. Several factories dumped chemical waste into the rivers in which workers bathed and from which they drank.[60]

In their factory visits inspectors expressed particular concern for working women because of the impact working conditions could have on the women's reproductive capacity, a common concern throughout the Americas.[61] The Department of Labor designed a series of factory talks aimed at improving women's reproductive health and their child-care skills. These talks were given in factories employing large numbers of women, including La Carolina textile factory, La Central match factory, and various clothing factories. In a talk given to a group of women in August 1922, Doctor Manuel Olea explained the reasons for protective labor legislation that provided maternity benefits to women. He told the women, "It is easier to avoid illness than to have to combat it. This is what in technical terms we call prophylaxis, terms I will avoid using as much as possible as my intention is to be easily understood by all of you, who have little special preparation." "Women," he told them,

and children, are physically weaker, and the damage done to them as a result of excessive work is much more intense. Women, due to the delicate nature of their sexual development, menstruation, pregnancy, and breast-feeding have a much weaker organism than that of men; and if we add to this the fact that before and after work they have to attend to housework and their children, it is easily understood that among them there are increasing reasons for their physical exhaustion, which also has a noxious influence on their children as well.[62]

Doctor Olea found that women and children shared similar physical traits, weaknesses in particular. While he recognized the exhausting effects of overwork, Doctor Olea also argued that women's physical uniqueness debilitated them. By placing women's physical characteristics at the heart of the problem of the health of children, he construed women to be an imperfect fit in the world of work.

Department of Labor concerns for the reproductive capacity of women also expressed themselves in interest in the physical positions in which women worked, especially those positions thought to "aggravate" the reproductive organs. Inspectors also feared the effects of humidity on female reproduction, as in the case of the seamstress who did finishing work sitting in a dark corner with only a petate between herself and the cold, humid cement floor.[63] More modern industries usually elicited a positive evaluation by inspectors. In the food processing industry, where women worked in the packaging of merchandise, one inspector commented favorably that "the jobs are simple and in none of them can we note any sign of afflictions this sort of work might produce. . . . The variety of positions in which they work allow the women to work and to rest."[64]

Though hygiene might seem to be a question of sanitation, and morality one of ethics, inspectors made no such distinction. One inspector reported that in sewing factories the most frequent illnesses suffered by the women were tuberculosis, anemia, genital congestion, and liver failure. But of all these illnesses, he wrote, the worst was "libertinism and dishonesty."[65] Another inspector of tortillerías summed up his findings in three categories:

> The first where hygienic conditions are good and the instruction, cleanliness and morality of the workers is acceptable . . . and among them there are few with vices; in the second, the conditions of the establishment and the workers is inferior to the first; and in the last, the filth of the establishment, the tools used in serving the public and persons of the workers are a constant danger to the public which frequents it. [The workers] are hardly lovers of work and the majority has many vices; they do not fulfill their obligations at home and furthermore lack any morality or instruction.[66]

In each of the categories he established in his report, the inspector correlated morality with dirt and a lack of education. In the words of yet another inspector, "The rules of hygiene are also the rules of morality."[67]

Inspectors' understanding of women challenged their attempts to treat workers' health in a uniform manner. In the process of inventorying female hygiene, inspectors developed a distinction between industrial-related ailments and ailments specific to the condition of being a woman. These conditions were referred to as "female ailments," "female ailments, not related to her profession," and ailments "inherent to the sex." This was a distinction of both the causes of disease and responsibility for its cure. The Department of Labor often would not hold industrialists responsible for conditions associated with being female. It was as if the body of a woman was separate from that body which performed the work.

Women countered these classifications by arguing that years of a body in service for an employer should qualify a woman for care. In 1920 an inspector of the Department of Labor argued on behalf of one woman, that because she had worked for La Abeja knitwear factory in Coyoacán for over twenty years, she deserved medical assistance, regardless of the fact that she suffered from "female ailments."[68] In the early 1920s inspectors worked more effectively to make sure that women labored in conditions that did not aggravate female health problems. As a means of achieving this, the Mexican government required a female minor seeking employment to have the permission of her father, or in his absence, that of her mother. She also had to have the approval of the Board of Arbitration and Conciliation. Finally, "to be able to work, all women of age must supply a medical certificate issued by a legally authorized representative justifying her state of health, in conformity with the last part of section II of Article 123."[69] The female body required special permission to enter the workplace.

While inspectors intermittently investigated questions of female health and morality, the Department of Labor took as one of its principal tasks investigations for the enactment of minimum wage laws. Factory inspection forms allowed inspectors to distinguish between the wages paid to men, women, and children. In 1921 the Department of Labor studied the cost of living among seamstresses, though the study did not lead to minimum wage legislation for the clothing industry. In 1923, however, the government did pass the By-Laws on Women's Work in Commercial Establishments, which established the vague criteria that "the minimum wage which the female employee should receive will be that considered sufficient for her indispensable needs."[70] In addition to assuming that the minimum wage language in the Constitution of 1917 did not include women, the By-Laws defined women's wages as for individual use, not the support of a household.

In their efforts to enforce Mexican labor law, Department of Labor inspectors ran up against the realities of the workplace for Mexican women. This was perhaps most obvious in their attempts to enforce the Sunday rest laws. As in other countries throughout the Americas, Mexico had a law requiring employers to provide a day of rest for their workers. Section IV of Article 123 stipulated that workers should receive one day off a week to "protect public health, conserve the race and the energies of the individual."[71] The government encouraged closings on Sundays. Owners of brothels, tortillerías, and commercial establishments that hired women to work sales counters were the ones that most frequently came into conflict with the Sunday rest law.

Employers often sought exemption from Sunday rest laws by arguing that women's work was more akin to domestic duties, and that the lack of morality of their workers disqualified them from protection of the law. When in 1924 Señor Argrove, the owner of several tortillerías, was repeatedly found in violation of the Sunday law, his case was taken to the Head of Conciliation. Argrove argued that it was never his intention to break the law. If, indeed, he had, he underlined, it was due to the nature of the product his shop produced. The tortilla—he pointed out—was considered an item of primary consumption, especially because it was inexpensive in comparison to bread. He argued that as the producer of an item essential to the Mexican diet an exception to the Sunday law should be made. However, Argrove focused less on the legal aspect of the conflict than on the behavior of the women he employed. To argue his point, Señor Argrove described his female employees as unreliable and of questionable morality. Argrove said the women rarely completed a continuous week of work and never brought their own tools. Argrove suggested that the women continually changed jobs "of their own accord," some of them working a few hours and then never showing their faces again. Because of the inconstancy of these women, he complained, he was continuously in need of workers. Given such conditions, Argrove portrayed himself as actually doing his workers a favor by employing them.

The inspectors who investigated the case agreed with Señor Argrove, pointing out that the women themselves argued against restrictions on their right to work. The inspector cited one woman as saying "that if it was the desire of her and her co-workers to work all day and they had the opportunity to do so, why did the Government prohibit them from doing so, that they needed the work in order to cover their financial obligations and that, if what they earned in eight hours of work was not sufficient to cover the cost of food, clothing, and rent, they would have to work longer hours whether it be in the tortillería or wherever God might provide them with work."[72] This tortilleras' comments reflected a work ethic founded upon insufficient earnings. If women's work habits did not fit the expectations of employers and the government, that was due to, and reinforced by, the poverty to which women working in tortillerías were relegated.[73] Women came and went from one place of work to another in order to combine various means of earning money. They also changed jobs in search of higher wages or better treatment.

The inspector reported his surprise that women wanted to work on Sundays. He thought the cultural and hygienic benefits of the law were obvious and of paramount importance. He wrote to the Section Head:

> Such arguments coming from the mouth of a worker did not cease to amaze me, because frankly I did not expect her to express herself in such terms. I made her see that the Government was not trying to take away anyone's right to work, that it was the law which determined work hours, with the intention of encouraging the worker to take advantage of the time she was not working to restore spent energies, as well as to give her the opportunity to better take advantage of her free time, above all Sundays, dedicating herself to personal hygiene and honest recreation, with friends or relatives, in the countryside or in the city; to which she responded that for them working Sunday mornings was relaxing, and that they'd take their day off whenever they felt like it, something which neither the Government nor their bosses could keep them from doing, because it is precisely for this reason that they work voluntarily, to be able to leave work of their own accord whenever they felt like it.[74]

Within the Department of Labor, opinions were divided. The Chief of the Conciliation and Arbitration Section used the woman's words to argue in favor of freedom of work, pointing out the mutual interests of workers and capital. He agreed that the tortilla should always be available and argued that because it was not the same person who worked six consecutive days in the tortillería there was no need to close on Sundays. In response, while the Section Head went on about the question of not closing on Sundays, he emphasized the importance of enforcing one day of rest. In a five-page memo he argued that the Chief of the Conciliation and Arbitration Section had relied on the words of the tortillera in question, without taking into consideration either the context in which her comments were made or the spirit of the law. The Section Head rightly pointed out that while the workers in nixtamal factories had contracts that included a minimum wage, the tortilleras had no such contract. What he failed to mention was that most nixtamal workers were men, while virtually all tortilleras were women. The Department of Labor was forced to contend with the fact that women had been left behind in the enforcement of minimum wage contracts, especially in piece-rate work. Employers paid tortilleras by the quantity they sold, and held them responsible for the cost of unsold dough and tortillas, while nixtamal workers were paid an hourly wage. Finally, the Section Head emphasized that the legal question at hand was not freedom to work, but the intention and enforcement of minimum wage laws.[75]

During the 1920s Department of Labor inspectors also turned to enforcing the provisions for maternity benefits stipulated in the Constitution of 1917. The Mexican government held up maternity benefits as a sign of the progressive nature of its labor legislation. Government representatives took prominent tourists and potential foreign investors to visit showcase factories to view nursing rooms for workers. For example, President Obregón converted a convent into a clothing factory with daycare facilities. While visiting the government sewing shop, Charlotte Cameron was treated to a tour of the "babies room" and kindergarten. Ms. Cameron also enjoyed a musical performance by the seamstresses' band—an honor, Ms. Cameron acknowledged, considering the women, who worked for piece rates, had taken the time away from their workday to play for her.[76]

Within Department of Labor records examples of such privileges actually granted to pregnant women and mothers of newborns are scarce. During the course of factory visits and census activities inspectors might ask about maternity provisions for female workers and make notes in the margins of their reports. However, at this time the Department of Labor made no systematic effort to enforce section V of Article 123. During the mid-1920s, industrialists largely disregarded maternity legislation. El Buen Tono cigarette factory did not provide a month of paid rest for women after they had given birth, and the factory still offered no adequate place to nurse children in 1920. At about this time, El Buen Tono employed 390 women, who among them had 123 children.[77] The owner of several tortillerías, a Señor Atherton, made no special provisions for pregnant women or recent mothers, which he justified by stating that his workers had never requested any sort of special treatment.[78] When further pressed by inspector Juan de Beraza as to why he did not provide any of the legally mandated services for women, Atherton replied with a question: "How is it possible that the factory must give assistance to women who are not legally married? Such assistance would be immoral given that many of the women lead irregular lives or live catch as catch can in this sense."[79] Thus, Atherton justified denying workers' rights to women of questionable sexual morality.

By the mid-1920s the Department of Labor recorded few investigations of, or conflicts regarding, the enforcement of Sunday rest laws, maternity benefits, or the protection of female hygiene. Rather, Luis Morones, as Secretary of Industry, Commerce, and Labor, leader of the CROM, and a leading force in the Partido Laborista, pushed several times for federal labor legislation. Conflict between the CROM and agraristas in Congress, as well as opposition from other labor organizations, doomed those efforts. It was not until the CROM fell out of favor with the federal government that Calles, during the presidency of Emilio Portes Gil (1928–1930), pushed for the passage of the Federal Labor Code. With the Federal Labor Code of 1931 Calles sought to curry favor with workers, drawing them into the newly formed Partido Nacional Revolucionario (PNR). The Mexican Congress was also interested in passing some measures that would address the consequences of international economic depression.[80] The 1931 Federal Labor Code built upon the efforts of Department of Labor inspectors to define the rights of working women.

Federal Labor Code 1931

The Mexican Constitution of 1917 had, via Article 123, established an impressive array of rights for Mexican workers. The details of those rights, and their enforcement, had been left to state and municipal authorities, with the exception of the Federal District, which remained under the federal jurisdiction of the Ministry of Industry, Commerce, and Labor.[81] A federal labor code would standardize the rights of workers throughout the country. The Ministry of Industry, Commerce, and Labor submitted the final labor code to the Chamber of Deputies in July and it went into effect in August 1931. Its enactment represented the increasing authority of the state to intervene in socioeconomic affairs. That authority built upon both the corpus of protective labor legislation that had developed over the previous decades, and on an increasing recognition of women's rights as workers. The Federal Labor Code established requirements for work hours, rest periods, and vacations, and addressed the question of workplace conditions, occupational accidents, illness, and work by women and minors.

Several articles of the Federal Labor Law were directed specifically at women, giving them more rights as workers. Most significantly, Article 21 recognized women as individuals by stating that a married woman did not need the permission of her husband in order to enter into a labor contract, exercise the rights derived from that contract, or participate in a union.[82] At the same time, the law continued to limit the rights of working women based on conceptions of female difference. This difference, as evidenced in the investigations of Department of Labor inspectors, was in part based on conceptions of female biology and morality. Article 77 of the Federal Labor Code prohibited women from engaging in night work, which was qualified as "antiphysiological . . . one hundred times more exhausting [than day work]."[83] Article 107 prohibited women from work in places that dispensed alcoholic beverages for immediate consumption, echoing similar legislation passed by Venustiano Carranza in 1919. Article 107 also prohibited women from dangerous or unhealthy work, except in cases where protective measures, as deemed by a judge, were installed.[84] The By-Laws on Unhealthy and Dangerous Work of 30 July 1934 further elaborated the definition of such work. Articles 83, 108, and 109 defined the term "dangerous or unhealthy" and prohibited women from either cleaning or repairing machinery and any moving parts, or working with any sort of saws. Women could not work underground, in submarines, in explosives factories, or in workplaces emitting dangerous gases, dust, continuous humidity, or other noxious emissions. Finally, the law enumerated compensation for workplace accidents, which was tied to a worker's wages. That women's wages were lower than those of men meant that such benefits would be unevenly distributed. The only explicit distinction in workers' compensation, however, related to those parts of the body conceived of as masculine and feminine, and which, it seems, were of different value. While a man under twenty years of age who lost a testicle would receive 90 percent of his salary, the loss of a breast was worth a mere 10 to 20 percent.[85]

The Federal Labor Law did establish important guidelines for the regulation of outwork, of particular importance to women. Chapter 18 of Article 213 required workers who labored outside of the factory to be paid an equal wage to those working inside. The law also held those who employed workers at home or in outwork to the same legal responsibilities as other employers. The law also stipulated that inspectors were required to investigate the conditions of domestic and outwork conditions on a periodic basis to assure compliance. These articles acknowledged problems that had existed for years within industries characterized by the persistence of outwork, such as in the clothing industry.[86]

The two pillars of Mexican labor law, the Constitution of 1917 and the Federal Labor Law (1931), as well as the By-Laws of Unhealthy and Dangerous Work (1934), were founded upon Department of Labor investigations. From the beginning, the Department of Labor had identified the working conditions of women as the combined result of labor relations, female poverty, and morality. Some of this legislation was either irrelevant to many women or led to conflict because of the actual position of women in the workforce.

Conclusion

Scholars have argued that the transition from the Porfiriato to the Revolution meant an increasing role for government in the lives of citizens.[87] In an important regard for working women, a continuity across these two periods existed. The ideological content of government intervention continued to include a concern for female sexual morality and motherhood. During the Porfiriato working women's activism led Porfirio Díaz and his wife Carmen Romero Rubio de Díaz to directly engage in labor disputes. While federal law made no distinction between male and female workers, mutual aid societies, vocational schools, and charitable activities provided by the Mexican government did. The distribution of resources was often predicated on the identification of working women with morality and maternity.

With the Mexican Revolution, women continued their activism for improved working conditions. The Department of Labor, in response, sought to mediate between working women and their employers. Both employers and Department of Labor officials frequently associated the rights of working women with morality. The contradictory efforts of the Department of Labor were most evident in the implementation of the Sunday rest law. Sunday rest laws, the burden of which fell largely on women, were proposed as a concession to workers and a means of protecting the Mexican "race." However, this benefit was unevenly extended to women working in tortillerías, brothels, and counter service jobs because these jobs were thought of as domestic work, and therefore outside the realm of labor policy. That the government had negotiated contracts for nixtamal workers and not for tortilleras, who were paid piece-rate wages, further complicated efforts to resolve this conflict. In addition, employers excused themselves from providing worker benefits by calling into question the morality of their female workers. The Federal Labor Code (1931) contained an increased recognition of the rights of working women based on their position in the workforce, including regulation of outwork. Nevertheless, with the Mexican Revolution older conceptions of female weakness found new life in protective labor legislation that limited where and when women could work.

Conclusion

Between 1879 and the late 1920s women made up approximately one-third of the Mexico City industrial workforce. By 1930, however, women made up only 24 percent of industrial workers, beginning a decline in female employment that was a reflection of national trends. Behind these modest shifts in aggregate numbers lay a sea change in the culture of women's work.

Though Mexican women had worked in modern textile factories since the 1830s, in late-nineteenth-century Mexico City the female-dominated cigarette and clothing industries filled the public imagination. Public discussion construed female-dominated workplaces as safeguards to women's morality. Women's declining position in cigarette production, both numerically and as a percentage of workers, and their entrance into an increasing variety of mixed-sex industries, raised important questions in this discussion. By the 1880s public concern regarding gender relations — "mixing the sexes" — had become increasingly tied to the language of class distinction. Both paternalism and middle-class paradigms relied upon the idea of female weakness, both moral and material. At the same time, the emerging identity of the middle class opened the possibility of "respectable" work as a safeguard for female sexual morality, for it kept women from resorting to prostitution. Nevertheless, sexual morality remained a defining concern in evaluating women and the conditions under which they labored. By the time of the Mexican Revolution women were pressing their work-related demands in unions and in the streets in the more narrowly defined terms of labor rights, now less closely tied to morality. Nevertheless, female sexuality, sexual morality, and honor continued to inform women's daily work well into the 1920s. The corpus of legislation that emerged during the Revolution built upon earlier associations of working women with compromised morality, though by the time of the Federal Labor Law (1931) formal recognition of women's rights was more concretely grounded in working conditions.

During the late nineteenth century, discursive constructions of female honor and sexual morality shaped Mexico City factories in both economic and cultural terms. Some industrialists built factories and disciplined workers based on ideas of female honor and sexual morality. Ernesto Pugibet, owner of El Buen Tono tobacco factory, was perhaps the most active in this regard. He cultivated the separation of the sexes in the work environment and encouraged a work culture that purported to protect female morality. Pugibet provided a church, schools, cinema, fêtes, and outings. Illustrating the impact of the female-dominated factory as an appropriate workplace for women, one observer suggested that the government remedy the lack of "respectable" work for women by employing them in silk factories like the one owned by Hipólito Chambón, who also cultivated a workplace which was seen as protecting the morality of female workers. While the fruits of Señor Pugibet's efforts served as the basis of a vibrant, work-centered culture, the female workspace he created turned out to be a double-edged sword. Surprisingly, Pugibet's efforts even allowed management to create a section within his factories where male workers produced cigarettes for a lower wage. Thus, gendered conceptions of honor and sexual morality contributed to differentiation not only between working men and working women but also in the wages they earned. While, at one point in time, male labor had been used to undercut women's wages, it was by and large gender distinctions at work that manifested themselves as lower wages for women.

Owners of small workshops and factories paid less attention to conceptions of female respectability in organizing production. However, as in larger factories, female honor could shape factory discipline. Ignacia Torres got a job with the understanding that, as she said, the clothing factory owner hired only "poor yet honorable people." The importance of honor and sexual morality persisted inside the factory walls. Interactions among the workers themselves — among mechanics, maestras, and obreras — could be altered with the insertion of ideas about female sexuality and sexual morality into work relations. In this regard, working women shared much in common with vendedoras. Women who worked on the street also had to contend with the way their rights were mitigated by conceptions of female sexual morality.

Where women worked shaped how they organized. During the late nineteenth century the concentration of women in female-dominated industries gave life to a rich labor culture. Cigarreras across Mexico City came together to improve their working conditions. Seamstresses, though they did not all work in the same factory, also came together over common concerns. As increasing numbers of women labored in the knitwear, processed food, and other consumer-goods industries, they too organized, loosely adhering to homosocial cultural practices. In their organizations, some women established ties with other women beyond the bounds of a single workplace, occupation, or industry. Because of the breadth and depth of this activity, working women figured centrally in Mexico City life, as workers and as participants in cultural and political events. Their strikes, demonstrations, and fêtes brought together people from different parts of the city, including women working in other industries, teachers, working men, and the President himself.

By the first decade of the twentieth century, women were moving away from homosocial labor organizations. The example of the city's seamstresses illustrates this point. Seamstresses had organized in all-female organizations during the Porfiriato. Following the 1911 "La Sin" strike, seamstresses had joined the Casa del Obrero Mundial. In so doing, they had allied themselves with tailors, as well as other working men and women. After the General Strike of 1916, working women, including seamstresses, joined the CROM, CGT, and other unions. In these unions women organized side by side with their male counterparts. At the same time, some of these organizations bore the legacy of homosocial labor organizing, evident in union names like Bonoteros y Bonoteras de La Perfeccionada.

Both the position of women in the workforce and the organizational culture that emerged shaped the entrance of working women into the public sphere. Historians, following Jürgen Habermas, define the public sphere as a realm of social life wherein individuals come together as a body to engage in conversations regarding issues of common concern.[1] This book contributes to the work of historians who have expanded the types of physical spaces and types of engagement we include in this definition. In Mexico City, that public sphere included the press, petitions, streets, plazas, and markets. The common conversation was about the moral and material implications of industrialization. Despite the relative lack of independence of the Porfirian-era press, newspapers and journals played an important role in fashioning public opinion.[2] Contributors frequently discussed the moral implications of women's working conditions, a strike, or of employers' treatment of workers. They addressed themselves to other newspapers, employers, and working women. Working women also participated in this conversation. Cigarreras, costureras, and women from across occupational backgrounds wrote letters to notable politicians, prominent women, and the press. Even when a letter was addressed to an individual, it was also sent to the press to be printed as a public statement and thus engage the public. Letter writing and the commentary regarding those letters served as an important public forum for discussing the legitimacy of working conditions and conflict. With the Revolution and until the 1930s, this space within the press contracted. Newspapers no longer printed workers' petitions; only the more disruptive strikes appeared in their columns.

Throughout the period under consideration, women used different discursive strategies to claim rights. Women like cigarreras and costureras frequently argued their cause by construing their labor demands as being in the public interest of protecting female morality. Other women argued their cause by differentiating between public and private morality. These women countered the idea that a woman's presence in a factory or public place compromised her sexual morality and therefore her rights. After 1911, working women continued to protest the association of sexual morality with their honor and rights as workers. And although unions did not provide the space for these protests, street demonstrations and petitions to the Department of Labor did. During the 1910s and 1920s working women demonstrated in the streets and petitioned the Department of Labor that their rights not be denied based on evaluations of their morality.

While Mexican historians have shown that women spoke of female weakness, they have not connected that language to women's participation in the public sphere.[3] Scholars portray discursive constructions of female weakness as cultural prejudice, vaguely defined, or as based in nineteenth-century conceptions of female biology. While these assessments are not wrong, it is also important to note both the historical and political nature of the language of female weakness. I have argued that during the nineteenth century Mexicans understood industrialization as both a moral and economic phenomenon. Within this context, Mexicans spoke of women's disadvantaged position within the workforce using the language of "weakness." This language conflated the material and moral weakness of women. And women themselves could use this language for political ends. Especially during the Porfiriato, working women's "reason," or means of legitimating their voices, was based in shared public concerns for the implications of industrialization for female virtue. In the face of the private political and economic power of employers, women empowered themselves with a language that allowed them to make their own labor concerns a matter of public concern. Regardless of whether working women "believed" that this language described their own reality, their subordinate position within society made using that language an important tool in their struggle. Women's use of the family metaphor, reminding statesmen and employers that their obligations to workers were like their obligations as fathers to children, created rights they did not have, either as workers or as women.

Important differences existed among women in terms of their participation in the public sphere. Vendedoras did not have access to the press or to upper- and middle-class patrons the way other working women did. Vendedoras' assertions of their rights occurred in public places and via petitions to municipal government, petitions written for them by public scribes. How do these petitions fit into the public sphere? Francois-Xavier Guerra includes rumor in his analysis of the public sphere; in a similar manner, petitions reflect larger conversations.[4] One could legitimately argue that rumor, or the petitions that evince them, reach a limited public, but such a judgment does not fully account for the way public conversations occur in countries with low literacy rates and different modes of communication. For that matter, the bourgeois public sphere that Habermas wrote about also engaged a limited audience.[5] Though the impact of petitions on public opinion may have been limited, petitions constituted, nevertheless, a positive space wherein vendedoras actively engaged the question of who constituted the public and the rights of that public. Their access to public scribes and their belief in the efficacy of petitioning put them in the public sphere. Vendedoras also engaged the public by the simple act of remaining on the streets, despite efforts on the part of municipal government to remove them and the disparagement of upper-class observers.

Scholars of Mexican women's history have debated whether the Revolution resulted in a greater public presence for women. While many characterize the Revolution as a "patriarchal event," others argue that it led to women's increasing public presence as professionals, suffragists, and peasants.[6] And what of working women? With the Mexican Revolution, as women became part of the larger working-class movement, working women's voices became louder. At the same time, their voices were more diffused, as the visibility of the women's letters, petitions, and female work-centered culture declined. In addition, women's fit in organized labor was an uneven one. The simultaneous efforts of the CROM to recruit unskilled female labor and to preserve skilled work for men exemplified this. The important shift in worker-state relations that characterized the Mexican Revolution was thus an ambivalent one for working women. Whether women's participation in public increased numerically is unclear. What is clear is that their voices were less distinct as working women.

Nevertheless, the Mexican Revolution heralded the formal abandonment of notions of working women as immoral. It also shifted where women found space to speak. The decline of associating working women with compromised morality, both in discourse and political rights, did not alter the power of morality in work relations. Women continued to contest the power of making their rights contingent upon morality and honor in disputes within the factory and in street demonstrations. In these spaces working women could speak to the specificity of their position in the workforce, their relationship with unions, and the persistent role of sexual morality at work.

The explanatory power of the Mexican Revolution also falls short in several other regards. First, the shift in women's employment: it was economic expansion beginning in 1890, and not the absence of men caused by civil war in the 1910s, that brought women into new occupations. The industries from which men left to join *la bola*—streetcars and electricity workers—did not hire women. Rather, it was the expansion of the consumer-goods industry and the breakdown of tasks in the production of consumer goods that opened up employment opportunities for women. Second, we need to look at the increased participation of women in organized labor.[7] What John Lear has shown to be true for organized labor more generally was also true for working women: the prominent role of workers during the Revolution was the result of a more extended process of mobilization that dated back to the previous century.[8] I would add that the move of women into mixed-sex workspaces in the 1890s played an important role in this process.

This book questions our understanding of class as both a material and cultural category in late-nineteenth- and early-twentieth-century Mexico City. More specifically, it explores how working women defined themselves, through their words and actions, in ways that challenge how we think of class in late-nineteenth- and early-twentieth-century Mexico City. Women's labor activists included workers from a wide range of occupations, both from inside and outside of the factory: cigarreras, costureras, and obreras joined with teachers, waitresses, counter service workers, street vendors, and telephone operators. Female teachers and counter service workers earned more than seamstresses and cigarreras, but their earnings only precariously supported a middle-class lifestyle. Though education may have contributed to their middle-class status, their participation in the struggles of cigarreras in the nineteenth century and with factory workers in the twentieth century suggests that they shared interests as women and as workers.[9]

While the shared interests of women from diverse occupations may have been in part economic and political, it may also have been cultural. Women from diverse backgrounds shared having to defend themselves against the association of their rights with sexual morality. Employers, overseers, and co-workers made sexual morality integral to factory discipline. Sexual morality also shaped how government officials dealt with working women and their employers. Mexican women, at work, in the streets, and in their dealings with organized labor and government officials, evolved in their responses to the association of their rights with sexual morality. Whereas during the Porfiriato many women utilized the language of female weakness to defend their rights as working women, by the 1920s they increasingly countered this language by redefining morality in legal and economic terms, thus distancing morality from their identity as working women. Inasmuch as this shared culture shaped women's labor protests, working women participated in creating an understanding, or consciousness, unique to their gender.

During the late nineteenth century Mexicans conceived of industrialization as both a material and cultural process, with political, financial, and moral implications. And while by the 1930s this was less the case, the legacy of the evolution of women's workforce participation meant that Mexican working women continued to be forced to contend with the conflation of their morality with their rights as workers. Labor practices in current-day maquiladoras are not so different.[10] Employers often cultivate a paternalistic relationship with workers and a work-centered culture that celebrates femininity with beauty pageants and roses on Mothers Day. Overseers play favorites as a means of enforcing factory discipline. While not necessarily the result of a continuous history, these examples do show the efficacy of controlling working women via discursive constructions of female sexual morality. Like many of the scholars who have studied these practices in maquiladoras, I hope my work contributes in some way to a demystification of this form of exploitation.

Notes

Introduction

1. Busto, *Estadística de la República Mexicana*, vol. 1.
2. This approach is inspired by debates both in Latin American and European labor history. For Latin America, see Van Young, "The New Cultural History Comes to Old Mexico"; for Europe, see Sewell, "Toward a Post-materialist Rhetoric for Labor History."
3. Haber, *Industry and Underdevelopment*, 18.
4. Colegio de México, *Estadísticas económicas del porfiriato*; Towner, "Monopoly Capitalism and Women's Work during the Porfiriato," 90–105. The trends found by Towner coincide with those found by Dawn Keremetsis (*La industria textil mexicana en el siglo XIX*, 220). In the 1970s Helieth Saffioti argued that the rapid expansion of the Brazilian economy forced industrialists to hire women (Saffioti, *A mulher na sociedade de classes*).
5. In part, those differences were determined by the occupations in which women were employed and by how census takers categorized those occupations.
6. Sheridan, *Mujer obrera y organización sindical*. See also Fowler-Salamini, "Gender, Work, and Coffee in Córdoba, Veracruz"; Chassen-Lopez, "'Cheaper Than Machines'"; and Fowler-Salamini and Vaughan, Introduction to *Women of the Mexican Countryside*.
7. Gutiérrez Álvarez, *Experiencias contrastadas*; García Díaz, *Un pueblo fabril del porfiriato*, 65–66.
8. Haber, *Industry and Underdevelopment*, 124; and Haber, "Assessing the Obstacles to Industrialization."
9. *Estadística de la Indústria*, AGN, RT600: 4 (1920).
10. México, Dirección General de Estadística, *Estadísticas sociales del porfiriato, 1877–1910*, 48, 55.
11. Garza, *El proceso de industrialización en la ciudad de México*, 94.
12. Ibid., 94, 100–103.
13. On New York City, see Stansell, *City of Women*, 105–29; on Detroit, see Jones, *Labor of Love, Labor of Sorrow*, 159.
14. Stansell, *City of Women*, 43. Anna Clark borrowed the term from Stansell; see Clark, *The Struggle for the Breeches*, 15.

15. Lear, *Workers, Neighbors, and Citizens,* 57–58. Also on the middle class in Mexico, see Knight, *The Mexican Revolution,* 1:43–44, 132.

16. For a critique of class as a direct manifestation of material conditions, see Canning, "Gender and the Politics of Class Formation"; and Sewell, "Toward a Post-materialist Rhetoric for Labor History," 27–32.

17. For a useful theory of class distinction and culture, see Bourdieu, *Distinction,* 7. On the Mexican middle class, see French, *A Peaceful and Working People,* 63–85. For Peru, see Parker, *The Idea of the Middle Class;* for Chile, see Barr-Melej, *Reforming Chile;* and for Brazil, see Owensby, *Intimate Ironies,* 103, 118. For a rich discussion of the volatile nature of discursive constructions of class and gender, see Scott, *Gender and the Politics of History,* 42–43, 60, 88; Scott's theoretical framework works well for Mexico, despite differences between French and Mexican industrialization.

18. Stevens, "Marianismo," 90–101; Tuñón Pablos, *Women in Mexico,* 47; Arrom, *The Women of Mexico City,* 259–66; Radkau, *"Por la debilidad de nuestro ser,"* 87–90. On masculinity and class in contemporary Mexico, see Gutman, *Meanings of Macho.* On both marianismo and machismo in contemporary Mexico, see Prieur, *Mema's House, Mexico City.* French and Daniels dismiss the relevance of "the cult of domesticity" for working women in Latin America, stating that such an ideology derives from different cultural, historical, and class circumstances (French and Daniels, *The Gendered Worlds of Latin American Women Workers,* 16–17).

19. Stern, *The Secret History of Gender,* 78; French and Daniels, *The Gendered Worlds of Latin American Women Workers,* 13.

20. Sex-segregation of the work force, sex-typing of occupations, and wage differentials based on sex are not unique to Mexico. On Brazil, see Besse, *Restructuring Patriarchy.* On the United States, see Goldin, *Understanding the Wage Gap,* 10–13, 76, 104; and Milkman, *Gender at Work.* For Europe, see Rose, *Limited Livelihoods,* 3, 201; and Downs, *Manufacturing Inequality.*

21. Prieur, *Mema's House, Mexico City,* 167–71; Farnsworth-Alvear, *Dulcinea in the Factory,* 27–28.

22. Twinam, *Public Lives, Private Secrets;* Caufield, *In Defense of Honor;* Klubock, *Contested Communities;* Picatto, *City of Suspects;* Stern, *The Secret History of Gender;* and Farnsworth-Alvear, *Dulcinea in the Factory.*

23. Bliss, *Compromised Positions;* Piccato, *City of Suspects;* Buffington, *Criminal and Citizen in Modern Mexico;* and Lear, *Workers, Neighbors, and Citizens.* For Mexican women's history which privileges the Mexican Revolution, see Macías, *Against All Odds;* Salas, *Soldaderas in the Mexican Military;* Soto, *The Emergence of the Modern Mexican Woman.*

24. Tenorio Trillo, "1910 Mexico City"; Lear, *Workers, Neighbors, and Citizens;* Lear, "Mexico City"; Jiménez Muñoz, *La traza de poder.*

25. Habermas, *The Structural Transformation of the Public Sphere;* Calhoun, *Habermas and the Public Sphere;* Guerra, Lempériere et al., *Los espacios públicos en Iberoamérica,* 10; Eley, "Nations, Publics, and Political Cultures"; Walker, *Smoldering Ashes.*

26. Ryan, "Gender and Public Access."

27. Studies that lack clarity include Deutsch, *Women and the City*. On the conflation of the term "the public sphere," see Fraser, "Rethinking the Public Sphere," 110.

28. Alexander, "Women, Class, and Sexual Differences in the 1830s and 1840s." Joan Landes argues that in Republican France women were construed as violating the norms of "universal reason" (Landes, *Women and the Public Sphere in the Age of the French Revolution*, 205).

29. See Eley, "Nations, Publics, and Political Cultures," 293; Ryan, "Gender and Public Access."

30. French, *A Peaceful and Working People*, 87.

31. On the rhetorical power of motherhood in Mexico, see Arrom, *The Women of Mexico City*; Soto, *The Emergence of the Modern Mexican Woman*; and Bliss, *Compromised Positions*. For the Southern Cone, see Lavrin, *Women, Feminism, and Social Change in Argentina, Chile, and Uruguay*; and for Brazil, Besse, *Restructuring Patriarchy*.

32. Roseberry, "Hegemony and the Language of Contention."

33. French and Daniels, *The Gendered Worlds of Latin American Women Workers*; James, "'Tales Told out on the Borderlands'"; Vecchia, "'My Duty as a Woman'"; and Farnsworth-Alvear, "Talking, Fighting, Flirting."

34. Scott, *Gender and the Politics of History*, 113–38; Hutchison, *Labors Appropriate to Their Sex*, 38.

35. E.g., see Cope, *The Limits of Racial Domination*. On the interdependence of ideologies of race, class, and gender, see Dias, *Power and Everyday Life*; Martínez-Alier, *Marriage, Class, and Color in Nineteenth-Century Cuba*; Burns, *Colonial Habits*, 15–18; Higginbotham, "African-American Women's History and the Metalanguage of Race." Gutman *(Meanings of Macho)* also emphasizes the interrelationship of gender and class.

36. E.g., in 1910, 43 percent of all working women were domestics.

37. Roseberry, "Hegemony and the Language of Contention," 355–66; Bourdieu, *Outline of a Theory of Practice*, 82–84; Fields, "Ideology and Race in American History."

38. Sonya Rose has described this approach as "discover rather than presume" (Rose, "Resuscitating Class"). See also Frader and Rose, *Gender and Class in Modern Europe*, 11–16.

39. Ramos, "Mujeres trabajadoras del porfiriato"; French, *A Peaceful and Working People*, 121; French and Daniels, *The Gendered Worlds of Latin American Women Workers*, 8.

40. Following Temma Kaplan, Lear shows that women protested against impediments to their capacity to provide for their families: inflation, food scarcity, and the insufficiency of the wages of their husbands (Lear, *Workers, Neighbors, and Citizens*, 8).

41. Middlebrook, *The Paradox of Revolution*.

42. Haber, *Industry and Underdevelopment*, 124.

43. For a similar argument regarding the persistent power of "outdated ideas," see Bliss, *Compromised Positions*, 7.

44. On reform more broadly in Mexico, see John Womack, "The Mexican Revolution, 1910–1920," 129. On women and reform in the Southern Cone, see Lavrin, *Women, Feminism, and Social Change in Argentina, Chile, and Uruguay*, 75–84. On the United States, see Kessler-Harris, *Out to Work*, 180–214.

Chapter 1

1. Basurto, *Vivencias femininas de la Revolución*, 17.

2. Ibid.

3. Carmen Ramos-Escandón states that gender ideology identified women with domestic skills such as ornamentation and self-denial, and shaped their entrance into the work force (Ramos-Escandón, "Mujeres trabajadoras del México porfiriano"). William French suggests women's occupations were an extension of female domestic duties (French, *A Peaceful and Working People*, 121). Lear acknowledges structural limitations on women's employment, but also states that women were concentrated in occupations that were an extension of domestic responsibilities (Lear, *Workers, Neighbors, and Citizens*, 73–76). Pioneering labor historians, interested in the relationship between workers and the government, infrequently included women (see González Casanova, *La clase obrera en la historia de México*; Tamayo, *La clase obrera en la historia de México*; Clark, *Organized Labor in Mexico*). More recently, historians interested in community and the workplace have included women (see García Díaz, *Un pueblo fabril del porfiriato*; Camarena and Fernandez A., "Los obreros-artesanos en las fábricas textiles de San Angel"; Radkau, *"La Fama" y la vida*; and Radkau, *"Por la debilidad de nuestro ser"*). Though Bliss *(Compromised Positions)* does not engage labor history, her study of prostitutes should also be included.

4. This approach approximates the one taken in recent European, U.S., and Latin American history. For the United States, see Blewitt, *Men, Women and Work*; Milkman, *Gender at Work*; and Goldin, *Understanding the Wage Gap*, 75–77. For Europe, see Downs, *Manufacturing Inequality*. For Columbia, see Farnsworth-Alvear, *Dulcinea in the Factory*.

5. On women in rural production and outmigration in Mexico, see Fowler-Salamini and Vaughan, *Women of the Mexican Countryside*; and Macías, *Against All Odds*, 30. Women have been the first to migrate to cities in search of wage labor in a variety of historical circumstances (see Hünefeldt, *Paying the Price of Freedom*, 91–96).

6. México, Secretaría de Fomento, Oficina Tipográfica, *Censo y división territorial del Distrito Federal*, 42; México, Dirección General de Estadística, *Tercer censo de población de los Estados Unidos Mexicanos*, vol. 1, ch. I–IV, pp. 57–58.

7. "Censo de la Población, 1900," *Boletín Municipal*, 19 July 1902.

8. Ibid.; México, Departamento de la Estadística Nacional, *Censo general de la República*, vol. 2, *Durango a Puebla*; México, Dirección General de Estadística, *V censo de población: Resumen general*.

9. Thompson, "Artisans, Marginals, and Proletarians," 307–24.

10. Costo de vida, AGN, RT287: 84 (1913).

11. On women's wage-earning activities in the 1930s, see Thompson, "Artisans, Marginals, and Proletarians," 307–24; and Rendón and Salas, "La evolución del empleo en México." See also Factory Inspection of La Perfeccionada, AGN, RT55: 8 (1921); AGN, RT287: 24 (1921); México, Comisión Investigadora de la Situación de la Mujer y de los Menores Trabajadoras, *Informe*, 10. Until the 1950s white working women in the United States were predominantly young and single; beginning in the 1950s an increasing number of married women worked, both prior to marriage and after children left the home (Goldin, *Understanding the Wage Gap*, 10–13). Most African American women always worked outside the home (Jones, *Labor of Love, Labor of Sorrow*, 8).

12. "El Trabajo en las Máquinas de Coser," *El Socialista*, 11 June 1876, 1; "Las Costureras," *El Socialista*, 11 September 1876; *La Convención Radical Obrera*, 5 March 1893.

13. Thompson, "Artisans, Marginals, and Proletarians," 307–24; on the prevalence of female-dominated households, see also Bach, "Un estudio del costo de vida."

14. Factory Inspection Report, AGN, RT32: 14 (1913); see also Factory Inspection Report, AGN, RT91: 4 (1914); Factory Inspection Report, AGN, RT162: 27, 35, 41, 42, 43, 35 (1914); and Factory Inspection Report, AGN, RT294: 15 (1920).

15. Infracciones de sastrerías, AHCM 2401–2402 (1919–1920); Infracciones de Talleres de Modas, AHCM 2404 (1919–1920).

16. González Angulo Aguirre, *Artesanado y ciudad a finales del siglo XVIII*, 30; Arrom, *The Women of Mexico City*, 157–65.

17. Carrera Estampa, *Los gremios mexicanos*, 76–78.

18. Arrom, *The Women of Mexico City*, 163–64.

19. Lombardo de Ruiz, "La real de tabaco," 38.

20. Deans-Smith, *Bureaucrats, Planters, and Workers*, 21, 100, 103, 179; Deans-Smith, "Working Poor and the Colonial State," 49; Ros, "La Real Fábrica de Tabaco," 100–103.

21. González Angulo Aguirre, *Artesanado y ciudad a finales del siglo XVIII*, 30.

22. Florescano and Sánchez, "La época de las reformas borbónicas," 220.

23. Ros, "La Real Fábrica de tabaco," 51–64.

24. Muriel, *Los recogimientos de mujeres*; Arrom, *Containing the Poor*.

25. On clothing production in Europe, see Jensen, "Needlework as Art, Craft, and Livelihood before 1900," 10; for the United States, see Stansell, *City of Women*, 142–43.

26. Iparraguirre, "Cuadros medios de origen artisanal." Although obrajes were not "factories in embryo," the gendered division of labor they contained presaged the labor arrangements that would come to characterize modern textile factories (see Salvucci, *Textiles and Capitalism in Mexico*, 43, 105; and Miño Grijalva, *La protoindustria colonial hispanoamericana*).

27. Gamboa Ojeda, *Los empresarios de ayer*, 25–33; Colón Reyes, *Los orígenes de la burguesía y el Banco de Avío*; Antuñano, "Ventajas políticas, civiles, fabriles y domésticos"; Leal, *Del mutualismo al sindicalismo en México*, 13.

28. The census did not distinguish the sex of minors; the figure for women as a percentage of workers excludes minors. See Busto, *Estadística de la República Mexicana*, 1:329–30; Keremetsis, *La industria textil mexicana en el siglo XIX*, 65. On female textile workers in the United States, see Dublin, *Women At Work*; Kessler-Harris, *Out to Work*.

29. Garza, *El proceso de industrialización en la ciudad de México*, 100–103. On similarities to early industry in Chile, see Palma, "External Disequilibrium and Internal Industrialization."

30. Sesto, *El México de Porfirio Díaz*, 94.

31. Figueroa Domenech, *Guía general descriptiva de la República Mexicana*, 178–79; Sanborn Map Company, *Insurance Maps of the City of Mexico*.

32. "Fábrica de Seda del Sr. Hipólito Chambón: Su Fundación," *El Obrero Mexicano*, 22 April 1910, 2; Busto, *Estadística de la República Mexicana*, 1:329–30; Colegio de México, *Estadísticas económicas del porfiriato*, 107–13; AGN, RT323: 13 (1921); Morgan, "Proletarians, Politicos, and Patriarchs," 154–56; Sanborn Map Company, *Insurance Maps of the City of Mexico*.

33. Factory Inspection Report, AGN, RT472: 12 (1915); Factory Inspection Report, AGN, RT70: 27 (1922); RT472: 12 (1922). On women in the U.S. clothing industry, see Butler, *Women and the Trades*, 104.

34. Factory Inspection Report, AGN, RT472: 12 (1922); see also Factory Inspection Report, AGN, RT162: 44 (1914); and "La Huelga de las Costureras de Munición," *Nueva Era*, 30 December 1911, 4.

35. Infracciones, Talleres de modas, AHCM 2404 (1919–1920); Factory Inspection Report, AGN, RT90: 33, 34 (1914); Sanborn Map Company, *Insurance Maps of the City of Mexico*

36. Infracciones, Talleres de Modas, AHCM 2404 (1919).

37. "La situación del obrero en México," *El Obrero Mexicano*, 13 May 1894.

38. Towner, "Monopoly Capitalism," 90–105; Rendón and Salas, "La evolución del empleo en México," 189–230.

39. Busto, *Estadística de la República Mexicana*, 1:329–30; Secretaría de Industria, Comercio y Trabajo, *Censo Industrial 1920*, AGN, RT600: 4 (1920). In 1895 in Mexico City women made up almost half of the total economically active population (México, INEGI, *Estadísticas históricas de México*; México, Dirección General de Estadística, *Estadísticas sociales del porfiriato, 1877–1910*).

40. Haber, *Industry and Underdevelopment*, 7, 59.

41. *Boletín del Archivo General de la Nación* 3, no. 3 (July–September 1979): 14–15.

42. On Ernesto Pugibet's investments, see Mexico, Department of Finance, *The Mexican Yearbook . . . 1912*, 421; Limones Ceniceros, "Las obreras del México porfiriano," 44; Anderson, *Outcasts in Their Own Land*, 22; El Buen Tono, AGN, Fototeca Nacional, G1–E2; Morgan, "Proletarians, Politicos, and Patriarchs," 154–56; Cosío Villegas, *Historia moderna de México*, 7:362.

43. AGN, RT31: 1 (1913); Colegio de México, *Estadísticas económicas del porfiriato*, 111–13.

44. México, Department of Finance, *The Mexican Yearbook . . . 1912*, 421; Camp, *Mexican Political Biographies*, 241.

45. Arturo M. Obregón argues that in the 1890s between twelve and fifteen tobacco manufactories in Mexico City employed an average of three hundred workers each. This contradicts the numbers I've used from Haber (see Obregón M., *Las obreras tabacaleras en la Ciudad de México*, 75; and Haber, *Industry and Underdevelopment*, 49; see also Censo Industrial, AGN, RT618: 1 [1921]).

46. "A Propósito del Viaje de Algunas Huelguistas de 'El Premio,'" *La Convención Radical Obrera*, 23 June 1893, 1. See also "El Trabajo de la Mujer," *La Convención Radical Obrera*, 17 March 1901, 1.

47. Figueroa Domenech, *Guía general descriptiva de la República Mexicana*, 178.

48. Report on complaints by workers at El Buen Tono, AGN, RT211: 17 (1920). See also the 1923 interview by Arturo Obregón M. with Doña Cholita (Obregón M., *Las obreras tabacaleras en la Ciudad de México*, 103–9). On occupational segregation by sex in U.S. tobacco factories, see Butler, *Women and the Trades*, 74–97.

49. Obregón M., *Las obreras tabacaleras en la Ciudad de México*, 103–9.

50. *La Gaceta del Trabajo*, AGN, RT332: 2 (1921); Factory Inspection Report, AGN, RT90: 33 (1914); Factory Inspection Report, AGN, RT332: 2 (1921).

51. In the colonial period there were 8 reales to a peso. The real circulated in Mexico until the mid–nineteenth century, when the country converted to a decimal system of account: 100 centavos per peso. Nevertheless, as late as the 1890s people still spoke of wages and prices in reales. At that time, the real would have been worth 12.5 centavos. The installation of steam-powered machinery began as early as 1881 at La Sultana (see *El Hijo del Trabajo*, 16 January 1881; *El Tiempo*, 28 October 1885, 3).

52. E.g., "La Huelga de las Cigarreras," in *El Tiempo*, 1 November 1885, 1, 4.

53. "La Retribución del Trabajo a las Obreras," *La Convención Radical Obrera*, 10 December 1893, 1; *La Convención Radical Obrera*, 23 July 1895, 3; "El Estanco del Tabaco," *La Convención Radical Obrera*, 12 May 1895, 1.

54. Busto, *Estadística de la República Mexicana*, 1:329–30; Censo Obrero, AGN, RT618: 1, 75–130 (1921); México, Secretaría de Industria, Comercio y Trabajo, Dirección de Publicaciones y Propaganda, *Monografía sobre el estado actual de la industria en México*, 150; Report on complaints by workers at El Buen Tono, AGN, RT211: 17 (1920).

55. México, Secretaría de Industria, Comercio y Trabajo, Dirección de Publicaciones y Propaganda, *Monografía sobre el estado actual de la industria en México*, 72–79, 150; Factory Inspection Report, AGN, RT300: 1, 653–69 (1921); Censo Industrial, AGN, RT618: 1 (1921); AGN, RT600: 4 (1921).

56. *El Hijo del Trabajo*, 27 May 1877.

57. *La Convención Radical Obrera*, 3 March 1901, 1.

58. Haber, *Industry and Underdevelopment*, 94. U.S. feminist labor historians have long worked from the premise that outwork formed an integral aspect of industrialization (see Stansell, *City of Women*, 107).

59. Conflictos, AGN, RT211: 18 (1920). The Barcelonette investment group established El Puerto de Liverpool and El Palacio de Hierro. León Signoret, a Barcelonette member, established Al Puerto de Veracruz in 1880 (Haber, *Industry and Underdevelopment*, 68, 74).

60. Conciliación y Arbitraje, AGN, RT1414: 1 (1928).

61. *La Convención Radical Obrera*, 3 March 1901, 1; *El Tiempo*, 1 November 1885, 4.

62. Factory Inspection Report, AGN, RT472: 12 (1923); México, Secretaría de Industria, Comercio y Trabajo, *Informe*, 58, 65. The 1936 study is perhaps the first use of the term *maquiladora* to refer to low-waged assembly work performed by women, and is therefore noteworthy. However, the working conditions that the term described, while similar to contemporary maquiladoras, should not be confused with current conditions in assembly factories in border industrialization zones.

63. Conciliación y Arbitraje, AGN, RT52: 1 (1913).

64. On import taxes and the purchase of sewing machines on credit, see Busto, *Estadística de la República Mexicana*, 1:25. On technology, see *El Socialista*, 11 June 1876. On wages, see *La Convención Radical Obrera*, 10 December 1893; and *La Convención Radical Obrera*, 24 February 1901.

65. AGN, RT101: 23 (1915).

66. *El Tiempo*, 10 September 1885; *El Socialista*, 26 April 1874; *El Socialista*, 11 June 1876, 1; Basurto, *Vivencias femininas de la Revolución*, 20; "El Nuevo Esquilmo de las Costureras de Munición," *La Convención Radical Obrera*, 24 February 1901, 1.

67. México, Departamento de Trabajo, *Boletín del Trabajo* 6 (December 1913): 539.

68. "La Retribución del Trabajo a las Obreras," *La Convención Radical Obrera*, 10 December 1893, 1.

69. *La Gaceta del Trabajo*, AGN, RT332: 2 (1921); Factory Inspection Report, AGN, RT90: 33 (1914); Factory Inspection Report, AGN, RT332: 2 (1921).

70. México, Comisión Investigadora de la Situación de la Mujer y de los Menores Trabajadoras, *Informe*, 58.

71. Parcero, *Condiciones de la mujer en México durante el siglo XIX*, 67–77; Busto, *Estadística de la República Mexicana*, 1:329–30; México, Dirección General de Estadística, *Censo general de la República Mexicana verificado el 28 octubre de 1900*; Basurto, *Vivencias femininas de la Revolución*, 66; "A Domicilio," AGN, RT15 (1920), 294.

72. México, Comisión Investigadora de la Situación de la Mujer y de los Menores Trabajadoras, *Informe*, 58.

73. Study of the Clothing Industry, *La Gaceta del Trabajo*, AGN, RT332: 2 (1921).

74. Study of the Clothing Industry, AGN, RT332: 2 (1921).

75. Study of the Clothing Industry, AGN, RT332: 15 (1921).

76. Study of the Clothing Industry, AGN, RT332: 2 (1921); México, Comisión Investigadora de la Situación de la Mujer y de los Menores Trabajadoras, *Informe*, 58.

77. Study of the Clothing Industry, AGN, RT332: 2 (1921), p. 9.

78. Study of the Clothing Industry, AGN, RT332: 2 (1921), p. 9; Factory Inspection Report, AGN, RT300: 1 (1921), pp. 653–69.

79. Study of the Clothing Industry, AGN, RT332: 2 (1921), p. 9.

80. In the period 1869–77 rarely more than 5.0 percent of the population of the Federal District had tuberculosis, but in the period 1890–98 at least 9.3 percent of the population suffered from this disease associated with poverty ("Campaña Contra la Tuberculosis," *Boletín Municipal*, November 1902, 1).

81. Ana María Hernández, "La mujer mexicana en la industria," *El Nacional*, 31 March 1939, 8; México, Comisión Investigadora de la Situación de la Mujer y de los Menores Trabajadoras, *Informe*, 111.

82. Garza, *El proceso de industrialización en la ciudad de México*, 94, 100–103.

83. Haber, *Industry and Underdevelopment*, 58, 157. San Antonio Abad was incorporated in 1892 (see México, Department of Finance, *The Mexican Yearbook . . . 1912*, 287).

84. Figures are from Colegio de México, *Estadísticas económicas del porfiriato*, 111–13.

85. Censo Obrero 1921, AGN, RT618: 1; Censo Industrial 1920, AGN, RT600: 4.

86. Haber, *Industry and Underdevelopment*, 161; Hernandez, *La mujer en la industria textil*, 118.

87. México, Secretaría de Industria, Comercio y Trabajo, Dirección de Publicaciones y Propaganda, *Monografía sobre el estado actual de la industria en México*, 34–57. Women never dominated the textile workforce in the same way they did during early industrialization in Europe and the United States. On women in the textile industry in Europe, see Valenze, *The First Industrial Woman*. For the United States, see Dublin, *Women at Work*; and Kessler-Harris, *Out to Work*.

88. *Censo Obrero 1921*, AGN, RT618: 1. This figure contrasts with estimates that women represented 13 percent of all Mexican textile workers during the nineteenth century (see Keremetsis, *La industria textil mexicana en el siglo XIX*, 209; Gonzalez Navarro, *Las huelgas textiles en el porfiriato*, 229).

89. *La Convención Radical Obrera*, 8 June 1890, and 10 April 1892.

90. Gonzalo de Quesada, "En la exposición de Chicago: La mujer de México," *El Partido Liberal*, 13 September 1893, 1–2; Census report, AGN, RT472: 12 (1923); AGN, RT405: 1 (1922); "Fábrica de Seda del Sr. Hipólito Chambón: Su Fundación," *El Obrero Mexicano*, 22 April 1910, 2; Census report, AGN, RT472: 12 (1922).

91. Chenut, "The Gendering of Skill as Historical Process," 77–110.

92. Factory Inspection Report, AGN, RT472: 12 (1922). In 1921, sixteen knitwear factories each employed from four to two hundred workers, 90 percent of them women (Censo Obrero, AGN, RT618: 1 [1921]). *Bonetería* comes from the French *bonneterie*, meaning "knitwear," and includes sweaters, socks, and other knitwear items, not bonnets. For misidentification of bonetería, see Bliss, *Compromised Positions*, 69.

93. BMLT, Recortes, Bonetería (1931).

94. *Boletín Municipal*, July 1902.

95. Centro de Estudios Históricos del Movimiento Obrera Mexicano, *La mujer y el movimiento obrero*, 148–61.

96. Censo Obrero, AGN, RT618: 1 (1921); AGN, Fototeca Nacional, Archivo Fotográfico Díaz, Delgado y García, 26:4 and 1:26; Emilia C. Viuda De Santa María et al., "Informe al Departamento de Investigación y Protección del Trabajo de la Mujer, 1914," *Boletín del Archivo General de la Nación* 3, no. 3 (July–September 1979), 1; Questionnaire for the Workers Census, AGN, RT782: 5 (1924); *Boletín del Archivo General de la Nación* 3, no. 3 (July–September 1979): 14–15.

97. Censo Industrial, AGN RT618: 1 (1920); and Censo Obrero, AGN, RT600: 4 (1921).

98. México, Secretaría de Industria, Comercio y Trabajo, *Ley Federal del Trabajo*, 49.

99. AGN, RT283: 123, pp. 1–30.

100. AGN, RT294: 15, pp. 1–109.

101. Iparraguirre, "Cuadros medios de origen artisanal," 45–63.

102. Radkau, *"La Fama" y la vida*, 78.

103. According to Fernando Rosenzweig, in 1902 the average wage for men was 1.45 pesos versus 80 centavos for women (Rosenzweig, "La industria," 413).

104. *El Tiempo*, 25 January 1893, 2.

105. Busto, *Estadística de la República Mexicana*, 1:329–30; Censo Obrero, AGN, RT618: 1 (1921).

106. Censo Obrero, AGN, RT618: 1 (1921); see also México, Secretaría de Industria, Comercio y Trabajo, Dirección de Publicaciones y Propaganda, *Monografía sobre el estado actual de la industria en México*, 34–57.

107. AGN, RT287: 23.

108. AGN, RT293: 1; Questionnaire for the Workers Census, AGN, RT782: 5 (1924).

109. México, Secretaría de Industria, Comercio y Trabajo, Dirección de Publicaciones y Propaganda, *Monografía sobre el estado actual de la industria en México*, 115–57.

110. Alicia Alva, "La mujer en el trabajo," *El Nacional*, 27 July 1933.

111. Ibid. At this time the growth of women in public administration was significant, from 171 to 6,000, while men increased from 14,000 to 41,000. In agriculture, women declined from 1,630 to 170, while men increased from 36,175 to 42,295. (México, Secretaria de la Economía Nacional, *Primer censo industrial de 1930*, vol. 3, bk. 1, *Textiles*).

112. México, Secretaría de la Economía Nacional, *Primer censo industrial de 1930*, vol. 3, bk. 1, *Textiles*. INEGI, *Estadísticas históricas de México*, 254.

113. Censo Obrero, Federal District, AGN, RT618: 1 (1921); Rastros y Mercados, Padrones, AHCM 3750 (1888–1918).

114. Factory Inspection Report, AGN, RT325: 5; Rosenzweig, "La industria," 364.

115. Bauer, "Millers and Grinders"; Keremetsis, "Del metate al molino"; AGN, RT117: 14, RT150: 1. The 1900 Federal District census counted 2,604 molenderas

(México, Dirección General de Estadística, *Estadísticas sociales del porfiriato, 1877–1910*).

116. Censo Obrero, AGN, RT618: 1 (1921).

117. "Tribuna Obrera," *El Renovador*, 29 July 1915, 3.

Chapter 2

1. Arrom, *The Women of Mexico City*, 261–62.

2. French, *A Peaceful and Working People*, 87–107.

3. Franco, *Plotting Women*; Castillo, *Easy Women*.

4. Molina Enríquez, *Los grandes problemas nacionales*, 361–70. See also Sesto, *El México de Porfirio Díaz*, 219–20.

5. Hale, *The Transformation of Liberalism in Late-Nineteenth-Century Mexico*, 211.

6. Tostado Gutiérrez, *El álbum de la mujer*, 2:121–22, 181, 190–920. See also Lavrin, "In Search of the Colonial Woman in Mexico," 25–59; and Courtier, "Women in a Noble Family," 129–49. On the culture of seclusion in Brazil, see Dias, *Power and Everyday Life*, 52–70; and Borges, *The Family in Bahia, Brazil*, 191–93. On the ways women's lives inhabited and challenged the ideal of seclusion, see Burns, *Colonial Habits*. On female homosocial culture in the United States, see Smith-Rosenberg, *Disorderly Conduct*, 53–75.

7. Hale, *The Transformation of Liberalism in Late-Nineteenth-Century Mexico*, 22; Payno, *Sobre mujeres, amores y matrimonios*; Arrom, *The Women of Mexico City*, 20–24, 264. On "republican motherhood" in the United States, see Hewitt, "Beyond the Search for Sisterhood." See also Macías, *Against All Odds*, 9–12.

8. Arrom, *The Women of Mexico City*, 27.

9. Antuñano, "Ventajas políticas, civiles, fabriles y domésticas."

10. Hale, *The Transformation of Liberalism in Late-Nineteenth-Century Mexico*, 249, 274.

11. "Prostitución Clandestina," *La Convención Radical Obrera*, 12 June 1887, 2.

12. Antuñano, "Ventajas políticas, civiles, fabriles y domésticas," 9. For a discussion of early U.S. industrialists' housing projects, see Kessler-Harris, *Out to Work*, 32–33.

13. Alvarado, *El siglo XIX ante el feminismo*. See also Molina Enriquez, *Los grandes problemas nacionales*; Gamboa, *La mujer moderna*, 58–100; and Hale, *The Transformation of Liberalism in Late-Nineteenth-Century Mexico*, 207, 251.

14. *La Convención Radical Obrera*, 23 June 1895, 1.

15. Elisa, "La mujer," *El Socialista*, 18 April 1886, 1–2.

16. Important exceptions existed (see *El Obrero Mexicano*, 4 August 1911).

17. Alvarado, *El siglo XIX ante el feminismo*, 113–15.

18. Ibid.

19. Ibid.

20. Ramos and Lau, *Mujeres y revolución*, 90, 155–58.

21. *El Progreso Latino*, 14 April 1906, 432. The newspaper was founded by Spaniard Román Rodríguez Peña (see Sesto, *El México de Porfirio Díaz*, 30).

22. *El Progreso Latino*, 14 April 1906, 432. See also "Faltan Trabajadores o Sobran Vagos?" *El Progreso Latino*, 28 February 1906, 226.

23. *El Progreso Latino*, 14 April 1906, 432.

24. Ibid.

25. Ibid.

26. Gonzalez Navarro, "La moral social," 383–86; Fernández de Lizardi, *El Periquillo Sarniento*; Garcia Cubas, *Libro de mis recuerdos*; Payno, *Los bandidos de Río Frío*. For selections on the middle sectors in nineteenth- and twentieth-century Mexico, see Pogolotti, *La clase media en México*. On Julio Guerrero, see Buffington, *Criminal and Citizen in Modern Mexico*, 51–54.

27. Bringas and Macareño, *Esbozo histórico de la prensa obrera en México*; Smith, "Contentious Voices Amid the Order."

28. Sesto, *El México de Porfirio Díaz*, 22.

29. E.g., *El Tiempo*, 28 August 1888.

30. Diocapo, "El trabajo de la mujer," *El Hijo del Trabajo*, 21 October 1883, 2.

31. "El porvenir de la mujer," *La Convención Radical Obrera*, 24 January 1897.

32. Anónimo, "Para las damas: Porvenir de la mujer," *La Convención Radical Obrera*, 22 April 1894, 2–3; 6 May 1894, 2.

33. Louis Büchner, "La bendición del trabajo," *El Socialista*, 13 September 1885, 1, 2; Anónimo, "El trabajo honrado y el porvenir de la mujer," *La Convención Radical Obrera*, 26 May 1901, 2; Anónimo, "Sed de instrucción en las obreras," *La Convención Radical Obrera*, 9 January 1898, 1.

34. Anónimo, "En favor de las obreras," *La Convención Radical Obrera*, 22 October 1893, 1; "El porvenir de Chihuahua," "El trabajo de la mujer," *La Convención Radical Obrera*, 8 October 1894, 2.

35. Felipe de J. Flores, "La obrera mexicana," *El Obrero Mexicano*, 1 July 1894, 1, 2; "El porvenir de Chihuahua," "El trabajo de la mujer," *La Convención Radical Obrera*, 8 October 1894, 2.

36. Anónimo, "La mujer en los talleres," *La Convención Radical Obrera*, 9 January 1898, 1.

37. Glantz, Introduction to *The Magic Lantern*; Barros and Buenrostro, *Las once y serenooo!*

38. For a more detailed discussion of the concept of imitation in French and Mexican studies, see Piccato, "La construcción de una perspectiva científica."

39. Lara y Pardo, *La prostitución en México*, 108–9.

40. Ibid., 108–13, 118.

41. Ibid., 114–15.

42. Ibid.

43. Ibid.

44. Ibid., 116.

45. "Prostitucion Clandestina," *La Convención Radical Obrera*, 12 June 1887, 2.

46. Ibid.

47. *La Convención Radical Obrera*, 12 June 1887, 2.

48. Lara y Pardo, *La prostitución en México*, 97.

49. "Señoritas Rateras," *El Tiempo*, 14 February 1893, 4.

50. "Campaña Contra las Cruzadoras," *El Demócrata*, 29 October 1914, 1.

51. *El Demócrata*, 2 May 1922, 1, 3.

52. Ibid., 1, 3.

53. Ibid., 7, 8.

54. For a more comprehensive treatment of Mexican feminist organizations, see Cano, "Revolución, feminismo y ciudanía en México (1915–1940)," 682; and Tuñón Pablos, *Mujeres que se organizan*.

55. Formoso de Santicillia Obregón, *La mujer mexicana en la organización social del país*; Alegría Garza, *Importancia de la asistencia social*; Romero Aceves, *La mujer en la historia de México*; Hernandez, *La mujer en la industria textil*; BMLT, Recortes, Mujeres–Trabajo (1929–1950).

56. Alicia Alva, "La Mujer en el Trabajo," *El Nacional*, 29 June 1933.

57. Scott, *Gender and the Politics of History*, 60.

Chapter 3

1. Historians who argue for a female ethic of protest include Lear, *Workers, Neighbors, and Citizens*, 362. The work of Temma Kaplan has been influential in supporting this thesis in Latin American and U.S. history (Kaplan, *Red City, Blue Period*). For brief mention of men's and women's shared reasons for protest, see Camarena and Fernández A., "Los obreros-artesanos en las fábricas textiles de San Angel," 192–96.

2. *El Tiempo*, 31 August 1888. Hall, "Urban Labor Movements," 196. On confraternities, see Bracho, *De los gremios al sindicalismo*; Illades, *República del trabajo*, 69–76; and Lear, *Workers, Neighbors, and Citizens*, 106–13.

3. *La Convención Radical Obrera*, 21 October 1887.

4. Industrias, AGN, RT1414: 1 (1923).

5. On 11 September 1910 the *liga feminil* "Josefa Ortiz de Domínguez" participated in protests against election fraud (see Tostado Gutiérrez, *El álbum de la mujer*, 2:232–35).

6. AGN, RT14: 12 (1914); RT128: 37 (1913).

7. "Fraternal 'El Fenix,'" *El Imparcial*, 26 July 1913, 7.

8. Ceballos Ramirez, *El catolicismo social*, 29; Schell, "An Honorable Vocation for Ladies"; Huitrón, *Orígines e historia del movimiento obrero en México*, 229.

9. Méndez de Cuenca, *Simplezas*, 89.

10. Illades, *República del trabajo*, 100.

11. *La Convención Radical Obrera*, 9 October 1887, 4; *La Convención Radical Obrera*, 20 May 1894, 3.

12. *La Convención Radical Obrera*, 24 July 1887.

13. González Navarro, *Las huelgas textiles en el porfiriato*, 298.

14. On cigarrera activism in Spain, see Radcliff, "Elite Women Workers and Collective Action."

15. Calderón, *La Convención Radical Obrera*, 1–6; Obregón, "El Segundo Congreso Obrero."

16. *La Convención Radical*, 18 September 1887, *La Convención Radical*, 15 January 1888; Vallens, *Working Women in Mexico during the Porfiriato*, 56.

17. Walker, "Porfirian Labor Politics"; Obregón, "El Segundo Congreso Obrero," 50–56.

18. Haber, *Industry and Underdevelopment*, 181–82.

19. *El Hijo del Trabajo*, 8 November 1881.

20. *El Tiempo*, 1 May 1884.

21. Florencia Mallon introduced the term "democratic patriarchy" to Mexicanists (borrowing it from Judith Stacey) (see Mallon, "Exploring the Origins of Democratic Patriarchy in Mexico," 5; and Stacey, *Patriarchy and Socialist Revolution in China*, esp. 116–17).

22. *La Convención Radical Obrera*, 7 August 1884.

23. Sesto, *El México de Porfirio Díaz*, 22.

24. *El Tiempo*, 1 November 1885, 3.

25. *El Tiempo*, 15 October 1885, 3.

26. "Las Cigarreras" and "Reducción de salarios a las costureras," in Rocha, *El álbum de la mujer*, 4:179–81, 191–92.

27. "La Cuestión de las Cigarreras," *La Convención Radical Obrera*, 14 August 1887, 1; González Navarro, "La moral social," 310; Vallens, *Working Women in Mexico during the Porfiriato*, 69.

28. "La Huelga de las Cigarreras," *El Tiempo*, 1 November 1885, 1; "Contratos y Contratistas," *El Tiempo*, 1 November 1885, 4; *El Tiempo*, 13 November 1885, 3.

29. *La Convención Radical Obrera*, 14 August 1887, 2.

30. "Letter to President Díaz," *El Tiempo*, 11 July 1887, 3.

31. *La Convención Radical Obrera*, 14 August, 1887, 2.

32. *La Convención Radical Obrera*, 24 July 1887. Dublán had served as an alternate senator from the Federal District from 1884 to 1886 (Camp, *Mexican Political Biographies*, 241).

33. *El Tiempo*, 30 December 1887.

34. "Obreras de la Cigarrería," *La Paz Pública*, 15 September 1887; "A la Señora Carmen Romero Rubio de Díaz," *La Paz Pública*, 16 September 1887.

35. Anónimo, "Nueva asociación," *La Paz Pública*, 11 December 1887; "Que Abuso," *El Tiempo*, 17 August 1887, 2.

36. Obregón, Introducción to *La convención radical*.

37. Anónimo, "Sociedad Hijas del Trabajo," *La Paz Pública*, 26 February 1888.

38. Anónimo, "El estandarte de las Hijas del Trabajo," *La Paz Pública*, 17 May 1888.

39. Ibid.

40. *El Tiempo*, 31 August 1888.

41. *El Tiempo*, 28 April 1895, 2; Parcero, *Condiciones de la mujer en México durante el siglo XIX*, 94.

42. Parcero, *Condiciones de la mujer en México durante el siglo XIX*, 70; Sesto, *El México de Porfirio Díaz*, 97; Galván, *La educación superior de la mujer en México*. Mary Kay Vaughan identifies female teachers in the 1920s as middle class (see Vaughan, *Cultural Politics in Revolution*, 27).

43. *El Tiempo*, 25 April 1895; *El Tiempo*, 28 April 1895; *La Convención Radical Obrera*, 19 May 1895, 3.

44. *El Tiempo*, 8 May 1895; *El Tiempo*, 12 May 1895.

45. "Las Obreras Huelguistas de 'El Premio,'" *La Convención Radical Obrera*, 16 June 1895, 2.

46. Hart, *Anarchism and the Mexican Working Class*, 51–53; Illades, *República del trabajo*, 99.

47. "Gacetilla: La Union de las Operarias de las Fabricas. —'Union y Alianza,'" *La Convención Radical Obrera*, 27 October 1895, 3; "Gacetilla: La Union de las Operarias de las Fabricas.—'Union y Alianza,' *La Convención Radical Obrera*, 27 October 1895, 3.

48. "Gacetilla: 'Representante de las obreras cigarreras,'" *La Convención Radical Obrera*, 20 October 1895, 3.

49. *El Imparcial*, 8 August 1906; Araiza, *Historia del movimiento obrero mexicano*, 1:95–98.

50. *El Tiempo*, 1 November 1885, 20.

51. "Sociedad Mexicana de Costureras," *El Universal*, 26 October 1888, 2. Carmen Romero Rubio de Díaz served as patroness of La Sociedad Mutualista Fraternal de Costureras, which should be distinguished from La Sociedad Mexicana de Costureras ("Sociedad Mutualista Fraternal de Costureras," *La Convención Radical Obrera*, 5 March 1893, 2).

52. *La Convención Radical Obrera*, 8 December 1895.

53. *La Convención Radical Obrera*, 1889.

54. *La Convención Radical Obrera*, 5 March 1893.

55. *La Convención Radical Obrera*, 22 January 1894.

56. "Sociedad Mutualista Fraternal de Costureras," *La Convención Radical Obrera*, 5 March 1893, 2.

57. See the article on the Gran Círculo de Obreros in *El Socialista*, 9 February 1882, 1.

58. *La Convención Radical Obrera*, 22 February 1894; *La Convención Radical Obrera*, 20 May 1894.

59. *La Convención Radical Obrera*, 24 January 1897.

60. *La Convención Radical Obrera*, 24 February 1901.

61. *La Convención Radical Obrera*, 3 March 1901.

62. *La Convención Radical Obrera*, 3 March 1901.

63. *La Convención Radical Obrera*, 10 March 1901.

64. Hernandez, *La mujer en la industria textil*, 35–38; Margarita Garcia Flores, "Adelina Zendejas: La lucha de las mujeres mexicanas," *Fem* 1 (October–December 1976); and Vidales, "Ni madres abnegadas ni adelitas."

65. *El Obrero Mexicano*, 3 June, 1910, 3; González Navarro, "La moral social," 351; Lear, "Workers, *Vecinos*, and Citizens," 80; Hernandez, *La mujer en la industria textil*, 50.

66. "Las Visitas del Señor Gobernador á las Fábricas," *El Obrero Mexicano*, 22 April 1910, 1.

67. "Las Visitas del Señor Gobernador á las Fábricas," *El Obrero Mexicano*, 29 April 1910, 1.

68. "A los Obreros," *El Obrero Mexicano*, 11 February 1910, 7.

69. "A qué Fabricas Pertenecen Los Obreros Inscritos," *El Obrero Mexicano*, 10 June 1910, 1. Most of these factories were female-dominated (see Busto, *Estadística de la República Mexicana*, 1:329–30; Censo Industrial, AGN, RT600: 4 [1921]; Censo Obrero, AGN, RT618: 1 [1920]; AGN, RT1449: 8 [1928]; AGN, RT918: 1 [1915]).

70. "Hijas de las Obreras," *La Convención Radical Obrera*, 1887, 3; Palavincini, *México*, 47–48; Betanzos Cervantes, "Las escuelas Casa Amiga de la Obrera," 149.

71. "A las obreras y los obreros," *El Obrero Mexicano*, 29 July 1910, 1.

72. *El Obrero Mexicano*, 7 January 1910.

73. "Despedida del Señor Don. Guillermo de Landa y Escandón," *El Obrero Mexicano*, 2 June 1911.

Chapter 4

1. For a more complete discussion of this transition, see Illades, *República del trabajo*; and Leal, *Del mutualismo al sindicalismo en México*.

2. Araiza, *Historia del movimiento obrero mexicano*, 1:79; *La Convención Radical Obrera*, 7 November 1895, 1.

3. "La Organización Obrera," *El Obrero Mexicano*, 8 December 1911, 1.

4. Ibid.

5. "La Huelga de las Costureras de Munición," *Nueva Era*, 30 December 1911, 4.

6. "Una carta al Presidente de la República," *Nueva Era*, 27 December 1911, 4.

7. "La Huelga de las Costureras de Munición," *Nueva Era*, 27 December 1911, 4.

8. Ibid.

9. "A las Costureras de la 'Sinaloense,'" *Nueva Era*, 13 January 1912, 2.

10. "Escándalo por Costureras en Huelga," *Nueva Era*, 16 January 1912, 2.

11. *Nueva Era*, 2 January 1912; *Nueva Era*, 3 January 1912; *Nueva Era*, 4 January 1912.

12. "'Nueva Era' ayudara a los Huelguistas," "Se Reducirán las Horas de Trabajo: No Admitirán Niños en los Talleres," and "Los Obreros en Huelga Piden Apoyo al Presidente Madero," *Nueva Era*, 7 January 1912, 1.

13. "Querían que abandonaran el trabajo todas las obreras," *Nueva Era*, 11 January 1912.

14. "Escándalo a las Puertas de una Fábrica," *Nueva Era*, 11 January 1912, 2.

15. Ibid.

16. *Nueva Era*, 13 January 1912.

17. *Nueva Era*, 29 January 1912.

18. Hernandez, *La mujer en la industria textil*, 128–36.

19. "Se Suspenden los Trabajos de la fábrica 'La Carolina,'" 18, 20 July 1913,

9. On the causes of shutdowns, see "La Casa C. Noriega y Companía Explica el Asunto del Algodón," *El Sol*, 27 June 1914, 3; and AGN, RT5: 4 (1912).

20. *El Imparcial*, 26 July 1913, 5; and AGN, RT41: 19 (1913).

21. "Se Solucionó la Huelga de las Obreras de Bonetería," *El Imparcial*, 18 July, 1913, 7; *Boletín del Trabajo* 1, no. 2 (1913).

22. Hernandez, *La mujer en la industria textil*, 144.

23. *El Sol*, 27 June 1914.

24. Guadarrama, *Los sindicatos y la política en México*, 31.

25. Ibid.

26. *El Imparcial*, 8 August 1913, 7.

27. *El Boletín del Trabajo* 1, no. 6 (1913).

28. *El Demócrata*, 3 October 1914.

29. Ibid.

30. Ibid.

31. "Va a Constituirse un Sindicato de Costureras," *El Demócrata*, 14 October 1914, 1; "Casa del Obrero," *El Imparcial*, 8 August 1913, 7.

32. AGN, RT70: 8 (April 1914); "Vida Obrera: Por la Casa del Obrero Mundial," *El Demócrata*, 31 October 1914, 3. This was not the first time that the Casa represented the interests of seamstresses (see *El Demócrata*, 3 October 1914, 2; and AGN, RT70: 8 [1914]).

33. *El Demócrata*, 31 October 1914.

34. AGN, RT70: 28 (1914).

35. Hernandez, *La mujer en la industria textil*, 52, 76, 85; Guadarrama, *Los sindicatos y la política en México*, 31.

36. Basurto, *Vivencias femininas de la Revolución*, 66.

37. "En la Casa del Obrero Mundial," *El Demócrata*, 13 October 1914, 2.

38. *El Demócrata*, 5 November 1915.

39. Huitrón, *Orígines e historia del movimiento obrero en México*, 275–92.

40. Hernandez, *La mujer en la industria textil*, 87. Esther Torres also helped found La Perfeccionada union (see *Historia Obrera* 2, no. 5 [1975]).

41. Basurto, *Vivencias femininas de la Revolución*, 24.

42. Ibid., 37.

43. Ibid., 38.

44. Huitrón, *Orígines e historia del movimiento obrero en México*, 294.

45. *El Demócrata*, 3 August 1916; *El Demócrata*, 28 August 1916.

46. On feminist conferences, see Soto, *The Emergence of the Modern Mexican Woman*, 107–8. *El Demócrata* and *El Universal* covered the conferences of 17–27 May 1923, 29 May 1925, and 7–15 July 1925. Cigarreras from El Buen Tono and La Tabacalera Mexicana, and women from the CROM and state worker's associations, as well as teachers, musicians, and students at the National Medical School, participated in the Union de Mujeres Ibero-Americanas conference in 1915 (see *El Demócrata*, 29 May 1925). For a remembrance by one of the participants, see the memoir by Artemisa Saenz Royo (*Historia político-social cultural del movimiento feminino*, 1914–1950, 50).

47. Hernandez, *La mujer en la industria textil*, 84–85.

48. Carr, *El movimiento obrero y la política en México*, 91–92.

49. Tamayo, *La clase obrera en la historia de México*, 116.

50. Obregón speech at La Tabacalera Mexicana, in Bassols Batalla, *El pensamiento político de Álvaro Obregón*, 148.

51. Lear, *Workers, Neighbors, and Citizens*, 350.

52. AGN, RT211: 25 (1920); AGN, RT418: 4 (1920).

53. *Vida Nueva*, 10 October 1920.

54. *El Comunista de México* 1, no. 3 (June 1920).

55. AGN, RT211: 25 (1920); AGN, RT418: 4 (1922). Dawn Keremetsis found that in Jalisco men replaced women in the work force. She argues that women chose to avoid the violence associated with male organized labor. However, her evidence shows the CROM made explicit efforts to displace female workers (Keremetsis, *La industria de empaques y sus trabajadoras*, 296–99).

56. Carr, *El movimiento obrero y la política en México*, 16.

57. Hernandez, *La mujer en la industria textil*, 87; Adelina Zendejas, "El Movimiento feminil en México," *El Día México*, 17 June 1975.

58. Tamayo, *La clase obrera en la historia de México*, 127–28; Taibo II, *Los Bolshevikis*, 114.

59. Tamayo, *La clase obrera en la historia de México*, 130; *El Demócrata*, 18 January 1922.

60. "No Sé Cuantos Hombres," *El Demócrata*, 2 May 1922, 1, 3; *El Demócrata*, 3 May 1922, 1; *El Demócrata*, 20 November 1920, 1. On women in preparation and thread departments, see AGN, RT287–88 (1921–1924).

61. *El Demócrata*, 2 May 1922, 1, 3.

62. Ibid.

63. Salazar and Escobedo, *Las pugnas de la glebe*, 65; see also Araiza, *Historia del movimiento obrero mexicano*, 1:98.

64. Araiza, *Historia del movimiento obrero mexicano*, 1:108–20.

65. Hernandez, *La mujer en la industria textil*, 119–20.

66. "Cuarenta Mil Tabaqueros Integran una Organización," *El Demócrata*, 28 May 1925, 5.

67. *El Demócrata*, 1 May 1925; *El Demócrata*, 6 May 1925; *El Demócrata*, 16 May 1925.

68. Rocha, *El album de las mujeres*, 4:255.

69. *El Demócrata*, 1 May 1925, 1.

70. Hart, *Anarchism and the Mexican Working Class*, 172.

71. "Fue Gigantesca la Manifestación Obrera de Ayer," *El Demócrata*, 6 May 1925; AGN, RT294: 25 (1921); and AGN, RT128: 28 (1913).

72. *El Demócrata*, 6 May 1925. To better understand the context within which such accusations could be made, see Gómez Izquierdo, *El movimiento antichino en México*.

73. "Fue Gigantesca la Manifestación Obrera de Ayer," *El Demócrata*, 6 May 1925.

74. *El Demócrata*, 16 May 1925; AGN, RT294: 25 (1921).

75. *El Demócrata*, 17 May 1925; Guadarrama, *Los sindicatos y la política en México*,

63; AGN, RT27: 1 (1928). Vendors outside of markets continued to organize, led by Romana O. de Cholico in the 1930s; on Cholico, see Saenz Royo, *Historia político-social cultural del movimiento femenino*, 25.

76. Hernandez, *La mujer en la industria textil*, 40–42.

77. Ibid., 42–43.

78. Ibid., 99–102.

79. México, Comisión Investigadora de la Situación de la Mujer y de los Menores Trabajadoras, *Informe*, 15.

80. Thompson, "Artisans, Marginals, and Proletarians," 307–24.

Chapter 5

1. Basurto, *Vivencias femininas de la Revolución*, 17. Patricia Galvão gives a fictional description of sexual morality as a condition of employment in a clothing shop in 1930s São Paulo, Brazil (see Galvão, *Industrial Park*, 43).

2. On the negotiation of public and private honor, see Twinam, *Public Lives, Private Secrets*, 34, 47.

3. Illades, *República del trabajo*, 197–205; Lear, *Workers, Neighbors, and Citizens*, 194–201; Hart, *Anarchism and the Mexican Working Class*, 57; Camarena and Fernández A., "Los obreros-artesanos en las fábricas textiles de San Angel."

4. Eileen Findlay (*Imposing Decency*) argues that an integral aspect of male honor was the capacity to dominate women.

5. Steve Stern argues that in colonial Mexico honor as social precedence predetermined honor as personal virtue—i.e., poor people did not have the economic wherewithal to lay claim to elite notions of honor (Stern, *The Secret History of Gender*, 15). In his work on crime in nineteenth- and twentieth-century Mexico, Pablo Piccato shows that honor was not reserved for upper-class white males, though he does argue that lower-class women did not defend a code of honor (Piccato, *City of Suspects*, 80–82, 110–11).

6. Twinam, *Public Lives, Private Secrets*, 31.

7. Caufield, *In Defense of Honor*, 4; Twinam, *Public Lives, Private Secrets*, 31; Klubock, *Contested Communities*, 7–8.

8. The important exception to the study of honor for male workers is Farnsworth-Alvear, *Dulcinea in the Factory*.

9. García Díaz, *Un pueblo fabril del porfiriato*, 63.

10. Anderson, *Outcasts in Their Own Land*, 59; Lear, *Workers, Neighbors, and Citizens*, 196–97.

11. Lear argues that women's demand for respect as women was "often both the initial demand and the last one to be surrendered" (Lear, *Workers, Neighbors, and Citizens*, 227). See also Factory Inspection Report, AGN, RT5: 14 (1914); Factory Inspection Report, AGN, RT172: 12 (1919).

12. Cuestionario de Trabajo a Domicilio, AGN, RT294: 15 (1921); Informe, AGN, RT684: 12 (1924).

13. AHCM 1735: 777 (1910).

14. Infracciones, AHCM 2401 (1919–1920).

15. "Las Obreras," *El Socialista*, 17 July 1882, 2.

16. Ibid.; Radkau, *"Por la debilidad de nuestro ser,"* 86.

17. Radkau, *"La Fama" y la vida*, 71–80. Latin American historians have used oral history to explore how female factory workers have negotiated their own experiences, or memory of those experiences, with the discourse of domesticity and conceptions of the factory as a dangerous space for women; see the essays by Teresa Vecchia, Ann Farnsworth-Alvear, and Daniel James, all in French and Daniels, *The Gendered Worlds of Latin American Women Workers*.

18. Radkau, *"La Fama" y la vida*, 71–80.

19. Ibid., 65, 71.

20. Ibid., 71–80.

21. Ibid.

22. Factory Inspection Report, AGN, RT163: 11 (1919).

23. AGN, RT438: 16 (1919).

24. AGN, RT648: 10 (1923).

25. Factory Inspection Report, AGN, RT172: 12 (1919).

26. AGN, RT162: 28 (1920).

27. Study of the Clothing Industry, AGN, RT332: 2 (1921).

28. *El Obrero Mexicano*, no. 10 (1894), reproduced in Centro de Estudios Históricos del Movimiento Obrera Mexicano, *La voz de los trabajadores*.

29. Cuestionario para el censo obrero, AGN, RT780: 6 (1924).

30. Morgan, "Proletarians, Politicos, and Patriarchs," 160.

31. *El Obrero Mexicano*, no. 10 (1894), reproduced in Centro de Estudios Históricos del Movimiento Obrera Mexicano, *La voz de los trabajadores*; Obregón M., 99.

32. El Buen Tono, AGN, RT211: 17 (1920).

33. AGN, RT672: 20 (February 1923); Parcero, *Condiciones de la mujer durante el siglo XIX*, 94.

34. Factory Inspection Report, AGN, RT90: 3 (1914).

35. Piccato states that honor as social precedence was not relevant to the lower classes (Piccato, *City of Suspects*, 80).

Chapter 6

1. AHCM 1730: 317 (1908).

2. Lear, "Mexico City"; Piccato, *"Urbanistas, Ambulantes*, and *Mendigos."* Anne Staples claims that by the early nineteenth century women had begun breaking down a public/masculine and private/feminine dichotomy; however, her evidence focuses on children and drunkards, without much consideration for gender (see Staples, "Policia y buen gobierno"; see also Voekel, "Peeing on the Palace").

3. Ryan, "Gender and Public Access," 264.

4. Habermas, *The Structural Transformation of the Public Sphere*, 31–35.

5. AHCM 608: 5 (1903).

6. AHCM 608: 5, 3643: 1471 (1903); AGN, Secretaría de Salubridad y Asistencia, 2 (1907).

7. AHCM, 646: 8, 608: 17 (1903).

8. AHCM 1732: 433 (1908); Busto, *Estadística de la República Mexicana*, 1:22; Martin, *Mexico of the Twentieth Century*, 127.

9. AHCM 1730: 298 (1908).

10. Yoma Medina and Martos López, *Dos mercados en la historia de la ciudad de México*; Lear, "Mexico City," 454–92.

11. AHCM 1729: 200 (1906); 646: 16 (1901–1906).

12. Lear, "Mexico City," 454–92; Martí, *Subsistence and the State*; Vanderwood, *Disorder and Progress*, 119–31.

13. AHCM 1727: 10 (1901–1916); AHCM 3750 (1885–1918).

14. AHCM 1727: 10 (1901–1916); AHCM 3750 (1885–1918).

15. AHCM 1727: 17 (1901); AHCM 3644: 1607 (1901).

16. AHCM 1732: 460 (1903).

17. AHCM 1729: 196 (1907).

18. AHCM 3644: 1698 (1911).

19. Reglamento de Carnicerías, AHCM (1904); Viqueira Albán, *¿Relajados o reprimidos?* 137.

20. AHCM 2394 (1919).

21. "Las Necesidades de México," *La Mujer Mexicana* 3 (1905), 10; *Boletín Municipal*, AHCM (1910); Pani, *La higiene en México*, 88.

22. For an example of this see AHCM 3640: 1206 (1898).

23. *Boletín Municipal*, 1 September 1902, AHCM.

24. *Boletín Municipal*, 1 September 1902, AHCM.

25. Positivism has been portrayed as a way of thinking cultivated by writers, philosophers, and a limited political clique, but it was also relevant to government at the municipal level (see Zea, *Positivismo en México*).

26. *Memorias, 1903–1914*, AHCM 608: 31 (1903).

27. *Memorias del Ayuntamiento, 1880*, 27, AHCM 1732: 460 (1908).

28. AHCM 608: 3 (1903); AHCM 1727: 8 (1901–1916).

29. Tuñón Pablos, *El álbum de la mujer*, 2:73, 88, 263–67.

30. García Cubas, *Libro de mis recuerdos*, 218–19.

31. *Boletín Municipal*, 15 March 1901, AHCM.

32. *Boletín Municipal*, 15 March 1901, AHCM.

33. AHCM 3644: 1607 (20 January 1903).

34. *El Tiempo*, 5 November 1885, 3.

35. *La Convención Radical Obrera*, 3 April 1887, 3.

36. "Las Reglas de la Calle," *Nueva Era*, 17 February 1912.

37. "Como una Inmensa Antorcha . . . El Soldado Vicente Sanchez. Cargado por La Ira, Dio Muerte a Una Mujer Vaciandole Un Bote de Petroleo y Prendiendole Fuego," *Nueva Era*, 22 January 1913, 1.

38. Ibid. For a discussion of the term *pelao* in contemporary Mexico, see Monsiváis, *Mexican Postcards*, 89, 98–99.

39. García Cubas, *Libro de mis recuerdos*, 202–6; Cope, *The Limits of Racial Domination*, 36–37. For Brazil, see Dias, *Power and Everyday Life*, 46–47, 71–94; for the United States, see Stansell, *City of Women*, 55–62.

40. Arrom, *The Women of Mexico City*, 191–92.

41. Viqueira Albán, *¿Relajados o reprimidos?* 137.

42. On the difficulties of accounting for women's economic participation, see Recchini de Lattes and Wainerman, "Unreliable Account of Women's Work."

43. AHCM 1729: 389 (1907).

44. Rastros y mercados, Padrones, AHCM 3750 (1885–1918); México, Secretaría de Fomento, Oficina Tipográfica, *Censo y División Territorial del Distrito Federal*.

45. AHCM 608: 5 (1903); AHCM 1730: 253 (1907–1908); AHCM 3618: 23 (1922); AHCM 3988: 199 (1922); México, Secretaría de Fomento, Oficina Tipográfica, *Censo y División Territorial del Distrito Federal*; México, Dirección General de Estadística, *Censo general de la República Mexicana verificado el 28 octubre de 1900*.

46. Stern, *The Secret History of Gender*, 256–58. For a similar argument regarding the United States, see Stansell, *City of Women*, 138.

47. AHCM 1737: 896, 904 (1901–1916).

48. AHCM 1729: 191 (1901–1916); AHCM 1737: 897, 903 (1901–1916); Yoma Medina and Martos López, *Dos mercados en la historia de la ciudad de México*, 59.

49. AGN, Secretaría de Asistencia Pública y Trabajo Social, s.1/311/372 (1932).

50. AHCM 1728: 76 (1903).

51. AHCM 3987: 115 (1922).

52. AHCM 1737: 905 (1901–1916).

53. AHCM 1731: 407 (1907).

54. AHCM 1731: 407 (1907).

55. AHCM 3728–41 (1880–1920); AHCM 3988: 115 (1922).

56. AHCM 1728: 126 (1904).

57. For similar arguments regarding the United States, see Ryan, "Gender and Public Access."

58. AHCM 1732: 675 (1909).

59. AHCM 1732: 675 (1909).

60. AHCM 1730: 329 (1908).

61. AHCM 1728: 49 (1902).

62. Roseberry, *Anthropologies and Histories*, 27.

63. Historians of colonial Latin America, and especially of Mesoamerica, have long noted the use of the phrase *desde tiempo inmemorial* by indigenous groups as a means of constructing and legitimating petitions to local and extra-local authorities. The connection between colonial practices and those of the late nineteenth and early twentieth centuries is provocative yet unclear. On the practice of petitioning and the use of the phrase *desde tiempo inmemorial*, see Kellogg, *Law and the Transformation of Aztec Culture*, 38–40; and Monsiváis, *Mexican Postcards*, 71–87.

64. AHCM 1728: 94, 49 (1902).

65. On the term *vecino*, see Warren, *Vagrants and Citizens*. See also AHCM 1728: 76 (1903).

66. Warren, *Vagrants and Citizens*.

67. AHCM 1730: 290, 317 (1908).

68. AHCM 3988: 158 (1919); AHCM 1735: 777 (1910); Viqueira Albán, *¿Relajados o reprimidos?* 137.

69. AHCM 1731: 395 (1907).

70. AHCM 1727: 17 (1901).

71. AHCM 1728: 8 (1901).

72. AHCM 1728: 8 (1901).

73. AHCM 1737: 894 (1910).

74. AHCM 1731: 395 (1907).

75. AHCM 1730: 335 (1908).

76. AHCM 1732: 625 (1909).

77. AHCM 1731: 389 (1907).

78. AHCM 1728: 76 (1903).

79. AHCM 1732: 475 (1908).

80. AHCM 1731: 355 (1908).

81. AHCM 3988: 199 (1922); *El Tiempo*, 20 September 1885, 3.

Chapter 7

1. Corrigan and Sayer, *The Great Arch*, 3–12.

2. Middlebrook, *The Paradox of Revolution*; Carr, *El movimiento obrero y la política en México*; Lear, *Workers, Neighbors, and Citizens*; and Guadarrama, *Los sindicatos y la política en México*.

3. For studies of Mexican welfare, see Betanzos Cervantes, "Las escuelas Casa Amiga de la Obrera." On the regulation of prostitutes, see Bliss, *Compromised Positions*. On cultural reform, see Knight, "Popular Culture and the Revolutionary State in Mexico." On welfare for working women in the Southern Cone, see Lavrin, *Women, Feminism, and Social Change in Argentina, Chile, and Uruguay*, 53–96.

4. Romero, *Mexico and the United States*, 511; Urbina Trueba, *La evolución de la huelga*; "Sentencia Contra las Cigarreras," *La Convención Radical Obrera*, 26 May 1895, 2.

5. Anderson, *Outcasts in Their Own Land*, 206–8; Radkau, *"Por la debilidad de nuestro ser,"* 1–10.

6. Ponce Alocer, *La elección presidencial de Manuel González*.

7. Betanzos Cervantes, "Las escuelas Casa Amiga de la Obrera," 148.

8. "Asilo para las Hijas de las Obreras," *La Convención Radical Obrera*, 6 November 1887, 2; Palavincini, *México*, 86–89.

9. Arrom, *The Women of Mexico City*, 44–45.

10. Lavrín, *Women, Feminism, and Social Change in Argentina, Chile, and Uruguay*, 80–82.

11. A daycare for the children of working women, La Buena Madre was founded in 1881, but little is known about its history (see *La Convención Radical Obrera*, 21 March 1897). See also Palavincini, *México*, 47–48; *La Convención Radical Obrera*, 21 March 1897; Baz, *Un año en México*, 206; Betanzos Cervantes, "Las escuelas Casa Amiga de la Obrera," 149, 153–56; "La Enseñanza en la Casa Amiga," *El Imparcial*, 13 July 1913, 3. A group of U.S. women also established the Casa Industrial y Amiga de la Obrera Florence Crittenton (Sesto, *El México de Porfirio Díaz*, 203).

12. *La Convención Radical Obrera*, 27 November 1887.

13. Anderson, *Outcasts in Their Own Land*, 78.

14. "El Asilo de Infancia y Regeneración de la Mujer," *La Convención Radical Obrera*, 9 May 1887.

15. "El Asilo de Infancia y Regeneración de la Mujer," *La Convención Radical Obrera*, 9 May 1887.

16. Palavincini, *México*, 85.

17. "Recibirán Alimentos más de 600 niños necesitados," *El Demócrata*, 18 August 1916. According to Douglas Richmond, Carranza established childcare facilities for working mothers (Richmond, "Carranza," 62).

18. Betanzos Cervantes, "Las escuelas Casa Amiga de la Obrera," 151. Moisés González Navarro states that the Casa Amiga closed due to a lack of funds in 1922 (González Navarro, *La pobreza en México*, 173).

19. González Navarro finds that the School of Arts and Vocations for Women existed during the presidency of Lerdo de Tejada. He suggests the central mission of the school was providing breakfast for poor women (González Navarro, *La pobreza in México*, 112).

20. "Proyecto de Reglamento de La Escuela Nacional de Artes y Oficios para Mujeres," APD44: 29, no. 017403 (1904).

21. "Escuelas de Artes y Oficios," *La Convención Radical Obrera*, 4 December 1887.

22. AGN, RT97: 270 (1910).

23. AGN, RT309: 5 (1912); AGN, RT312: 8 (1913).

24. Ana María Hernandez, writing in *Eficiencia: Revista de Economía Política*, October 1930.

25. Knight, *The Mexican Revolution*, 1:445.

26. *Nueva Era*, 14 January 1912; *Nueva Era*, 22 January 1912.

27. *Nueva Era*, 29 January 1912.

28. *Nueva Era*, 9 February 1912.

29. Gonzalez Navarro, *La pobreza en México*, 148, 152, 157.

30. AGN, RT61: 9, RT59: 2 (1913–1914). On the U.S. Department of Labor (1913) and the Women's Bureau (1918), see Orleck, *Common Sense and a Little Fire*, 137.

31. Knight, *The Mexican Revolution*, 2:62.

32. México, Departamento de Trabajo, *Boletín del Trabajo* 1, no. 6 (December 1913): 541. See also, e.g., AGN, RT606: 3, RT31: 4; and Meyer, *Huerta*, 173.

33. AGN, RT56: 1 (1913).

34. AGN, RT56: 1 (1913).

35. AGN, RT56: 1 (1913); AGN, RT175: 31 (1919).

36. Soto, *The Emergence of the Modern Mexican Woman*, 63–65.

37. AGN, RT90: 5, RT90: 7, RT90: 17 (1914).

38. AGN, RT68: 1; RT91: 4 (1914); AGN, RT59: 3, RT90: 10. For a provocative argument regarding the influence of women on the U.S. government, see Baker, "The Domestification of Politics," 89.

39. AGN, RT91: 3 (17 July 1914).

40. AGN, RT91: 3 (17 July 1914).

41. AGN, RT61: 9 (1913–1914); Meyer, *Huerta*, 208.

42. AGN, RT61: 9 (27 July 1914).

43. AGN, RT61: 9 (27 July 1914).

44. *El Demócrata*, 8 October 1914.

45. For the United States, see Baker, *Protective Labor Legislation*; Kelley, *The Development in the United States of Legislation*; Kessler-Harris, *Out to Work*; Lehrer, *Origins of Protective Labor Legislation for Women*.

46. Knight, *The Mexican Revolution*, 2:475.

47. Richmond, *Venustiano Carranza's Nationalist Struggle*, 165–71; Knight, *The Mexican Revolution*, 2:503.

48. Knight, *The Mexican Revolution*, 2:320, 475.

49. AGN, RT83: 6 (1914).

50. *Boletín del Trabajo* 1, no. 1 (1913); *Boletín del Trabajo* 1, no. 2 (1913); *Boletín del Trabajo* 1, no. 5 (1913); *Boletín del Trabajo* 1, no. 7 (1913).

51. For Title VI, section VIII, see Congreso Constituyente, *Diario de los debates*, 1:362, 834.

52. México, Congreso Constituyente, *Diario de los debates*, 1:1012.

53. *Nueva Era*, 29 January 1912.

54. Congreso Constituyente, *Diario de los debates*, 1:975.

55. Congreso Constituyente, *Diario de los debates*, 1:362.

56. "Reglamento para el Trabajo de las Mujeres en Establecimientos Comerciales: 1923," *Boletín del Archivo General de la Nación* 3, no. 3 (July–September 1979): 21.

57. México, Departamento de la Estadística Nacional, *Economía social: La estadística del trabajo*, 47; Congreso Constituyente, *Diario de los debates*, 1:834; González Navarro, *La pobreza en México*, 142. In Brazil, President Vargas passed similar maternity protection legislation in the early 1930s (see Besse, *Restructuring Patriarchy*, 141). On Chile, Argentina, and Uruguay, see Lavrin, *Women, Feminism, and Social Change in Argentina, Chile, and Uruguay*, 87–90.

58. During this period, first Plutarco Elías Calles (1919–1920) and then Luis Morones (1924–1928) served as Secretary of Industry, Commerce, and Labor (see Carr, *El movimiento obrero y la política en México*, 131).

59. Middlebrook, *The Paradox of Revolution*, 48; Lear, *Workers, Neighbors, and Citizens*, 185.

60. Factory Inspection Report, AGN, RT324: 11 (1919); Factory Inspection Report, AGN RT324: 16 (1919); Factory Inspection Report, AGN, RT323: 9 (1919); Factory Inspection Report, AGN: RT175: 31 (1919); articles from *El Globo*, AGN, RT323: 18; and AGN, RT323: 4.

61. Guy, *Sex and Danger in Buenos Aires*; Lavrin, *Women, Feminism, and Social Change in Argentina, Chile, and Uruguay*, 97–124.

62. AGN, RT498: 10 (1922). Doctor Olea was contracted to give eight conferences a month. After giving only four in six months, his contract was cancelled.

63. Factory Inspection Report, AGN, RT90: 32, 34 (1914).

64. Factory Inspection Report, AGN, RT324: 19 (1921).

65. Factory Inspection Report, AGN, RT472: 12 (1923).

66. Factory Inspection Report, AGN, RT684: 12 (1924).

67. Factory Inspection Report, AGN, RT684: 12 (1924).

68. Factory Inspection Report, AGN, RT223: 32 (1920).

69. "Reglamento para el Trabajo de las Mujeres en Establecimientos Comerciales: 1923," *Boletín del Archivo General de la Nación* 3, no. 3 (July–September 1979): 21.

70. "Reglamento para el Trabajo de las Mujeres en Establecimientos Comerciales: 1923," *Boletín del Archivo General de la Nación* 3, no. 3 (July–September 1979): 22.

71. *Proyecto de Exposición de Motivos para la Ley Sobre Descanso Semanal*, AGN, RT132: 15 (1918). Regarding Sunday rest laws and prostitutes, see Bliss, *Compromised Positions*, 81–82.

72. *Proyecto de Exposición de Motivos para la Ley Sobre Descanso Semanal*, AGN, RT132: 15 (1918).

73. In the United States and Brazil women frequently changed their place of work in an attempt to improve their working conditions (see Wolf, *Working Women and Working Men*, 33).

74. AGN, RT684: 12 (1924).

75. AGN, RT684: 12, 95–99 (1924).

76. Cameron, *Mexico in Revolution*, 161–62.

77. AGN, RT211: 17 (1920); RT782: 5 (1924).

78. AGN, RT684: 12 (1924).

79. AGN, RT684: 12 (1924).

80. Middlebrook, *The Paradox of Revolution*, 51.

81. Ibid., 47–48.

82. México, Secretaría de Industria, Comercio y Trabajo, *Ley Federal del Trabajo*, 49.

83. Alianza de Mujeres de México, *La situación jurídica de la mujer mexicana*, 145; México, Secretaría de Industria, Comercio y Trabajo, *Ley Federal del Trabajo*, 45.

84. During the 1930s several doctoral students at the National Autonomous University of Mexico wrote their theses on the physical impact of work on the female body, as well as on questions of maternity leave and women's legal rights as workers; see, e.g., Herrera Gonzalez, "Breves consideraciones."

85. Cámara Nacional de la Ciudad de México, *Reglamento de labores peligrosos o insalubres para mujeres y menores*; Alianza de Mujeres de México, *La situación jurídica de la mujer mexicana*, 146. See also *Diario Oficial*, 11 August 1934; Camara Nacional de la Ciudad de México, *Reglamento de labores peligrosos o insalubres para mujeres y menores*, 55–63; México, Secretaría de Industria, Comercio y Trabajo, *Ley Federal del Trabajo*, 77.

86. México, Secretaría de Industria, Comercio y Trabajo, *Ley Federal del Trabajo*, 45.

87. Knight, "Popular Culture and the Revolutionary State in Mexico."

Conclusion

1. Eley, "Nations, Publics, and Political Cultures," 289.

2. The lack of independence of the press is important to Habermas's analysis of the transformation of the public sphere during the nineteenth century (see Habermas, *The Structural Transformation of the Public Sphere*, 203).

3. Lear, *Workers, Neighbors, and Citizens*, 227; Radkau, *"Por la debilidad de nuestro ser,"* 80.

4. Guerra, Lempériere et al., *Los espacios públicos en Iberoamérica*, 9.

5. Eley, "Nations, Publics, and Political Cultures," 289.

6. These scholars include Fowler-Salamini and Vaughan, *Women of the Mexican Countryside*, 106–24; Bliss, *Compromised Positions*, 8; and Salas, *Soldaderas in the Mexican Military*, 101.

7. Lear, *Workers, Neighbors, and Citizens*, 280.

8. Ibid., 359.

9. On education as a marker of middle-class status, see, on Chile, Barr-Melej, *Reforming Chile*; on Peru, Parker, *The Idea of the Middle Class*; and on Brazil, Owensby, *Intimate Ironies*.

10. Iglesias Prieto, *Beautiful Flower of the Maquiladora*; Fernández-Kelly, *For We Are Sold, I and My People*; Cowie, *Capital Moves*.

Glossary

ambulante itinerant vendor

aprendiza female apprentice

atole non-alcoholic grain beverage of pre-Columbian origin

bonetería knitwear (also known as tejidos de punto)

buscona female petty thief, pilferer, or streetwalker

Casa Amiga de la Obrera Friend of the Working Woman House

cecina cured meat

cigarrera cigar or cigarette maker, female

colchonero/a mattress maker

costurera seamstress

cruzadora woman shoplifter

engargolado cigarette machine

envolvedora cigar wrapper, female

Escuela de Artes y Oficios School of Arts and Vocations

escuelas nocturnas night schools

fabricanta female factory worker

fraternal fraternal society or sorority

gabanes a wrap, like a serape

gorditas common street fare made of corn meal

guacales wooden carts

maestro/a master worker, teacher

mesero/a waiter/waitress; also a salesclerk

mozo boy; also a term suggesting subservience

mujer woman

munición military apparel and goods such as tents

mutualista mutual aid society

obrero/a factory worker

petate mat woven of palm leaves used for a variety of purposes including sleeping and working

portales an architectural structure, arches

pulquería pulque shop

revoltura pressing, grading, and sorting

serape wrap; traditional Mexican attire

tipo type or character

tortillera tortilla maker or vendor

tortillería tortilla shop

trapería rag processing shop

trapero/a ragpicker

vendedero/a vendor

vendedero/a ambulante itinerant vendor

zacates woven mats

Bibliography

Archives

Archivo General de la Nación, Mexico City [AGN]
  Beneficencia
  Departamento Autónomo del Trabajo [DAT]
  Fototeca Nacional
  Ramo del Trabajo [RT]
Archivo Histórico de la Ciudad de México, Ex-Ayuntamiento [AHCM]
Biblioteca Miguel Lerdo de Tejada, Mexico City [BMLT]
Archivo Porfirio Díaz, Universidad Iberoamericana, Mexico City [APD]
Centro de Estudios de História de México (CONDUMEX), Mexico City
  [CEHM]
Hemeroteca Nacional, Fondo Reservado, Mexico City

Newspapers and Periodicals

Album de Damas (Mexico City)
Boletín del Archivo General de la Nación (Mexico City)
Boletín Municipal (Mexico City)
El Comunista de México (Mexico City)
La Convención Radical Obrera (Mexico City)
El Correo de las Señoras (Mexico City)
El Dia México
Diario Oficial (Mexico City)
El Demócrata (Mexico City)
Eficiencia: Revista de Economía Política
Fem (Mexico City)
El Gráfico (Mexico City)
El Hijo del Trabajo (Mexico City)
La Mujer Mexicana (Mexico City)
El Nacional (Mexico City)
Nueva Era (Mexico City)
El Obrero Mexicano (Mexico City)

La Paz Pública (Mexico City)
El Socialista (Mexico City)
El Tiempo (Mexico City)
El Trimestre Económico (Mexico City)
El Universal (Mexico City)
Vida Nueva

Published Sources

Adelson, S. Lief "Clase y comunidad: Los estibadores de Tampico." In *Comunidad, cultura y vida social: Ensayos sobre la formación de la clase obrera.* Excerpts from the "Seminario de Movemiento Obrero y Revolución Mexicana." Mexico City: INAH, 1991.

Aguirre, Carlos A., and Robert Buffington, eds. *Reconstructing Criminality in Latin America.* Wilmington, Del.: Scholarly Resources, 2000.

Aguirre, Jorge. *Artesanado y ciudad a finales del siglo XVIII.* Mexico City: Fondo de Cultura Económica, SEP/Ochentas, 1983.

Alegría Garza, Paula. *Importancia de la asistencia social en relación con la mujer trabajador.* Mexico City: UNAM, 1943.

Alexander, Sally. "Women, Class, and Sexual Differences in the 1830s and 1840s: Some Reflections on the Writing of Feminist History." *History Workshop Journal* 17 (1984).

Alianza de Mujeres de México. *La situación jurídical de la mujer mexicana.* Mexico City, 1953.

Alonso Gutiérrez del Olmo, José Félix. "De la caridad a la asistencia." In *La atención materno infantil: Apuntes para su historia.* Mexico City: Secretaría de Salud, 1993.

Alvarado, Lourdes. *El Siglo XIX ante el feminismo: Una interpretación positivista.* Mexico City: UNAM, 1989.

Anderson, Rodney. *Outcasts in Their Own Land: Mexican Industrial Workers, 1906–1911.* Dekalb: Northern Illinois University, 1976.

Antuñano, Esteban de. "Ventajas políticas, civiles, fabriles y domésticas, que por dar ocupación también a las mugeres en las fábricas de maquinaria moderna que se están levantando en México, deben recibirse." Puebla: Oficina del Hospital de San Pedro, 1837.

Araiza, Luis. *Historia del movimiento obrero mexicano.* Vol. 1. Mexico City: Ediciones Casa del Obrero, 1975.

Arizpe, Lourdes, and Carlota Botey. "Mexican Agricultural Development Policy and Its Impact on Rural Women." In *Mexican Agricultural Development.* Boulder, Colo.: Westview Press, 1987.

Arizpe, Lourdes, and Josefina Aranda. "The 'Comparative Advantage' of Women's Disadvantages: Women Workers in the Strawberry Export Agribusiness in Mexico." *Signs* 7, no. 2 (1981): 453–73.

Arrom, Silvia. *The Women of Mexico City, 1790–1857.* Stanford, Calif.: Stanford University Press, 1985.

————. *Containing the Poor: The Mexico City Poor House, 1774-1871*. Durham, N.C.: Duke University Press, 2000.

Bach, Federico. "Un estudio del costo de vida." *El Trimestre Económico* 2, no. 5 (1935): 21-22.

Baker, Elizabeth Faulkner. *Protective Labor Legislation with Special Reference to Women in the State of New York*. New York: Columbia University Press, 1925.

Baker, Paula. "The Domestification of Politics." *American Historical Review* 89 (June 1984): 620-47.

Barr-Melej, Patrick. *Reforming Chile: Cultural Politics, Nationalism, and the Rise of the Middle Class*. Chapel Hill: University of North Carolina Press, 2001.

Barros, Cristina, and Marco Buenrostro. *Las once y serenooo!: Tipos mexicanos, siglo XIX / Introducción, selección de textos e investigación iconográfica*. Mexico City: Fondo de Cultura Económica, 1994.

Bassols Batalla, Narciso. *El pensamiento político de Álvaro Obregón*. Mexico City: Editorial Nuestro Tiempo, 1970.

Basurto, Jorge. *Vivencias femininas de la Revolución*. Mexico City: INEHRM, 1993.

Bauer, Arnold J. "Millers and Grinders: Technology and Household Economy in Meso-America." *Agricultural History* 64, no. 1 (winter 1990): 1-17.

Baz, Gustavo. *Un año en México, 1887*. Mexico City: E. Dublán y Cía Editores, 1887.

Besse, Susan. *Restructuring Patriarchy: The Modernization of Gender Inequality in Brazil, 1914-1940*. Chapel Hill: University of North Carolina Press, 1996.

Betanzos Cervantes, Irma. "Las escuelas Casa Amiga de la Obrera." In *La Atención materno infantil: Apuntes para su historia*. Mexico City: Secretaría de Salud, 1993.

Blewitt, Mary. "The Sexual Division of Labor and the Artisan Tradition in Early Industrial Capitalism: The Case of New England Shoe Making, 1780-1860." In *"To Toil the Live Long Day,"* edited by Carol Groneman and Mary Beth Norton. Ithaca, N.Y.: Cornell University Press, 1987.

————. *Men, Women, and Work: Class, Gender, and Protest in the New England Shoe Industry, 1780-1910*. Urbana: University of Illinois Press, 1988.

Bliss, Katherine E. *Compromised Positions: Prostitution, Public Health, and Gender Politics in Revolutionary Mexico City*. University Park: Pennsylvania State University Press, 2001.

Boris, Eileen. *Home to Work: Motherhood and the Politics of Industrial Homework in the United States*. New York: Oxford University Press, 1994.

Boris, Eileen, and Cynthia R. Daniels, eds. *Homework: Historical and Contemporary Perspectives on Paid Labor at Home*. Chicago: University of Illinois Press, 1989.

Borges, Dain. *The Family in Bahia, Brazil, 1870-1945*. Stanford, Calif.: Stanford University Press, 1995.

Bourdieu, Pierre. *Distinction: A Social Critique of the Judgement of Taste*. Translated by Richard Nice. Cambridge: Harvard University Press, 1984.

————. *Outline of a Theory of Practice*. Translated by Richard Nice. Cambridge: Cambridge University Press, 1977.

Bracho, Julio. *De los gremios al sindicalismo*. Mexico City: UNAM, 1990.

Bray, Francesca. *Technology and Gender: Fabrics of Power in Late Imperial China*. Berkeley: University of California Press, 1997.

Bringas, Guillermina, and David Macareño. *Esbozo historico de la prensa obrera en México*. Mexico City: UNAM, 1988.

Buffington, Robert M. *Criminal and Citizen in Modern Mexico*. Lincoln: University of Nebraska Press, 2000.

Burns, Kathryn. *Colonial Habits: Convents and the Spiritual Economy of Cuzco, Peru*. Durham, N.C.: Duke University Press, 2000.

Busto, Emiliano. *Estadística de la República Mexicana*. Vols. 1, 3. Mexico City: Imprenta de Ignacio Cumplido, 1879.

Butler, Elizabeth Beardsley. *Women and the Trades: Pittsburgh, 1907-1908*. Pittsburgh: University of Pittsburgh Press, 1984.

Calderón, Liborio Villalobos. *La convención radical obrera: Antología de prensa*. Mexico City: Centro de Estudios del Movimiento Obrero Mexicano, 1978.

Calhoun, Craig, ed. *Habermas and the Public Sphere*. Cambridge, Mass.: MIT Press, 1992.

Calvi, Giulia. "Women in the Factory: Women's Networks and Social Life in America (1900-1915)." In *Sex and Gender in Historical Perspective: Selections from Quaderni Storici*, edited by Edward Muir and Guido Ruggiero. Baltimore, Md.: Johns Hopkins University Press, 1990.

Cámara Nacional de la Ciudad de México. *Reglamento de labores peligrosas o insalubres para mujeres y menores*. Mexico City, 1934.

Camarena, Mario, and Susana A. Fernández A. "Los obreros-artesanos en las fábricas textiles de San Angel, 1920-1930." In *Comunidad, cultura y vida social: Ensayos sobre la formación de la clase obrera*. Excerpts from the "Seminario de Movimiento Obrero y Revolución Mexicana." Mexico City: INAH, 1991.

Cameron, Charlotte, O.B.E., F.R.G.S. *Mexico in Revolution*. London: Seeley, Service, and Co., 1925.

Camp, Roderic. *Mexican Political Biographies, 1884-1934*. Austin: University of Texas Press, 1991.

Canning, Kathleen. "Gender and the Politics of Class Formation: Rethinking German Labor History." *American Historical Review* 87 (June 1992): 736-68.

Cantu Corro, Pbro. José. *La mujer através de los siglos*. Mexico City: Editorial Jose Cantu Corro, 1900.

Cano, Gabriela. "Revolución, feminismo y ciudanía en México (1915-1940)." In *Historia de las mujeres en occidente*, edited by George Duby and Michelle Perrot. Madrid: Taurus Ediciones, 1993, 685-95.

Carr, Barry. *El movimiento obrero y la política en México, 1910-1929*. Mexico City: ERA, 1981.

Carrera Estampa, Manuel. *Los gremios mexicanos: La organización gremial en Nueva España, 1521-1861*. Mexico City: Edición y Distribución Ibero Americana de Publicaciones, S.A., 1954.

Castillo, Debra A. *Easy Women: Sex and Gender in Modern Mexican Fiction*. Minneapolis: University of Minnesota Press, 1998.

Caufield, Sueann. *In Defense of Honor: Sexual Morality, Modernity, and Nation in Early-Twentieth-Century Brazil*. Durham: Duke University Press, 2000.

Ceballos Ramírez, Manuel. *El catolicismo social: Un tercero en discordia. Rerum Novarum, la "cuestión social" y la movilización de los católicos mexicanos (1891-1911)*. Mexico City: Colegio de México, 1991.

Centro de Estudios Históricos del Movimiento Obrero Mexicano. *La mujer y el movimiento obrero: Prensa obrera del siglo XIX*. Mexico City: CEHSMO, 1975.

————. *La voz de los trabajadores: Periódicos obreros del siglo XIX*. Mexico City: CEHSMO, 1975.

Chassen-Lopez, Francie R. "'Cheaper Than Machines': Women and Agriculture in Porfirian Oaxaca, 1880-1911." In *Women of the Mexican Countryside, 1850-1990*, edited by Heather Fowler-Salamini and Mary Kay Vaughan. Tucson: University of Arizona Press, 1994.

Chávez Orozco, Luís. *El Banco de Avío y el fomento de la industria nacional: Colección de documentos para la historia del comercio exterior de México*. 2d series, vol. 3. Mexico City: Publicación del Banco Nacional de Comercio Exterior, S.A., 1966.

Chenut, Helen Harden. "The Gendering of Skill as Historical Process: The Case of French Knitters in Industrial Troyes, 1880-1939." In *Gender and Class in Modern Europe*, edited by Laura Frader and Sonya Rose. Ithaca, N.Y.: Cornell University Press, 1996.

Clark, Anna. *The Struggle for the Breeches: Gender and the Making of the British Working Class*. Berkeley: University of California Press, 1995.

Clark, Marjorie Ruth. *Organized Labor in Mexico*. Durham: University of North Carolina Press, 1934.

Coatsworth, John H. *Growth Against Development: The Economic Impact of Railroads in Porfirian Mexico*. DeKalb: Northern Illinois University Press, 1981.

Colegio de México. *Estadísticas económicas del porfiriato: Fuerza de trabajo y actividad económica por sectores*. Proceedings of the Seminario de historia moderna de México. Mexico City: Colegio de México, 1965.

Colón Reyes, Linda Ivette. *Los orígenes de la burguesía y el Banco de Avío*. Mexico City: Ediciones El Caballito, S.A., 1982.

Comité Ejecutico del Partido Revolucionario Institucional. *La Lucha política de las mujeres*. Mexico City: Archivo General de la Nación, 1990.

Cooper, Patricia A. *Once a Cigar Maker: Men, Women, and Work Culture in American Cigar Factories, 1900-1919*. Urbana: University of Illinois Press, 1987.

Cope, R. Douglas. *The Limits of Racial Domination*. Madison: University of Wisconsin Press, 1994.

Corrigan, Phillip, and Derek Sayer. *The Great Arch: English State Formation as Cultural Revolution*. London: Verso, 1990.

Cosío Villegas, Daniel. *Historia moderna de México*. 8 vols. in 9. Mexico City: Editorial Hermes, 1955-74.

Cott, Nancy. *The Bonds of Womanhood: Woman's Sphere in New England, 1780-1835*. New Haven, Conn.: Yale University Press, 1977.

Courtier, Edith. "Women in a Noble Family: The Mexican Counts of Regla,

1750–1830." In *Latin American Women: Historical Perspectives*, edited by Asunción Lavrin. Westport, Conn.: Greenwood Press, 1978.

Cowie, Jefferson. *Capital Moves: RCA's Seventy-Year Quest for Cheap Labor*. Ithaca, N.Y.: Cornell University Press, 1999.

Deans-Smith, Susan. *Bureaucrats, Planters, and Workers: The Making of the Tobacco Monopoly in Bourbon Mexico*. Austin: University of Texas Press, 1992.

———. "Working Poor and the Colonial State." In *Rituals of Rule, Rituals of Resistance: Public Celebrations and Popular Culture in Mexico*, edited by William Beezley, Cheryl English Martin, and William E. French. Wilmington, Del.: Scholarly Resources, 1994.

Deutsch, Sarah. *Women and the City: Gender, Space, and Power in Boston, 1870–1940*. New York: Oxford University Press, 2000.

Diaz, Maria Elena. "The Satiric Penny Press for Workers in Mexico, 1900–1910: A Case Study in the Politicization of Popular Culture." *Journal of Latin American Studies* 22, no. 3 (1990): 497–526.

Dias, Maria Odila Silva. *Power and Everyday Life: The Lives of Working Women in Nineteenth Century Brazil*. Translated by Ann Frost. New Brunswick, N.J.: Rutgers University Press, 1995.

Doré, Elizabeth, and Maxine Molyneux, eds. *Hidden Histories of the State in Latin America*. Durham, N.C.: Duke University Press, 2000.

Downs, Laura Lee. *Manufacturing Inequality: Gender Division in the French and British Metalworking Industries, 1914–1939*. Ithaca, N.Y.: Cornell University Press, 1995.

Dublin, Thomas. *Women at Work: The Transformation of Work and Community in Lowell, Massachusetts, 1826–1860*. New York: Columbia University Press, 1979.

Eley, Geoff. "Nations, Publics, and Political Cultures: Placing Habermas in the Nineteenth Century." In *Habermas and the Public Sphere*, edited by Craig Calhoun. Cambridge, Mass.: MIT Press, 1992.

Farnsworth-Alvear, Ann. "Talking, Fighting, Flirting: Workers Sociability in Medellín Textile Mills, 1935–1950." In *The Gendered Worlds of Latin American Women Workers: From Household and Factory to the Union Hall and Ballot Box*, edited by John French and James Daniels. Durham, N.C.: Duke University Press, 1998.

———. *Dulcinea in the Factory: Columbia's Industrial Experiment, 1905–1960*. Durham, N.C.: Duke University Press, 2000.

Fernández de Lizardi, José Joaquín. *El Periquillo Sarniento*. Mexico City: Editorial Porrúa, 1969.

Fernández-Kelly, María Patricia. *For We Are Sold, I and My People: Women and Industry in Mexico's Frontier*. Albany: State University of New York Press, 1983.

Fields, Barbara J. "Ideology and Race in American History." In *Region, Race, and Reconstruction: Essays in Honor of C. Vann Woodward*, edited by J. Morgan Kousser and James McPherson (New York: Oxford University Press, 1982).

Figueroa Domenech, J. *Guía general desciptiva de la República Mexicana*. 2 vols. Mexico City, Barcelona (España): R. de S. N. Araluce, [1899].

Findlay, Eileen. *Imposing Decency: The Politics of Sexuality and Race in Puerto Rico, 1870–1920*. Durham, N.C.: Duke University Press, 1999.

Florescano, Enrique, and I. Gil Sánchez. "La época de las reformas borbónicas." In vol. 2 of *Historia general de México*. Mexico City: El Colegio de México, 1977.

Formoso de Santicillia Obregón, Adela. *La mujer mexicana en la organización social del país*. Mexico, 1939.

Fowler-Salamini, Heather. "Gender, Work, and Coffee in Córdoba, Veracruz, 1850–1910." In *Women of the Mexican Countryside, 1850–1990*, edited by Heather Fowler-Salamini and Mary Kay Vaughan. Tucson: University of Arizona Press, 1994.

Fowler-Salamini, Heather, and Mary Kay Vaughan. Introduction to *Women of the Mexican Countryside*, edited by Heather Fowler-Salamini and Mary Kay Vaughan. Tucson: University of Arizona Press, 1994.

Fowler-Salamini, Heather, and Mary Kay Vaughan, eds. *Women of the Mexican Countryside, 1850–1990*. Tucson: University of Arizona Press, 1994.

Frader, Laura, and Sonya Rose, eds. *Gender and Class in Modern Europe*. Ithaca, N.Y.: Cornell University Press, 1996.

Franco, Jean. *Plotting Women*. New York: Columbia University Press, 1988.

Fraser, Nancy. "Rethinking the Public Sphere: A Contribution to the Critique of Actually Existing Democracy." In *Habermas and the Public Sphere*, edited by Craig Calhoun. Cambridge, Mass.: MIT Press, 1992.

French, John, and James Daniels. *The Gendered Worlds of Latin American Women Workers: From Household and Factory to the Union Hall and Ballot Box*. Durham, N.C.: Duke University Press, 1998.

French, William. *A Peaceful and Working People: Manners, Morals, and Class Formation in Northern Mexico*. Albuquerque: University of New Mexico Press, 1996.

Galván, Luz Elena. *La educación superior de la mujer en México: 1876–1940*. Mexico City: CIESAS, 1985.

Galvão, Patricia. *Industrial Park: A Proletarian Novel*. Lincoln: University of Nebraska Press, 1993.

Gamboa, Ignacio. *La mujer moderna*. Hoctún, Yucatán: Imprenta Gamboa Guzmán, 1906.

Gamboa Ojeda, Leticia. *Los empresarios de ayer*. Puebla: UAP, 1985.

García Cubas, Antonio. *Libro de mis recuerdos*. Mexico City: Imprenta de A.G.C. Sucesores Hermanos, 1905.

Garcia Diaz, Bernardo. *Un pueblo fabril del porfiriato: Santa Rosa, Veracruz*. Mexico City: Fondo de Cultura Economica, 1981.

———. *Textiles del Valle de Orizaba (1880–1925)*. Mexico City: IIESES, 1990.

Garza, Gustavo. *El proceso de industrialización en la ciudad de México, 1821–1970*. Mexico City: El Colegio de Mexico City, 1985.

Glantz, Margo. Introduction to *The Magic Lantern: Having a Ball and Christmas Eve*, by José Tomaás de Cuéllar. Translated by Margaret Carson, edited and with an Introduction by Margo Glantz. Oxford: Oxford University Press, 2000.

Goldin, Claudia. *Understanding the Wage Gap: An Economic History of American Women*. New York: Oxford University Press, 1990.

Gómez Izquierdo, José Jorge. *El movimiento antichino en México (1871–1934)*. Mexico City: INAH, 1991.

Gomezjara, Francisco A. *María de la O. y Benita Galeana: Precursoras del feminismo socialista en Guerrero.* Mexico City: Universidad Autónoma de Guerrero, 1982.

Gonzalez Angulo Aguirre, Jorge. *Artesanado y ciudad a finales del siglo XVIII.* Mexico City: Fondo de Cultura Economica, SEP/Ochentas, 1983.

Gonzalbo Arizpuru, Pilar. *Las mujeres en la Nueva España: Educación y vida cotidiana.* Mexico City: El Colegio de México, 1987.

González Casanova, Pablo. *La clase obrera en la historia de México en el primer gobierno constitucional (1917-1920).* Mexico City: Siglo Veintiuno Editores, 1980.

González Cossío, C. General Manuel. *Discurso leído el 1o de enero de 1888.* Mexico City: Imprenta de F. D. de L., 1889.

Gonzalez Navarro, Moisés. *Las huelgas textiles en el porfiriato.* Puebla and Mexico City: Editorial José M. Cajica Jr., S.A., 1970.

———. "La moral social." In *Historia moderna de México*, by Daniel Cosío Villegas, Vol. 4, *El porfiriato: La vida social*, by Moisés Gonzalez Navarro. Mexico City: Editorial Hermes, 1957.

———. *La pobreza en México.* Mexico City: Colegio de México, 1985.

Gordon, Linda. *Pitied but Not Entitled.* Cambridge, Mass.: Harvard University Press, 1994.

Gruening, Ernest. *Mexico and Its Heritage.* New York: Greenwood Press, 1968.

Guadarrama, Rocío. *Los sindicatos y la política en México: La CROM.* Mexico City: ERA, 1981.

Guerra, François-Xavier, Annick Lempériere, et al. *Los espacios públicos en Iberoamérica: Ambigüedades y problemas. Siglos XVIII-XIX.* México: Fondo de Cultura Económica, 1998.

Guerrero, Julio. *La génesis del crimen en México: Estudio de psiquiatría social.* París: Librería de la Vda. de Ch. Bouret, 1901.

Gutierrez Álvarez, Coralia. *Experiencias contrastadas: Industrialización y conflictos en los textiles del centro-oriente de México, 1884-1917.* Mexico City: El Colégio de México, 2000.

Gutman, Mathew C. *The Meanings of Macho: Being a Man in Mexico City.* Berkeley: University of California Press, 1996.

Guy, Donna. *Sex and Danger in Buenos Aires: Prostitution, Family, and Nation in Argentina.* Lincoln: University of Nebraska Press, 1991.

Haber, Stephen H. *Industry and Underdevelopment: The Industrialization of Mexico, 1890-1940.* Stanford, Calif.: Stanford University Press, 1989.

———. "Assessing the Obstacles to Industrialization: The Mexican Economy, 1830-1940." *Journal of Latin American Studies* 24, no. 1 (Jan. 1992): 1–32.

Habermas, Jürgen. *The Structural Transformation of the Public Sphere.* Cambridge: MIT Press, 1992.

Hale, Charles A. *The Transformation of Liberalism in Late-Nineteenth-Century Mexico.* Princeton, N.J.: Princeton University Press, 1989.

Hall, Catherine. *White, Male, and Middle Class: Explorations in Feminism and History.* New York: Routledge, 1992.

Hall, Linda B. *Álvaro Obregón: Power and Revolution in Mexico, 1911-1920.* College Station: Texas A & M University Press, 1981.

Hall, Michael M. "Urban Labor Movements." In *Latin America Economy and Society, 1870–1930*, edited by Leslie Bethell. Cambridge: Cambridge University Press, 1989.

Hart, John Mason. *Anarchism and the Mexican Working Class, 1860–1931*. Austin: University of Texas Press, 1978.

——. *Revolutionary Mexico: The Coming and Process of the Mexican Revolution*. Berkeley: University of California Press, 1987.

Hernandez, Ana María. *La mujer en la industria textil*. Mexico City: Tipografía Moderna, 1940.

Herrera Gonzalez, Jose G. "Breves consideraciones acerca de la influencia del trabajo industrial sobre el organismo de la mujer." Doctoral thesis, UNAM, 1933.

Hewitt, Nancy. *Women's Activism and Social Change: Rochester, New York, 1822–1872*. Ithaca, N.Y.: Cornell University Press, 1984.

Hewitt, Nancy A. "Beyond the Search for Sisterhood: American Women's History in the 1980s." *Social History* 10, no. 3 (October 1985): 299–321.

Higginbotham, Evelyn Brookes. "African-American Women's History and the Metalanguage of Race." *Signs* 17, no. 2 (winter 1992): 251–74.

Huitrón, Jacinto. *Orígenes e historia del movimiento obrero en México*. Mexico City: Editores Mexicanos Unidos, 1984.

Hünefeldt, Christine. *Paying the Price of Freedom: Family and Labor among Lima's Slaves, 1800–1854*. Berkeley: University of California Press, 1994.

Hutchison, Elizabeth Quay. *Labors Appropriate to Their Sex: Gender, Labor, and Politics in Urban Chile, 1900–1930*. Durham, N.C.: Duke University Press, 2001.

Iglesias Prieto, Norma. *Beautiful Flower of the Maquiladora*. Austin: University of Texas Press, 1997.

Illades, Carlos. *República del trabajo: La organización artisanal en la ciudad de México, 1853–1876*. Mexico City: Colegio de México, 1996.

Iparraguirre, Hilda. "Moroleón: Procesos de trabajo y comunidad, 1840–1920." In *Comunidad, cultura y vida social: Ensayos sobre la formación de la clase obrera*. Mexico City: INAH, 1991.

——. "Cuadros medios de origen artisanal—maestros, captaces, y encargados—en el proceso de industrialización y proletarización en México en la segunda mitad del siglo XIX y primeras décadas del XX." *Cuicuilco* 2, no. 4 (May–August 1995): 45–63.

James, Daniel. "'Tales Told out on the Borderlands': Doña María's Story, Oral History, and Issues of Gender." In *The Gendered Worlds of Latin American Women Workers: From Household and Factory to the Union Hall and Ballot Box*, edited by John French and James Daniels. Durham, N.C.: Duke University Press, 1998.

Jensen, Joan M. "Needlework as Art, Craft, and Livelihood before 1900." In *A Needle, a Bobbin, a Strike*, edited by Joan M. Jensen and Sue Davidson. Philadelphia: Temple University Press, 1984.

Jiménez Muñoz, Jorge H. *La traza de poder: Historia de la política y los negocios urbanos en el Distrito Federal*. Mexico City: CODEX, 1993.

Jones, Jacqueline. *Labor of Love, Labor of Sorrow: Black Women, Work, and the Family, from Slavery to the Present*. New York: Basic Books, 1985.

Joseph, Gil, and Daniel Nugent, eds. *Everyday Forms of State Formation: Revolution and the Negotiation of Rule in Modern Mexico*. Durham, N.C.: Duke University Press, 1994.

Kaplan, Temma. *Red City, Blue Period: Social Movements in Picasso's Barcelona*. Berkeley: University of California Press, 1992.

Keesing, Donald. "Mexico's Changing Industrial Structure." *Journal of Economic History* 24, no. 4 (1969): 717–38.

Kelley, Florence. *The Development in the United States of Legislation Concerning Women's Remunerative Work in Gainful Occupations: A Study*. Columbus: Central Ohio Alumnae Chapter, Pi Lambda Theta, 1939.

Kellogg, Susan. *Law and the Transformation of Aztec Culture, 1500-1700*. Norman: University of Oklahoma Press, 1995.

Keremetsis, Dawn. *La industria textil mexicana en el siglo XIX*. Mexico City: Sep/ Setentas 67, 1973.

———. "Del metate al molino: La mujer mexicana, 1910-1940." *Historia Mexicana* 13, no. 2 (October–December 1983): 285–302.

———. *La industria de empaques y sus trabajadoras: 1910-1914*, unpublished ms. located at the library of the Programa Interdisciplinario de Estudios de la Mujer, El Colegio de México, n.d., 296–99.

Kessler-Harris, Alice. *Out to Work: A History of Wage-Earning Women in the United States*. New York: Oxford University Press, 1982.

Klubock, Thomas Miller. *Contested Communities: Class, Gender, and Politics in Chile's El Teniente Copper Mine, 1904-1951*. Durham, N.C.: Duke University Press, 1998.

Knight, Alan. *The Mexican Revolution*. 2 vols. Lincoln: University of Nebraska Press, 1986.

———. "Popular Culture and the Revolutionary State in Mexico, 1910-1940." *Hispanic American Historical Review* 74, no. 3 (1994): 393–443.

Landes, Joan B. *Women and the Public Sphere in the Age of the French Revolution*. Ithaca, N.Y.: Cornell University Press, 1988.

Lara y Pardo, Doctor Luis. *La prostitución en México*. Mexico City: Librería de la Viuda de Ch. Bouret, 1908.

Lavrin, Asunción. "In Search of the Colonial Woman in Mexico: The Seventeenth and Eighteenth Centuries." In *Latin American Women: Historical Perspectives*, edited by Asunción Lavrin. Westport, Conn.: Greenwood Press, 1978.

———. "Investigación sobre la mujer de la colonia en México, siglos XVII y XVIII." In *Las mujeres latinoamericanas: Perspectivas históricas, México*. Mexico City: Fondo de Cultura Económica, 1985.

———. *Women, Feminism, and Social Change in Argentina, Chile, and Uruguay, 1890-1940*. Lincoln: University of Nebraska Press, 1995.

———, ed. *Latin American Women: Historical Perspectives*. Westport, Conn.: Greenwood Press, 1978.

Leal, Juan Felipe. *Del mutualismo al sindicalismo en México: 1843-1910.* Mexico City: El Caballito, 1991.

Lear, John. "Workers, *Vecinos*, and Citizens: The Revolution in Mexico City, 1910-1917." Ph.D. diss., University of California at Berkeley, 1993.

———. "Mexico City: Space and Class in the Porfirian Capital, 1884-1910." *Journal of Urban Studies* 22, no. 4 (1996): 454-92.

———. *Workers, Neighbors, and Citizens: The Revolution in Mexico City.* Lincoln: University of Nebraska Press, 2000.

Lehrer, Susan. *Origins of Protective Labor Legislation for Women, 1905-1925.* Albany: State University of New York Press, 1987.

Limones Ceniceros, Georgina Mayela. "Las obreras del México porfiriano: Trabajo, organization y conflictos laborales, 1880-1900." Ph.D. diss., UANM, 1993.

Lombardo de Ruiz, Sonia. "La real de tabaco: Un ejemplo de la construcción arquitectónica en el siglo XVIII en la ciudad de México (1793-1807)." In *Seminario de Historia Urbana: Investigaciones sobre la historia de la Ciudad de México,* coordinated by Alejandra Moreno Toscano. Mexico City: Instituto Mora, 1983.

Lombardo Toledano, Vicente. *Sin mujeres no hay democracia.* Mexico City: Editorial Combatiente, Talleres Gráficos Miguel Hernández González, 1984.

Loyo, Gilberto. "Notas sobre la evolucíon demográfica de la Ciudad de México." *Boletín de la Sociedad Mexicana de Geografía y Estadística* 45 (1933).

Macías, Ana. *Against All Odds: The Feminist Movement in Mexico to 1940.* Westport, Conn.: Greenwood Press, 1982.

Mallon, Florencia. "Exploring the Origins of Democratic Patriarchy in Mexico: Gender and Popular Resistance in the Puebla Highlands, 1850-1876." In *Women of the Mexican Countryside,* Heather Fowler-Salamini and Mary Kay Vaughan. Tucson: University of Arizona Press, 1994.

Martí, Judith E. "Subsistence and the State: The Case of Porfirian Mexico." In *The Economic Anthropology of the State,* edited by Elizabeth M. Brumfiel. Lanham, Md.: University Press of America, 1994.

———. *Subsistence and the State: Municipal Government Policies and Urban Markets in Developing Nations. The Case of Mexico City and Guadalajara, 1877-1900.* Ann Arbor: University Microfilms, 1990.

Martin, Percy F. *Mexico of the Twentieth Century.* London: Edward Arnold, 1907.

Martínez-Alier, Verena. *Marriage, Class, and Color in Nineteenth-Century Cuba: A Study of Racial Attitudes and Sexual Values in a Slave Society.* Ann Arbor: University of Michigan Press, 1989.

Melville, Roberto. *Crecimiento y rebelión: El desarrollo económico de las haciendas azucareras en Morelos (1880-1910).* Mexico City: Editorial Nueva Imagen, 1979.

Méndez de Cuenca, Laura. *Simplezas.* Mexico City: Instituto de Bellas Artes, 1983.

Metz, Brígida von. *Pueblos de indios, mulatos y mestizos, 1770-1870: Los campesinos y las transformaciones protoindustriales en el poniente de Morelos.* Mexico City: CIESAS, 1988.

México. Comisión Investigadora de la Situación de la Mujer y de los Menores Trabajadoras. *Informe sobre las labores de la Comisión Investigadora de la Situación de la Mujer y de los Menores Trabajadores.* Mexico City: Departamento del Trabajo, 1936.

————. Congreso Constituyente, 1916–1917. *Diario de los debates del Congreso Constituyente.* Mexico City: Imprenta de la Cámara de Diputados, 1922.

————. Congreso Nacional de Comerciantes. *Reseña y memorias del primer Congreso Nacional de Comerciantes y de la Asamblea General de Cámaras de Comercio de la República, reunidos en la Ciudad de Mexico City bajo el patrocinio de la Secretaría de Industria y Comercio.* Mexico City: Talleres gráficos de la Secretaría de Comunicaciones, 1917.

————. Congreso Nacional de Industriales. *Reseña y memorias del primer Congreso de Industriales reunido en la ciudad de México bajo el patrocinio de la Secretaría de Industria, Comercio y Trabajo.* Mexico City: Departamento de Aprovisionamientos Generales, Dirección de Talleres Gráficos, 1918.

————. Department of Finance. *The Mexican Yearbook: A Financial and Commercial Handbook, compiled from Official and Other Returns, 1912.* Mexico City: Department of Finance, 1912.

————. Departamento de la Estadística Nacional. *Censo General de la República,* Vol. 2, *Durango a Puebla* (verificado el 30 noviembre de 1921). Mexico City: Dirección General de Estadística, 1921(?).

————. Departamento de la Estadística Nacional. *Economía social: La estadística del trabajo.* Mexico City: Imprenta del "Diario Oficial," 1924.

————. Departamento de Trabajo. *Boletín del Trabajo* 6 (December 1913).

————. Dirección General de Estadística. *V censo de población: Resumen general.* Mexico City, 1930.

————. Dirección General de Estadística. *Segundo censo industrial de 1935.* Mexico City: [D.A.P.P., 1936?]–[1938].

————. Dirección General de Estadística. *Estadísticas sociales del porfiriato, 1877–1910.* Mexico City: Talleres Gráficos de la Nación, 1956.

————. Dirección General de Estadística. *Censo general de la República Mexicana verificado el 28 octubre de 1900 conforme a las instrucciones de la Dirección General de Estadística a cargo de Dr. Antonio Peñafiel.* Mexico City: Oficina Tipográfica de la Secretaría de Fomento, 1901–1906.

————. Dirección General de Estadística. *Tercer censo de población de los Estados Unidos Mexicanos, verificado el 27 de octubre de 1910. Secretario de Agricultura y Fomento, Dirección de Estadística.* Mexico City: Dirección de Estadística, 1918.

————. Instituto Nacional de Estadística, Geografía e Informática (INEGI). *Estadísticas históricas de México.* 3d ed. Aguascalientes: INEGI, 1994.

————. Secretaría de la Economía Nacional. *Primer censo industrial de 1930: Resúmenes generales por industrias,* Vol. 3, bk. 1, *Textiles.* Mexico City, 1934.

————. Secretaría de Educación Pública (SEP). *Folleto de la Escuela Nocturna de Artes y Oficios para Señoritas.* Mexico City: Editorial Cultura, 1928.

————. Secretaría de Educación Pública (SEP). *Memoria de trabajo realizados por el*

Departamento de Enseñanza durante la administración de Plutarco Elías Calles (1924-1928). Mexico City: SEP, 1928.

———. Secretaría de Fomento. Oficina Tipográfica. *Censo y división territorial del Distrito Federal, verificados en 1900*. México: Oficina Tipográfica de la Secretaría de Fomento, 1901.

———. Secretaría de Industria, Comercio y Trabajo. *Ley Federal del Trabajo*. Mexico City: Talleres Gráficas de la Nación, 1931.

———. Secretaría de Industria, Comercio y Trabajo. Dirección de Publicaciones y Propoganda. *Monografía sobre el estado actual de la industria en México*. Mexico City: Talleres Gráficos de la Nación, 1929.

Meyer, Michael C. *Huerta: A Political Portrait*. Lincoln: University of Nebraska Press, 1972.

Milkman, Ruth. *Gender at Work: The Dynamics of Job Segregation by Sex during World War II*. Urbana: University of Illinois Press, 1987.

———. "New Research in Women's Labor History." *Signs* 18, no. 2 (1993): 376-88.

Miller, Simon. "Mexican Junkers and Capitalist Haciendas, 1810-1910: The Arable Estate and the Transition to Capitalism between Insurgency and the Revolution." *Journal of Latin American Studies* 22 (May 1990): 251-52.

Middlebrook, Kevin J. *The Paradox of Revolution: Labor, the State, and Authoritarianism in Mexico*. Baltimore, Md.: Johns Hopkins University Press, 1995.

Miño Grijalva, Manuel. *La protoindustria colonial hispanoamericana*. Mexico City: El Colegio de México, 1993.

Molina Enríquez, Andrés. *Los grandes problemas nacionales*. 4th ed. Preface by Arnoldo Córdova. Mexico City: Ediciones Era, 1983.

Monsiváis, Carlos. *Mexican Postcards*. New York: Verso, 1997.

Morales Jurado, Alvarado. "La Mujer Campesina Mexicana." Licenciatura en Derecho, UNAM, 1954.

Morgan, Tony. "Proletarians, Politicos, and Patriarchs." In *Rituals of Rule, Rituals of Resistance: Public Celebrations and Popular Culture in Mexico*, edited by William Beezley, Cheryl English Martin, and William E. French. Wilmington, Del.: Scholarly Resources, 1994.

Moser, C. "Informal Sector or Petty Commodity Production? Dualism or Dependence in Urban Development?" *World Development* 6, no. 9/10 (1978): 1041-64.

Muriel, Josefina. *Los recogimientos de mujeres: Respuesta a una problemática social novohispana*. Mexico City: UNAM, IIH, 1974.

Obregón, Arturo. "El Segundo Congreso Obrero, 1879." In *Historia Obrera*, vol. 7. Mexico: CEHSMO, 1977.

———. Introduction to *La convención radical: Antología*, revision and thematic classification by Liborio Villalobos Calderón. Mexico City: CEHSMO, 1978.

Obregón M., Arturo. *Las obreras tabacaleras en la Ciudad de México, 1764-1925*. Mexico City: CEHSMO, 1982.

Orleck, Annelise. *Common Sense and a Little Fire*. Chapel Hill: University of North Carolina Press, 1995.

Owensby, Brian P. *Intimate Ironies: Modernity and the Making of Middle-Class Lives in Brazil*. Stanford, Calif.: Stanford University Press, 1999.

Palavincini, Felix F. *México: Historia de su evolución constructiva*. Mexico City: Distribuidora Editorial "Libro, S. de R.L.," 1945.

Palma, J. G. "External Disequilibrium and Internal Industrialization: Chile, 1914–1935." In *Latin America, Economic Imperialism, and the State: The Political Economy of the External Connections from Independence to the Present*, edited by C. Abel and C. M. Lewis. London: Published for the Institute of Latin American Studies, University of London [by] Althone, 1985.

Pani, Alberto J. *La higiene en México*. Mexico City: Ballescá, 1917.

Parcero, María de la Luz. *Condiciones de la mujer en México durante el siglo XIX*. Mexico City: Colección Científica, 1992.

Parker, D. S. *The Idea of the Middle Class: White-Collar Workers and Peruvian Society, 1900–1950*. University Park: Pennsylvania State University Press, 1998.

Pateman, Carole. "Feminist Critiques of the Public/Private Dichotomy." In *The Disorder of Women*. Stanford, Calif.: Stanford University Press, 1989.

Payno, Manuel. *Los bandidos de Río Frío*. Mexico City: Editorial Ars, 1888.

———. *Sobre mujeres, amores y matrimonios*. Mexico: Premia Editora Instituto de Bellas Artes, 1984.

Percy, Martin F. *Mexico in the Twentieth Century*. London: E. Arnold, 1907.

Piccato, Pablo. "La construcción de una perspectiva científica: Miradas a la criminalidad." *Historia Mexicana* 47, no. 1 (1997): 133–81.

———. *"Urbanistas, Ambulantes, and Mendigos*: The Dispute for Urban Space in Mexico City, 1890–1930." In *Reconstructing Criminality in Latin America*, edited by Carlos A. Aguirre and Robert Buffington. Wilmington, Del.: Scholarly Resources, 2000.

———. *City of Suspects: Crime in Mexico City, 1900–1931*. Durham, N.C.: Duke University Press, 2001.

Pogolotti, Marcelo. *La clase media en México*. Mexico City: Editores Diogenes, 1972.

Ponce Alocer, María Eugenia Patricia. *La elección presidencial de Manuel González, 1878–1880 (preludio de un presidencialismo)*. Mexico City: Universidad Iberoamericana, 2000.

Prado de la Piedra, Carlos E. "Regimen de protección a la mujer obrera: Seguro de maternidad." Ph.D. diss., UNAM, 1932.

Prieur, Annick. *Mema's House, Mexico City: On Transvestites, Queens, and Machos*. Chicago: University of Chicago Press, 1998.

Radcliff, Pamela. "Elite Women Workers and Collective Action: The Cigarette Makers of Gijón, 1890–1930." *Journal of Social History* 27, no. 1 (fall 1993): 85–108.

Radkau, Verena. *"La Fama" y la vida: Una fábrica y sus obreras*. Cuadernos de la Casa Chata, no. 108. Mexico City: CIESAS, 1984.

———. *"Por la debilidad de nuestro ser": Mujeres 'del pueblo' en la paz porfiriana*. Cuadernos de la Casa Chata, no. 168. Mexico City: CIESAS, 1989.

Ramos-Escandón, Carmen. "Mujeres trabajadoras del porfiriato: 1876–1911." *La*

Revista Europea de Estudios Caribeños y Latinoamericanos y del Caribe 48 (June 1990): 27–44.

Ramos, Carmen, and Ana Lau. *Mujeres y revolución, 1900–1917*. Mexico City: IN-HERM, 1993.

Recchini de Lattes, Zulma, and Catalina H. Wainerman. "Unreliable Account of Women's Work: Evidence from Latin American Census Statistics." *Signs* 11, no. 4 (1986): 740–50.

Redclift, Nanneke, and Enzo Mingione. *Beyond Employment: Household, Gender, and Subsistence*. New York: Basil Blackwell, 1985.

Rendón, Teresa, and Carlos Salas. "La evolución del empleo en México, 1895–1980." *Estudios Demográficos y Urbanos* 2, no. 2 (May–August 1987): 189–230.

Richmond, Douglas W. "Carranza: The Authoritarian Populist." In *Essays on the Mexican Revolution: Revisionist Views of the Leaders*, edited by William Beezley. Austin: University of Texas Press, 1979.

———. *Venustiano Carranza's Nationalist Struggle, 1893–1920*. Lincoln: University of Nebraska Press, 1983.

Rocha, Martha Eva, ed. *El album de las mujeres: Antología ilustrada de las mexicanas*. In *El porfiriato y la Revolución*, vol. 4. Mexico City: INAH, 1991.

Romero, Matías. *Mexico and the United States: A Study of Subjects Affecting their Political, Commercial, and Social Relations, Made with a View to Their Promotion*. G. P Putnam's Sons, 1898.

Romero Aceves, Ricardo. *La mujer en la historia de México*. Mexico City: Costa-Amic Editores, 1982.

Romougnac, Carlos. *Criminales en México: Ensayo de psicología criminal*. Mexico City: Tipografía "El Fénix," 1904.

Ros, Maria Amparo. "La Real Fábrica de Tabaco: Apuntes acerca de la organización del trabajo." In *Seminario de Historia Urbana: Investigaciones sobre la historia de la Ciudad de México*, edited by Alejandra Moreno Toscano. Mexico City: INAH, 1976.

———. "La Real Fábrica de Tabaco." *Historias* 10 (July–September 1985): 51–64.

Rose, Sonya O. *Limited Livelihoods: Gender and Class in Nineteenth-Century England*. Berkeley: University of California Press, 1992.

———. "Resuscitating Class." *Social Science History* 22, no. 1 (spring 1998): 19–27.

Roseberry, William. *Anthropologies and Histories: Essays in Culture, History, and Political Economy*. New Brunswick, N.J.: Rutgers University Press, 1989.

———. "Hegemony and the Language of Contention." In *Everyday Forms of State Formation*, edited by Gilbert M Joseph and Daniel Nugent. Durham, N.C.: Duke University Press, 1994.

Rosenzweig, Fernando. "La industria." In *Historia moderna de México*, Vol. 7, *El porfiriato: La vida económica*, edited by Daniel Cosío Villegas. Mexico City: Editorial Hermes, 1957.

Ryan, Mary P. *The Cradle of the Middle Class: The Family in Oneida County, New York, 1790–1856*. New York: Cambridge University Press, 1981.

———. "Gender and Public Access: Women's Politics in Nineteenth-Century

America." In *Habermas and the Public Sphere*, edited by Craig Calhoun. Cambridge, Mass.: MIT Press, 1992.

Saenz Royo, Artemesia N. *Historia político-social cultural del movimiento femenino, 1914-1950*. Mexico City: Imprenta M. Leon Sanchez, 1954.

Saffioti, Heilieth I. B. *A mulher na sociedade de classes: Mito e realidade*. Petropolis: Voces, 1976.

Salas, Elizabeth. *Soldaderas in the Mexican Military: Myth and Reality*. Austin: University of Texas Press, 1990.

Salazar, Rosendo, and José Escobedo. *Las pugnas de la glebe*. Mexico City: UNAM, 1978.

Salvucci, Richard. *Textiles and Capitalism in Mexico: An Economic History of the Obrajes, 1539-1840*. Princeton, N.J.: Princeton University Press, 1987.

Sanborn Map Company. *Insurance Maps of the City of Mexico*. New York: The Company, 1905.

Santicillia Obregón, Adela Formoso de. *La mujer mexicana en la organización social del país*. Mexico, 1939.

San Vicente Tello, Victoria (coordinadora general). *Tiempos y espacios laborales*. Mexico City: Honorable Cámara de Diputados, 1994.

Schell, Patience. "An Honorable Vocation for Ladies: The Work of the Mexico City Unión de Damas Católicas Mexicanas, 1912-1926." *Journal of Women's History* 10, no. 4 (winter 1998-99): 78-103.

Scott, Joan W. *Gender and the Politics of History*. New York: Columbia University Press, 1988.

Sesto, Julio. *El México de Porfirio Díaz*. Mexico City: Valencia, F. Dempere y Cia, 1910.

Sewell, William H., Jr. "Toward a Post-materialist Rhetoric for Labor History." In *Rethinking Labor History*, edited by Lenard R. Berlanstein. Urbana: University of Illinois Press, 1993.

Sheridan, Cecilia. *Mujer obrera y organización sindical: El sindicato de obreras desmanchadoras del café, Coatepec, Veracruz: Un estudio histórico-monográfico*. Cuadernos de la Casa Chata, no. 76. Mexico City: CIESAS, 1983.

Smith, Phyllis S. "Contentious Voices Amid the Order: The Opposition Press in Mexico City, 1876-1911." *Journalism History* 22, no. 4 (winter 1997): 138-45.

Smith-Rosenberg, Carroll. *Disorderly Conduct*. New York: Oxford University Press, 1985.

Soto, Shirlene. *The Emergence of the Modern Mexican Woman: Her Participation in Revolution and Struggle for Equality, 1910-1940*. Denver: Arden Press, 1990.

Stacey, Judith. *Patriarchy and Socialist Revolution in China*. Berkeley: University of California Press, 1983.

Stansell, Christine. *City of Women: Sex and Class in New York, 1780-1860*. Urbana: University of Illinois Press, 1982.

Staples, Anne. "Policía y buen gobierno." In *Rituals of Rule, Rituals of Resistance: Public Celebrations and Popular Culture in Mexico*, edited by William H. Beezley, Cheryl English Martin, and Willian E. French. Wilmington, Del.: Scholarly Resources, 1994.

Stern, Steven. *The Secret History of Gender: Women, Men, and Power in Late Colonial Mexico*. Chapel Hill: University of North Carolina Press, 1995.

Stevens, Don. *Origins of Instability in Early Republican Mexico*. Durham, N.C.: Duke University Press, 1991.

Stevens, Evelyn P. "Marianismo: The Other Face of Machismo in Latin America." In *Female and Male in Latin America: Essays*, edited by Anne Pescatello. Pittsburgh: University of Pittsburgh Press, 1973.

Taibo II, Paco Ignacio. *Los Bolshevikis: Historia narrativa de los orígenes del comunismo en México*. Mexico City: Joaquín Mortíz, 1987.

Tamayo, Jaime. *La clase obrera en la historia de México en el interinato de Adolfo de la Huerta y el gobierno de Álvaro Obregón (1920-1924)*. Mexico City: Siglo Veintiuno Editores, 1987.

Tenorio Trillo, Mauricio. "1910 Mexico City: Space and Nation in the City of the Centenario." *Journal of Latin American Studies* 28 (1): 75–104.

Thompson, Lanny. "Artisans, Marginals, and Proletarians: The Households of the Popular Classes in Mexico City, 1876-1950." In *Five Centuries of Mexican History / Cinco siglos de historia de México*, edited by Virginia Guedea and Jaime E. Rodriguez O. Mexico City: Instituto de Investigaciones Dr. José María Luis Mora; Irvine: University of California, Irvine, 1992.

Topik, Steven. "The Emergence of Finance Capital in Mexico." In *Five Centuries of Mexican History / Cinco siglos de historia de México*, edited by Virginia Guedea and Jaime E. Rodriguez O. Mexico City: Instituto de Investigaciones Dr. José María Luis Mora; Irvine: University of California, Irvine, 1992.

Tostado Gutiérrez, Marcela. *El álbum de la mujer*. Vol. 2, *Época colonial*. Mexico City: INAH, 1991.

Towner, Margaret. "Monopoly Capitalism and Women's Work during the Porfiriato." In *Women in Latin American History: An Anthology from "Latin American Perspectives,"* by Eleanor B. Leacock et al. Riverside, Calif.: Latin American Perspectives, 1979.

Tuñón, Julia. *El álbum de la mujer: Antología ilustrada de las mexicanas*, Vol. 3, *El siglo XIX (1821-1880)*. Mexico City: INAH, 1991.

Tuñón Pablos, Enriqueta. "La lucha política de la mujer mexicana por el derecho al sufragio y sus repercusiones." In *Presencia y transparencia: La mujer en la historia de México*, edited by Centro de Estudios Históricos del Movimiento Obrero Mexicano. Mexico City: Colegio de México, 1987.

Tuñón Pablos, Esperanza. *Mujeres que se organizan: El frente único pro derechos de la mujer, 1934-1938*. Mexico City: Miguel Angel Porrua, 1992.

Tuñón Pablos, Julia. *Women in Mexico: A Past Unveiled*. Translated by Alan Hynds. Austin: University of Texas Press, 1999.

Twinam, Ann. *Public Lives, Private Secrets: Gender, Honor, Sexuality, and Illegitimacy in Colonial Spanish America*. Stanford: Stanford University Press, 1999.

Urbina Trueba, Alberto. *La evolución de la huelga*. Mexico City: Ediciones Botas, 1950.

Valenze, Deborah. *The First Industrial Woman*. Oxford: Oxford University Press, 1995.

Vallens, Vivian M. *Working Women in Mexico during the Porfiriato, 1880-1910*. San Francisco: R & E Research Associates, Inc., 1978.

Vanderwood, Paul. *Disorder and Progress: Bandits, Police, and Mexican Development*. Lincoln: University of Nebraska Press, 1981.

Van Young, Eric. "The New Cultural History Comes to Old Mexico." *Hispanic American Historical Review* 79, no. 2 (May 1999): 211-47.

Vaughan, Mary Kay. *Cultural Politics in Revolution: Teachers, Peasants, and Schools in Mexico, 1930-1940*. Tucson: University of Arizona Press, 1997.

Vecchia, Teresa. "'My Duty as a Woman': Gender Ideology, Work, and Working-Class Women's Lives in São Paulo, Brazil, 1900-1950." In *The Gendered Worlds of Latin American Women Workers: From Household and Factory to the Union Hall and Ballot Box*, edited by John French and James Daniels. Durham, N.C.: Duke University Press, 1998.

Vidales, Susana. "Ni madres abnegadas ni adelitas." *Críticas de la economía política*, no. 14-15. Mexico City: El Caballito, 1980.

Viotti da Costa, Emilia. "Experience versus Structure: New Tendencies in the History of Labor and the Working Class in Latin America—What Do We Gain? What Do We Lose?" *International Labor and Working-Class History* 36 (fall 1989): 3-24.

Viqueira Albán, Juan Pedro. *¿Relajados o reprimidos?* Mexico City: Fondo de Cultura Económica, 1987.

Voekel, Pamela. "Peeing on the Palace: Bodily Resistance to Bourbon Reforms in Mexico City." *Journal of Historical Sociology*, 5, no. 2 (June 1992): 183-208.

Walker, Charles F. *Smoldering Ashes: Cuzco and the Creation of Republican Peru, 1780-1840*. Durham, N.C.: Duke University Press, 1999.

Walker, David. "Porfirian Labor Politics: Working Class Organizations in Mexico City and Porfirio Diaz, 1876-1902." *The Americas* 37, no. 3 (January 1980): 257-90.

Warren, Richard A. *Vagrants and Citizens: The Politics of the Masses in Mexico City from Colony to Republic*. Wilmington, Del.: Scholarly Resources, 2001.

Wolf, Joel. *Working Women and Working Men: São Paulo and the Rise of Brazil's Industrial Working Class, 1900-1955*. Durham, N.C.: Duke University Press, 1993.

Womack, John. "The Mexican Revolution, 1910-1920." In *Mexico Since Independence*, edited by Leslie Bethell. Cambridge: Cambridge University Press, 1991.

Yoma Medina, María Rebeca, and Luis Alberto Martos López. *Dos mercados en la historia de la ciudad de México: El Volador y La Merced*. Mexico: Colección Divulgación, INAH, 1990.

Zea, Leopoldo. *Positivismo en México*. Norman: University of Oklahoma Press, 1963.

Index

Espinosa Mireles, Gustavo, 109–10
ethnicity, xxi

fabricanta, 122, 125
factory as sexualized space, 53,
  62–63, 70, 132
factory worker, female. *See* obrera;
  fabricanta
family wage, 57, 79, 118
Federación Comunista del Proletariado, 111
Federal District penal code (1871),
  161
Federal Labor Code (1931), 32, 43,
  159–60, 184–86; Article 107, 185;
  Article 21, 184
Federation of Thread and Cloth
  Workers of the Federal District,
  107
Federation of Worker's Unions of
  the Federal District, 97, 107, 108,
  110, 117–18
female ailments, 179–80
female consciousness, 74, 154
female dependency, 61
female-dominated industry. *See*
  industry: female-dominated
femininity: paradigms of, xix; normative and factory discipline, xx;
  women define, 147–48
feminism, 69–70, 112, 172–73; and
  cigarreras, 211n. 46; positivism
  and, 55–57; and teachers, 211n. 46
Folsa Viuda de Menocal, L., 171
foreigners, criticism of, 56, 62, 67,
  68, 71, 80, 128, 166, 173
foreign investment, 21–22, 31, 38, 40
Franco, Jean, 51
Fraternal de Costureras, 75
French, William, xix, 51
Frente Regional de Obreros y Campesinos, women in, 117
Frías, Catalina, 90–91, 116
Frías, María del Carmen, 90–91,
  111–12, 116, 117

Galindo, Rafaela, 84
Gamboa, Ignacio, 57–58
García Cubas, Antonio, 143
gender: concept of, xv–xvii; in com-
  parative perspective, 196n. 20;
  paradigms, xix, 51. *See also* class:
  and gender
gender confusion, 56, 58–59
General Strike (1916), 108–9, 173
General Workers Confederation
  (Confederación General de Tra-
  bajadores), 97, 109, 112
Gomez, María, 90
González Cosío, Manuel, 22, 88, 162
La Gran Liga de Torcedores de
  Tabacos de los Estados Unidos
  Mexicanos, 86
Guerra, François-Xavier, xviii
Guerrero, Francisca, 84
Guerrero, Isabel, 84
guilds, 8, 74, 52

Haber, Stephen, xxv
Habermas, Jürgen, xviii, 189
head of household: female, 6–7, 37,
  89, 151, 153–55, 171; male, 150;
  and wages, 180
Hernández, Ana Maria, 70, 167
Hernández, Dolores, 81
Las Hijas de Anahuac, 90–91, 107
Las Hijas del Trabajo, 82
El Hijo del Trabajo, 60
homework, industrial. *See* outwork
honor: xx, xvii, 164, 187; concept
  of, 121–22; defined by working
  women, 119–24, 129–33; and male
  workers, 121–22; at work, 4, 126
Honorat, Signoret, Sr., 170
Huerta, Victoriano, 104, 159, 168,
  169, 173
hygiene, 130, 179–80

identity, 122–24
imitation, 64
El Imparcial, 60

industrialization: historical definition of, xii, 71; of Mexico City, compared to other regions, xii–xiv; porfiriato, xii–xiv, 15; and technology, 21; and vendors, 146; and women in comparative perspective, xiv

industrial segregation by sex, 10–13

industry: defined, xii–xiii, 13–14, 46–47; female-dominated, xiii, 13–14, 18, 19, 38, 94, 188; links between, 31, 46–47

inspectors, female, 169–73

Islas, Gabriel María, 82

Jesus de Huerta, María, 75

Juárez, Benito, 76

Juárez de Sánchez, Felícitas, 88

Justa, Doña, 125

Kaplan, Temma, 197n. 40, 207n. 1

Keremetsis, Dawn, 13, 212n. 55

Knight, Alan, 167

knitwear, 40–41, 203n. 92; protest, 101–4. *See also* unions: Union of Knitwear Working Men and Working Women; wages, knitwear

Knitwear Working Men and Working Women of the Federal District, 107

Labor Exchange (Bolsa de Trabajo), 169

labor force: children in, 10–13; cigarette workers, 25; clothing, 37–38; knitwear, 40–41, 203n. 92; markets, 146–47; molenderas, 204n. 115; needle trades, 35; pushed out of, 22; rural workforce, 5–6, 204n. 111; shifts in, 19, 41–43; textile industry, 38–39, 203n. 88; women in, xii–xiv, xxv, 8–9, 13–14, 41–46, 198n. 3, 200n. 39, 204n. 111

Landa y Escandón, Don Guillermo, 91–93

Landes, Joan, 197n. 28

Lara y Pardo, Doctor Luis, 60, 63–67

Lavrin, Asuncion, 163

leadership: women in, 107, 109, 116–17; decline of, 113–14

Lear, John, xv, xvii, 192, 197n. 40, 207n. 1, 213n. 11

legal rights, of working women, porfiriato, 160–61

legislation: Madero promises, 101; married women, 184; maternity, 183; minimum wage, 174–75, 180; night work, 175–76, 184–85; outwork, 185; protective labor legislation, 174, 184; Sunday rest 240–43; vending, 134, 138, 140, 142

León de la Barra, Francisco, 168

liberal political philosophy and gender, 51–52

Libreta (identity card), 123

Lira, Carlota, 90

literacy, of working women, 35

Llamedo, Señor, 87–88

Longa, Valeriana de la, 128

Lugo, José Inocente, 174

Macedo, Pablo, 22

Macías, Ana, 69

Macías, José Natividad, 174

Madero, Francisco I., 99, 101, 159, 167–68, 173; workers support, 91, 92

Madero, Mercedes (Gutiérrez), 167

Madero, Sara Perez de, 167

Madero de González Trevino, Prudencia, 167

maestras, 84, 111, 128–32

Mallon, Florencia, 78, 208n. 21

Mancera, Gabriel, 76

maquiladoras, 32, 193–94, 202n. 62

marianismo, xvi

market reform, resistance to, 139–42, 150–51, 156–57

markets: ad hoc, 136–37, 142; ambulantes (itinerant peddlers), 137; colonial, 146; comideras, 139; description of, 135–37; La Lagunilla, 136; La Merced, 135, 139, 146; reorganization of, 137–40, 146–47; San Juan, 136, 144; Tepito, 137, 148; women and men in, 146; Zócalo, 136, 140, 144–45

Martí, Senator, 175

Mateos, Juan A., 82

maternity benefits, 176

May Day (1913), 104; (1925), 114

mechanics, 127–28

Méndez, Luis, 104

metropolitan industrialization, xiv

Metropolitan Tailors Union, 104

Mexican Communist Party, 111

Mexican Revolution: and public discourse, xix–xx, 50, 68–71, 131; significance of for women, xvii, xxv, 68–69, 70–71, 191–92; as turning point, 117–18, 159, 186–87, 189–92; and vendors, 158

Mexico City: compared to other cities, 38; defined, xvii–xviii; employment of women in, 3; and industrialization, xvii, 15–19; transformation of, 15–20, 133–34

middle class, xv; identity, xv, 50, 59–66, 71, 89, 132, 143, 166

migration, 6

military, apparel production, 98–99; support striking workers, 82, 85

minimum wage, 174–75, 180, 182. *See also* legislation: minimum wage

Ministry of Industry, Commerce, and Labor, 176–77, 184

mixing the sexes, 50, 53, 70, 176

Moheno, Querido, 168–69

Molina Enríquez, Andrés, 51

morality, 58–59, 119–20, 129–32, 187–90; in discourse, xx, 53–54, 62, 89, 94–95, 118; and education, 165–66, 171–73; informs government programs, 169, 175–76; and hygiene, 178–79; public, 54, 92; and women's labor; and women's rights, 181, 183; working women define, 73–73, 79, 114–15, 129–32, 147–51; in the work place, 20–24

Morgan, Anthony, 129

Morones, Luis, 110, 113, 183–84

motherhood, 50–51, 75, 92–93, 169, 171–73, 178; charity for, 163–64

Múgica, Francisco J., 116

mujer: as job description, 45

Mujeres, 116

La Mujer Mexicana, 142

municipal government, 138–40

mutual aid societies: Catholic, 76, 91–93; cigarette workers, 77–86; compared, 87, 94–95; elite patronage of, 81–82, 88; as homosocial organizations, 74–93; named, 75–76, 82; seamstresses, 87–90; and transition to unions, 95, 97–98, 104; women in, 73–77, 91–94; women's compared to men's, 75

nationalism, 87, 97–98, 108

The Needle Strike, 105–6

newspapers, discussion of, 60

night schools, 165

night work. *See* legislation: night work

nixtamal, molinos de, 47, 182

Nueva Era, 100

obrajes, 54

Obregón, Álvaro, 105–6, 110, 159, 168, 176

obrera (female factory worker), 38–46; defined, 122; as discursive category, xiv–xx, 51, 56, 68–71, 94, 119, 126

El Puerto de Veracruz, 31, 170
Pugibet, Ernesto, 15, 21, 83, 188,
    128–29
pulquerías, 151; and vendors, 136;
    legislation regarding, 140

race, 58, 115–16, 155
Radkau, Verena, 125
Rag processors, 46–47
Ramos-Escandón, Carmen, 198n. 3
recojimientos, 10
Red Brigades, 106
Red Cross, 168
redemption, 62, 105, 164, 167
Regional Confederation of Mexi-
    can Workers. *See* Confederación
    Regional de Obreros Mexicanos
    (CROM)
religion, 70; and charity, 162–64;
    and factory discipline, 129–31;
    instruction in, 171–73. *See also*
    Catholic church
respectability, xv, 39, 61–63, 164
Revista Positivista, 56
Rio Blanco (1907), invoked, 99
Romero, Jacobita, 128
Romero Rubio, Manuel, 76
Roseberry, William, xx, 152, 154
Rouaix, José, 174
Ryan, Mary P., xviii

Salado Alvarez, Ana, 70
Santa María, Paula, 81
Sarabia, Juan, 98
savings bank (caja de ahorros), 90
Scott, Joan, 71, 196n. 17
scribers. *See* public scribes
seamstresses, 10, 13, 16–19, 28–38,
    45, 48–49; compared to other
    working women, 87, 90, 94–95; in
    Convención General de Trabaja-
    dores, 111–12; strike, 98–101. *See
    also* mutual aid societies; unions
seclusion, 51–52
Señorita, term discussed, 126

separate spheres, ideology of, 93
service sector, xiv
Sesto, Julio, 15
sewing agencies, 88–89
sex typing of occupations, 22–23,
    39, 45, 61–63, 88; in curriculum,
    166
Sierra, Justo, 86
La Sinaloense, 30–31, 98–101
skilled labor, women as, 38, 40, 45,
    110–11
El Socialista, 60
Sociedad de Costureras Sor Juana
    Inés de la Cruz, 88
Sociedad Filantrópica Mexicana, 88
Sociedad Instructiva y Recreativa
    Guillermo Landa y Escandón,
    92, 104
Sociedad Mexicana de Costureras,
    88
Sociedad Mutualista y Moralizadora
    Landa y Escandón, 92–93, 103
Soto, Shirlene, 69
source, discussion of, xx–xxi, 19, 41,
    46–48, 146, 200n. 28
Stansell, Christine, xiv
state, concept of, 160, 162
Stern, Steven, 213n. 5
Stevens, Evelyn P., xvi
strikes: cigarette workers, 77–86;
    knitwear, 101–4; mutual aid soci-
    eties and, 76; porfiriato, 91, 101–
    2, seamstresses, 98–101; women
    in, 69
subcontracting, 31–32
suffrage, 56
sweat shops, 32, 35, 53

La Tabacalera Mexicana, 16, 21, 92,
    167, 211n. 46
tailors, 32, 36
teachers, 84, 91; in Casa de Obrero
    Mundial, 107
technology, 70; and labor disputes,
    110–11; and occupational seg-

technology (*continued*)
  regation by sex, 22–23; sewing
  machines, 33
Telephone and Telegraph Company
  strikes, 173
Tenorio, Mauricio, xvii
textile industry, 10–13, 16, 38–39;
  women in, compared to other
  countries, 13n. 28
Thompson, Lanny, 7
El Tiempo, 60, 79
tipos, 63, 67, 143
tobacco industry, 8–10, 13–16, 20–28
Torres, Esther, 107–8
Torres, Ignacia, 126
Torres Viuda de Alvarez, Ignacia,
  3–4
tortillerías, 42, 47, 179–83
Towner, Margaret, xii–xiii, 19
tradition, 134, 152–54
Tron, Enrique, 22
Tron, Justino, 106
Tuñón Pablos, Esperanza, 69

unions: Catholic, 110–11; women
  in, 97; named, 107, 111–12, 116–
  17; Union of Anarchist Women,
  113; Union of Knitwear Working
  Men and Working Women, 107,
  117; Union de Mujeres Ibero-
  Americanas, 211n. 46; La Union
  Obrera, 85; Union of Vendors
  from Outside Markets, 116;
  Union of Workers and Employees of Eriksson Telephone, 111
unskilled labor, men as, 25, 78–79;
  women as, 47, 97

Vargas, Elvira, 70
vecinas, 153
Vega, Justa, 90
Vega, Lina, 84
vendors, union, 116
Vicario, Leona, 75

Villareal, Leopoldo, 140
vocational training, 172–73. *See also*
  Escuelas de Artes y Oficios

wages, 43–46, 79, 204n. 103; cigarette industry, 25–26, 78–81,
  83–84; clothing industry, 33–
  38; conflict over, 87–90; family
  wage, knitwear, 41; legislation
  regarding women's, 180; and
  occupational segregation by sex,
  47; and technology, 34, 44; textile industry, 44–45; vendors,
  148–49; women's and men's compared, 45–46, 204n. 103; women's
  compared, 33–34
Waiters Union, 115–16
waitresses, 47–48, 114–16
weakness, xvi–xvii, xx, 57–58, 150,
  187, 190. *See also* debilidad; desvalida; respectability
White Cross, 167, 168
widows, 6, 89, 175
worker consciousness, 80, 120, 123–
  24, 132
worker organizations, employer-
  sponsored, 87
working conditions: accidents, 185;
  cigarette industry, 78–79, 81;
  clothing industry, 32–33; described by women, 83; factories,
  177; nixtamal mills, 177; production quotas, 24–25; separation of
  sexes, 9, 22–23, 24, 25, 39. *See
  also* industry: female-dominated;
  occupational segregation by sex;
  wages
working women compared, 73, 117,
  134, 158, 186, 188–91, 212n. 55;
  compared to other countries,
  199n. 11, 203n. 87. *See also* obrera
work stoppages (closures), 102–3

Zetina, Carlos B., 168

About the Author

Susie S. Porter is Assistant Professor in the Department of History and the Gender Studies Program at the University of Utah, Salt Lake City. She received her Ph.D. in History from the University of California, San Diego in 1997.

Professor Porter is the author of "Juana Belén Gutiérrez de Mendoza (1875–1942): Woman of Words, Woman of Action," in *The Human Tradition in Mexico*, edited by Jeffery Pilcher (Wilmington, Del.: Scholarly Resources, 2003); and of "And that it is custom makes it law": Class Conflict and Gender Ideology in the Public Sphere, Mexico City, 1880–1910," *Social Science History* 24, no. 1 (spring 2000). Her current research continues to explore the relationship between gender and class in Mexico. At the University of Utah she has been involved in developing a program in comparative women's history.